BEAT NOT
THE POOR DESK

BEAT NOT
THE POOR DESK

Writing:
What to Teach,
How to Teach It, and Why

MARIE PONSOT
and
ROSEMARY DEEN

BOYNTON/COOK PUBLISHERS, INC.

Acknowledgments

For "Leda and the Swan"
Reprinted with permission of Macmillan Publishing Co., Inc.
from *Collected Poems* by William Butler Yeats. Copyright 1928 by
Macmillan Publishing Co., Inc., renewed 1956 by Georgie Yeats.

For "Leonardo's Knot" (cover)
Reprinted with permission of the Trustees of the British Museum.

Library of Congress Cataloging in Publication Data

Ponsot, Marie.
    Beat not the poor desk.

    Includes index.
        1. English language—Study and teaching
    2. English language—Rhetoric.   I. Deen,
    Rosemary.   II. Title.
    PE1404.P6   808'.042'.071073   81–15519
    ISBN 0-86709-009-X   AACR2

For information address Boynton/Cook Publishers, Inc.
Box 860, Upper Montclair, New Jersey 07043

ISBN: 0-86709-009-X

Printed in the United States of America

        85 86 10 9 8 7 6 5 4 3

for Leonard Deen
"a sublime energizer"

To this perfection of nature in our poet we require exercise of those parts, *exercitatio*, and frequent. If his wit will not arrive suddenly at the dignity of the ancients, let him not yet fall out with it, quarrel, or be over hastily angry, offer to turn it away from study in a humor; but come to it again upon better cogitation, try another time with labor. If then it succeed not, cast not away the quills yet, nor scratch the wainscot, beat not the poor desk, but bring all to the forge and file again; turn it anew. There is no statute law of the kingdom bids you be a poet against your will or the first quarter; if it comes in a year or two, it is well.

Ben Jonson, *Timber*

Preface

For teachers this is a book about imagining writing so that their students will learn to generate writing that has a shape. It differs from other books by setting forth an organized way of teaching writing inductively. And by *inductively* we mean that writers discover not simply a personal experience but a coherent set of essential skills, and discover them in the act of writing.

If we expressed our ideas as a manifesto, we would say our book proposes:

- The assertion that elemental skills are teachable.
- The promise that to learn skill is to take on power proper to us.
- Ways to begin with writing rather than with teachers' analytic conclusions.
- A way of teaching elemental skills as a whole set so as to save time and effect lasting change.
- A core of useful work that can't be done wrong.
- Raising writing to skill by putting process to work with its coordinate, product.
- The development of skill not by drill but by incremental repetition.
- Consequential syllabi rooted in principles and developed without waste.
- The growth of expository writing as a literary skill through assignments designed as literary structures.
- The return of teaching to teachers, as writing to writers, by counting on teachers' own skills as writers and expert readers of literature.

The principles in this are not new. Principles can never be new; only radical consistency in working them out can be new or make a difference. Consistency implies chosen limits. Here is how we would contrast our limits with those other teachers choose.

We might begin by agreeing that learning is economically based on method and order, repetition, discovery, and success. But method and discovery are usually found to be incompatible.

Most teachers assume that a systematic way of teaching makes an analysis of the material to be learned and of what students don't know, decides on an order of priority or of difficulty, and then presents the material in that order step by step. The difficulties of this way are accepted by conscientious teachers because it is thought to be the only systematic way.

The difficulties are that it rides over individual differences, that everything depends on explaining the teacher's analysis, that it orients itself by what students don't know, and that the steps are valid only if learners are homogeneous. Despite its difficulties, this way of beginning with the material and teaching it as a subject step by step will always be the way most systematic teaching is done, because for university-trained people, it's easier to make the general particular than it is to make experience coherent and negotiable.

But the requirement that students be homogeneous so that material will be easier to teach will always provoke reactions in societies which value democracy. In a writing class this requirement means twisting things around to make writing the subject of the course, while the student writers, the true subjects, become objects. There is nothing to be gained, however, by reactions which turn simply to spontaneity and impulse. The small muscles are valuable, but not for long. Impulse has no staying power; step by step survives.

This book presents another way of learning systematically which makes a resource of individual differences and what students know, not step by step but by beginning with the whole and repeating it incrementally. The whole must be the nucleus: the constituent elements, related as a set. The method is incremental repetition; the process is developing the nucleus (growth). Repeating an elemental structure with individual differences — among different writers and within each writer's different experiences — leads to individual and systematic development.

But the elemental always looks simple-minded to the inexperienced writer or teacher — perhaps even to those sensitive to prestige. The elemental *is* simple. It constitutes. And it passes the initiative for completion and development to the learner. Mastery — or even endurance — depends on the habitual exercise of the elemental. Skills are neither process nor product, but the power to carry on one and achieve the other. So a course of writing such as we propose, consisting of a set of elemental skills (the potency), a set of exemplary shapes (images of the product), and ways to repeat, as a set, writing/reading/listening/observing/rewriting (the process) can profit writers at any level of experience, whether they are ninth graders or professional writers — or teachers who would like to teach and write better.

The first chapter is an overview of what we teach and why. Most of the following chapters are generally practical. Chapter 15 is concretely practical: a day-by-day bringing of essay writing into practice in the greenest writers. Two chapters step back from practice to take a more detached view of teaching: "Reading Writing" and "Polar Powers: Abstract & Concrete." We use the *we* of our agreement throughout the book, but drop into *I* where it is occasionally appropriate. We have used *he* and *she* in alternate chapters for any general reference to the single person. Since it seems condescending to identify literary references as we go along, we have indexed them for the reader's convenience.

Prefaces must be acts of thanksgiving. We thank:

- our students for what they taught us about writing, mind, and the varieties of experience;
- our colleagues who understood us right away with welcome and prolific intelligence, especially Betsy Kaufman and Bette Weidman;
- colleagues who were curious and brave enough to try it, especially Dominic Yezzo and Virginia Hlavsa;
- Leo Rockas for his *Modes of Rhetoric* and for himself, exemplar of kindness and intelligence;
- colleagues who kept saying, "But *why*?" "But *what* difference does it make?" until we articulated what and why, especially Bob Lyons, Sandra Schor, Don McQuade, and Sue Shanker.
- our team teachers for their right good will and for helpful shop talk, especially Margaret Shirk, Sandra Brettler, Kate Sotiridy, and Catherine Deen (who made our ideas her own);
- Mimi Eisenberg for superior typing even on short notice;
- the Fund for the Improvement of Post-Secondary Education, and its embodiment in Robert Fullilove, for a two-year grant to the Queens English Project, which, among its other deeds, disseminated and tested our principles and some strategies. Marie Ponsot taught writing seminars not only to Queens College colleagues, but also to public high school chairpersons and teachers who transferred them into practice in their own ways in classes at Beach Channel, Flushing, Grover Cleveland, John Adams, and John Bowne high schools;
- Barbara Richter for her investigations of the place in exposition of metaphor and other imaginative work;
- our parents for the start of everything and for nurturing us in the love of language, and our children for having made us parental and for trying to take away our selfish hearts;
- Neal Bruss for being the clear mind, the imagined reader for whom several chapters were rewritten;

- Ann Berthoff for spontaneous and noble help when the bottom drawer was about to swallow it up;
- Robert Boynton for being his own man and the right man: a lover of literature and teaching.

Contents

1 | Elemental Skills

Writing is one of the great human pleasures and is done in the energy of that pleasure. There is great professional pleasure in teaching it, especially in its beginnings.

Yet the difficulty and stresses of teaching writing to inexperienced students seem to be the facts of doing it. Students who come in knowing how to write, leave knowing how to write. But the students we labored over, when we meet them later or when our colleagues meet them, appear to have gone right back to their old ways. Our increased efforts — whether to be more kindly and enthusiastic, or to work harder and make students work harder at writing — always seem to run against student passivity or the shortage of time in one semester to work any real change.

There are inert students, and no semester is long enough to accomplish all we desire. But we want to separate the passivity we can't do anything about, the shortage of time we can't control, from what we can change. It is right to begin with the problems that seem most antithetical and external, so that we can understand more truly which are really internal and within our power to change. To begin with, we want to get more learning time out of the time we have. Though we can't slow the passing sun, there is a sense in which humans invent time; and better ways of working re-invent time. Here's how we do it.

We cut out the time for this:

1) Explanations and instructions. (That eliminates writers' "doing it wrong." How do we know that we aren't laboring away to correct faults that our assignments have induced?)

2) Class discussions. (That eliminates a class divided into those who can/will talk and those who can't/won't.)

3) Teacher-selected subjects and topics. (That eliminates arbitrary class apathy about subjects, and student failure to prepare assignments because they "couldn't think of anything.")

in order to have time for this:

1) For writers to work inductively (from the experience we design) and imaginatively (from their own images of the models we present).

2) For writers to read all their writing and write observations about what they hear.

3) To assign structures that pull writers' subjects out of their minds.

4) Teacher-selected texts.
(That eliminates unnecessary reading problems.)

4) For writers to learn how to pay attention to their own and their colleagues' writing. Writers write their own "texts," and in studying them learn the vocabulary of literary criticism.

5) Teacher emphasis on "good" writing.
(That eliminates writer paralysis.)

5) Writer emphasis on good writing.

6) Drills, exercises, workbooks, anything that isn't writing.

6) For writers to acquire the habit of writing by practicing a core of writing that can't be done wrong.

7) Teachers' analytical criticism.
(That eliminates writers' attempts to form their own syntheses out of someone else's analysis.)

7) For the formation of the writers' authority over their own writings: comparing their own writing with the writing of others, and drawing inferences from the observations they hear and make.

In general, we saved the time it takes to do all our work as separate tasks: work on grammar, paragraphing, reasoning, reading, explaining, starting, stopping, changing.

We freed all this time by and for doing all our work as a whole set of skills, shifting emphasis whenever writing/reading required it, and moving forward in incremental steps. After the first week of classes, we introduce nothing new; the rest is development.

How can we facilitate writing? The best way to make something easy is to make it a habit. If we cut out everything in class except the practice of essential skills, we could practice them enough to make a difference. The experienced writer too needs the elemental, though he has mastered it, in the sense that it works from within as the initiating power of his writing. By what characteristics do we know these elements?

An elemental skill 1) can be practiced directly, 2) can be repeated, 3) perfects itself through use, 4) without being measured, and 5) proliferates.

1) To be done directly means without any explanation, lecture, discussion, or persuasion. It is the need to work directly that drives teachers to set exercises in work books. But such work, though direct enough, is not writing.

2) The elemental is repeatable. Skills must be practiced, and we work by practicing them.

3) Elemental skills perfect themselves through use — as everyone knows who has watched a baby learn to walk.

4) . . . perfect themselves through use without being measured. An elemental skill cannot be done wrong. Its products can be measured, but the skills may not, because skill is potency.

5) Skills truly elemental proliferate. The sustained balance on two legs that achieves walking may also accomplish running, skipping, jumping and leaping, climbing and descending, vaulting, dancing, uncountable skills, among which some have counted thinking. Moreover, skills, being essentially constructive, are not essentially remedial. Skills develop us and develop out of our ongoing life.

Teachers who skip the practice of these skills and work only with the product are working with experienced writers, or they must supply the absence of the writers' power directly with their own, and present the art of composition as a study by lectures, composition texts, explanations, persuasion, or discussion.

Some teachers assign the process of writing an essay and spend the semester completing two or three short essays. They lecture about the process. But the process of essay writing still assumes the elements of writing, and — in fact — such assignments mean that teachers exercise still more control over students' writing, encroaching on the writer's initiative even in the forming process, and extending the students' passivity back into the realm of thinking itself. Moreover,if the process takes up most of the semester, and the products are few, teachers must grade the process itself. What the norm is for evaluating process, we don't know, but it looks as though it would be moral rather than intellectual.

The desirable condition, as we see it, is to use the class periods to practice together the elemental skills, and to assign for homework a respectable number of essays (one a week for beginning classes), most of these to be rewritten, a process which only the writer can supervise, for a grade, which only the teacher can properly give.

We may seem to have got away from the idea of time, but we must not talk simply about clock time but about mind time, which expands when writers are active and diminishes when they are passive. The problems of the passivity of students and of the shortage of time are really one. The solution to both is the same: shifting from the passivity of the student to the activity of the writer.

Here are the five elemental skills for writers. The first two are the central ones.

1) Prolific writing: generates and sustains writing. Writers need the prolific power, where language may be pleasure and play, in order to begin writing at once, and to get out a body of language in which to find the true language they need for the work at hand. Practiced, prolific writing keeps language and perceptions flowing past the fidgets, self-distractions, and bogeys that the mind occasionally throws out when it doesn't care to work.

2) Beginning writing for others with the whole structure. The *whole* is the imagined form, the image or plot of any composition. One might begin with the structure of the sonnet (in any of its various models), with an "Old Comedy" plot, a "Sleeping Beauty" plot, or an image (not a visual image but a mental vision, which has structure) like "the marvelous voyage," "the paradise garden," "the nadir." While there are no useful names for the structures of the discursive essay, there are plenty of structures.

The usual way to get at them is by class reading of book essays, class analysis and explanation, and student imitation. The difficulty here is that there is a hidden step. Students are not really asked to imitate what they read; they are to write the college expository essay. This may be a literary form, but if it is, we ourselves cannot teach it because we don't have any literary models for it in our heads. As students we had to write it, and we did this by trying to imagine the model teachers had in *their* heads for it and then writing it with as much dash and flow as possible.

Teachers can cut out the steps from reading to analysis in any writing course where they want more time for writing, or want to teach reading by writing, in this way: First, using their own knowledge of literature, they abstract useful structures for class essays. Second, they present these structures in seed sentences for writers to imagine in their own versions. For example, the structure of the passage in *Walden* beginning, "If I should attempt to tell how I have desired to spend my life in years past . . ." can be presented by the sentence: "Once I was _____; now I am _____." Writers imagine their own predicates and write seed sentences for an essay, like this: "Once I played soccer as if a fire were in me; now I study all the time and smoke two packs a day." Some sentences are almost models to begin with. Usually these are epigrammatic and need only a slight revising or recasting to serve as models. "A man sits as many risks as he runs," suggests a three-part structure: "Risks: running them, sitting them."

The idea of epigrams points the way to the oral tradition of literature, the seminary of structures, where the forms of written literature come from in the first place. And glancing at this tradition reminds us that this is a body of literature all our students have in their heads and bring with them along with their native language into class. It is the same ready compendium of structures for composition that it ever was.

It's a congenial task for teachers to work out useful models for discursive essays from oral literature. Fables, riddles, sermons, curses, epitaphs, prayers, anecdotes, proverbs, spells and charms, laws, invective — all are quintessential structures. We present in some of the chapters that follow structures that we have developed models for, tested and organized into courses of writing.

We say that these two skills are central because they represent the polar powers of language, which must belong also to writing: plenteousness and the structuring power of language. Polar they are certainly; one won't support a writer long without the other.

3) *Making observations and separating them from inferences:* a skill essential not only to writing but to the successful working together of writers. Writers read everything they write to their colleagues and learn from each other. The teacher holds writers to the requirement of publicly recognizable observations.

We do this first by banning all adverse criticism, because it creates competition and stress. These conditions are appropriate for heroes but antithetical to community. Writing is not heroic work, just one sort of ordinary enterprise. Essentially, however, class criticism is impertinent because criticism pertains to the author.

What we ask for from those who listen to the essays is written observations, not opinions, not even legitimate inferences. Authors can draw their own inferences when they realize what listeners have remembered and noticed. By *inference* we mean a statement like, "The essay is sentimental." By *observation* we mean a statement like, "Many words in the essay name emotions." Because observations are true and limited, they help writers. The obligation to write observations teaches listeners to pay attention to writing.

4) *Writing both abstractly and concretely:* encourages keeping to perception (rather than generalization) as the ground of writing. The concrete is the perception of sense; the abstract is the perception of structure. Encouraging perception is the elemental way all writers exercise and strengthen imagination, "the prime agent of all human perception."

5) Rewriting: is the "fallen power," the skill lost to writers who go to school, because in schools it is always used remedially. (We are distinguishing between re-writing and the more drastic re-vision, a writing that represents a seeing-again.) Writers need rewriting in order to think about the most important parts of their essays by recasting key sentences to open up or unpack their meaning. Writers try new orders or patterns, new words, or perhaps, as Leo Rockas suggests, a conversion of abstract to concrete, or concrete to abstract, to keep the blood flowing through the heart of what they mean and support the growth of the idea they have in mind.

All other writing skills are perfections of these skills.

How is it that these skills work directly for writers without the sort of explanation we are giving here for readers? We discuss techniques for making them work in the chapters that follow. Most of us begin something unaccustomed by trying the very techniques that an experienced person has tried; but as we sense the interplay of skills, we develop our own techniques to suit our own timing and our experience of how we ourselves help writers.

But before techniques, there are principles that make the skills work. We don't call these "learning theory," because there is nothing theoretical about them. But they are principles: that from which the rest proceeds. They test the actual practices and techniques teachers develop. Whenever, for example, a technique becomes what Blake calls "The Accusation of Sin," it invades the principle that the practice of skills cannot be done wrong and abrogates itself as a useful technique. Or whenever techniques, even for a kindly purpose, turn these practices away from their imaginative foundation, away from perception to passive instruction, or away from what constructs literature to the remedial or therapeutic, they cease to be techniques for the teaching of these skills.

1) The practice of these skills cannot be done wrong. The final version of the essay is going to be judged and graded. But the class training that enables writers to compose that essay is a process whose products are free.

Practicing that process is what is right. Error-free work in class enables all writers to work, each at his own capability. One can't expect even good students to practice anything wholeheartedly in fear and trembling.

2) Writing is energizing, pleasure-full, self-evidently constructive. (As a principle, this reason comes first, but psychologically the fact that these practices are free comes first.)

The pleasure for writers of rousing the mind by writing is as direct as feeling the sun on your cheek in April. I have seen a teacher who knew how to teach classical Greek enroll a class of 25 students, work them to the top of their bent every day, and bring them back for the second semester, though most of them were accounting majors who had signed up in the first place because they knew a little modern Greek and thought the class would be easy. That was their mistake — not so much in thinking it would be easy, but in thinking that taking it easy could compare with the pleasure of learning.

3) All these practices are limited. We set a lower limit, which in a way is our limit, as if we said, "I only have five minutes to give you to do this." We say, "You write as many observations as you can in five minutes." Lower limits are supporting and liberating: we can do anything for 20 minutes, even if it's writing without stopping.

4) Practicing even one skill of a whole set makes the others easier to come at. For example, structures enable writers to find their material and listeners to make observations about completed essays. Structure makes rewriting easier for the writer.

5) What makes this practicing possible right on the spot is that everyone (including the teacher) is writing. A kind of alive concentration expands the time in the room then. ("There is a moment in each day that Satan cannot find.")

6) The variety of skills means that different writers find in themselves different aptitudes. It frequently happens that a poor essay writer has an excellent small skill. One such student, for example, turned out to be a cracker-jack rewriter. I had to laugh with delight whenever I saw one of his golden sentences on the board. Other writers were minded to try parallel construction and images when they saw what he could do with them.

But though success and talent are encouraging, we keep our eye on the main point: it is steady practice, the creation of a body of skills, that makes writers. We all know those who write well who are not writers. "Just as in the Olympic Games, the prize does not go to the strong and beautiful but only to those who enter the games — for it is some of those who win the crown; so those who act win, and rightly win, the good and noble things in life." (*Nicomachean Ethics,* I, 8, 1099a)

The teachers' part is that we are trained students of literature. Because we know what literature is, we ought to be able to set up an elementary writing course on elemental literary principles. (cf. Frye, "Elementary Teaching and Elemental Scholarship," *The Stubborn Structure,* 90.)[1] We bring to our students' writing all our reading of literature — not to pick amateurs apart, but to help them define how their work is part of the literature of our language. We don't have to starve ourselves of literature just because we are teaching inexperienced writers. We can use all we know to teach them. But *not* directly.

All the things we know can be submerged, implied in the skills we teach, embodied in the conduct and organization of the class hour, the structure of each assignment and of the course of assignments, and in our reading of student writing. When we have submerged what we know into a course of training in writing, it isn't visible any more as coming from us, from a distance that has to be explained to writers. It is present, as a body of experience for them to work through. In this way it is not the teacher whose wonderful labors carry students through the course. Nor the wonderful class of responsive students who carry the teachers through their labors. What carries us all is the structure and power of language and literature.

This brings us to the question of motivation. We have never thought it possible to "motivate" others. But we are always asked about motivation, and this is the right point to address it. All composition texts, we notice, start out with arguments intended to persuade students that what is coming will be good for them. But any elementary good is self-evidently good.

Susanne Langer gives us a useful definition of motivation:

> The only way an external influence can produce an act is to alter the organic situation that induces acts; and to do this it must strike into a matrix of ongoing activity, in which it is immediately lost, replaced by a change of phase in the activity.... This indirect causation of acts via the prevailing dynamic situation is 'motivation.'[2]
>
> (*Mind,* I, 283)

This suggests that the writing teacher's real job is not to "motivate" students but to make writing prevail. We do this by setting up a matrix of ongoing activity: the practice of the essential writing skills. Now comes the external influence in the form of assignments which we have abstracted from literature and present as models. These strike into the matrix of working skills, in which they are immediately lost (as external influence — the teacher's idea) because each writer takes the model and imagines his own version of it. The next change of phase is that the working skills become an essay, then the essay read to others, the essay observed, the essay rewritten, and, if we are all lucky, the essay revised.

It would certainly be hard to persuade students that writing is a good when they look around them and see how little a part it plays in what they often call "real life." The ten years we have been working on the ideas of this book have seen the disappearance of the customer business letter. We have been called by a "prestigious" brokerage firm and asked to give an *oral* recommendation for a prospective employee. Students won't often meet good writers in college. And as for writing classes, what actually goes on in them every day? Talk and more talk. What can anyone say to students about the importance of writing that the very conduct of these classes does not cry out against? No. The implicit lesson of such classes is clear: "Writing teachers aren't writers and don't know how to write. They just talk about writing and teach their students to talk about it."

But if we said to students: "I would give you a skill, a power over yourself. You will have authority over it. No one will ever be able to take it away from you. It's an ordinary thing, a human thing, like learning to talk, and you already know most of what you need to do it. You learn it in the company of others. And at every step of the way to learning it, the power of it will be there as part of the pleasure of learning it." How many takers do you think we'd get? Of course, the productive good of writing is thinking. But we don't say either of these things to writers. Any elemental good is self-evidently good.

The key to all we have said is this: for the sake of the integrity of both teacher and writer, we begin with the whole.

Negatively, that means we do not begin with analysis presented in lecture or explanation. A person need not become a student before becoming a writer. Even the sequence: reading/analysis/imitation assumes that analysis puts the model in mind. But it never did that yet. The model perceived is the image. The imagination, the power to make images, puts the model in the mind. To begin with the whole, then, means to begin with the imaginative synthesis of the writer.

Behind this, and what keeps it from being random or arbitrary, is the whole with which the teacher begins: the whole tradition of literature in English, as it bears on the whole purpose of the expository essay, as submerged in the structure of assignments forming the body of the writing course. We could not expect writers to work inductively unless there were a deductive framework that selects and supports their experience. To say that teachers submerge their knowledge of literature in the framework of a course of writing means that they too have imagined what they know, realized it in one of its visible forms.

What follows is one such form: what we have imagined and practiced to help inexperienced writers master fundamental writing skills. The heart of this (Chapter 15) is an intensive writing course described in a week-by-week, hour-by-hour model in which writers draw entirely on their own experience, learning as they write how much there is to their lives after all and how much skill makes of a life.

In the book we give both principles and practice, not because one is binding on the other, but in the interest of laying all our cards out.

> Es geht auch anders
> Aber so geht es auch.
> (You can do it other ways
> But you can also do it this way.)

Our principles express the consistency of how we teach writing. Our deepest conviction is that we are not different from our students in any important way. We have tried to make our teaching of writing conform to our experience of writing.

2 | Structures: The Fable

In ordinary terms, to know about something is to have experienced it particularly, often enough so that the mind senses in it the form which it conceals and recognizes it by that form. Beneath the experiences of what we know by it, the form recurs. The richer our experiences, the better we can detect the form, even when concealed in instances of marked intricacy or brilliance. Often the mind is satisfied to sense the presence of an underlying form without acting to abstract and recognize, even to itself, what it senses.

Sometimes we go a step further. From any set of experiences, the mind may choose to derive and distinguish the idea of that hidden form. We may see what it is that underlies the similarity among the experiences and enables us to view them as members of a set.

When we want to tell someone else about that idea, we find that memory has stored it in words that are few compared to the many it would take to narrate even one of the experiences from which it was derived. As a way to organize and memorize experience, our minds search out form, not only in objects (oak, apple, beech: tree) but in common actions (the washing of hands, perhaps, or sharpening a knife, giving a party, or driving a car) and simple estimates (unfairness, joking).

That mental act is what is meant, we suppose, by the truisms, "We learn from experience," or "Experience is the best teacher." And for writers there is the corollary, "We write best when we write about what we know."

Writers are formalists. There is only by courtesy any such thing as informal writing. Alphabetic letters are forms assigned — over millenia of human consciousness by heaven only knows what alchemy of mind — to signal certain sounds. They are learned as abstract symbols for concrete vocal utterances by those who are entering upon literacy. Words are forms, imploded units of repeatable, recognizable, memorable meaning. Writing is a mystery, but that mystery is not amorphous. It abounds in active forms and conventions.

We realize that we are talking about matters to which specialists in disciplines narrower than literature have devoted competent and systematic thought. We are not developing an epistemology, a psychology of knowledge, or an anthropological report on the transmission of culture. What we want is to describe here, as eyewitnesses, in an ordinary way, what is apparent about one kind of knowledge in ordinary experience.

"Form," you might say. "Does it mean shape? pattern? structure? design? order? organic wholes? virtual life? force fields? a web, a net, a cluster, a fruit, a whole?" Yes. It means whichever of these terms you find to be the least exclusive. We want to avoid collision with special systems, but by speaking more commonly than they, not by creating jargon of our own.

Hugh Kenner says, "We allude to the 'structure' of just about everything, from a Shakespearean song to Jefferson's foreign policy, heedless of the intuitions bottled up in the word Structure." We too allude to structure, because of how much it does bottle up of what we observe about reading and writing. We will try to decant from the bottle with steady hands, knowing we've had to guess at how many glasses we should set out.

Writing teachers are concerned with a humming mandala of structures. The semester has a structure. Each class and each class meeting has a structure. The human mind, the English language *langue et parole*, literature as a whole and in its each instance, have structures.

We cannot afford to ignore any of these in teaching writing. The semester, the class, and the classroom hour are so submerged in experience we seldom think to separate out the shapes of their structures, so well do we know how they work. Yet we may now and then separate them out, first to assent to or adapt them by choice rather than blindly; second, to make our conscious minds attentive to better ways to use them. In actual practice, as far as students are concerned, they remain submerged.

The structures of written language are our central concern. Clearly, the structures of literature operate at full strength only when submerged in the written work. It is there that they are organic to the virtual life of the work. Once a writer knows by experience the live literary structures submerged in what she has written, it is useful for her to separate them out, first to assent to them and second to imagine better ways to use them.

How we teach what we perceive about structures is governed by one principle: To discover a structure where it underlies experience is to fix it in the active memory as a ready implement.

We therefore must stand out of the light, so that our students may make their own discoveries, from their writing and that of their peers, about what they know of structure and what they can do with it. So wherever possible — and taking thought usually makes it possible — we keep the structures we have chosen to teach submerged. We ask students to write papers which exploit a single structure, without first giving them rules or hints or definitions or descriptions or examples of the structure, or convention. We know no two papers will be alike, and we want the particular piece of writing that each writer will make of the form. We want the group to hear each different piece and experience the same embodied structure over and over in their own and their colleagues' papers. Only after that kind of repetition are we certain they are ready to derive and articulate the singular structure that the many-voiced papers contain.

The Fable

In a writing class, three ways of working at writing begin at once: structured writing, free writing, and immediate response to these as students read them aloud and make observations on what they hear. They are equally important; they parallel and implement each other. Their effects on writers overlap, yet they stress three different aspects of writing which are enabling and teachable.

We want to bring the structures of literature out of our students' writing and into daylight, under their conscious control. We want them to discover what they can do with what they (not their instructors) know about the larger shapes of effective language.

So we start where literature starts, with some of what literature records of the structures of oral tradition. Among the orally developed structures we have tried are those of the fable, the parable, the curse, the complaint, the riddle, the song of praise or aversion, the myth, the romance, the cautionary tale, the catalogue.

We who teach have, of course, encountered and recognized these forms in the literature, but that is not where we expect students in a writing class to find them. Instead we plan, while keeping them submerged, to evoke them in the students' own writing where students will themselves discover them.

This chapter, therefore, describes how we move: through developing awareness of the need for structure by means of these strong and classic shapes, to structures that incorporate choices of the kind everyone is accustomed to make, but argued from evidence, inference, and conscious awareness of them.

Since the how and the why of this all-at-once juggling act are not more separate than are, say, body and mind, these chapters on structures describe our practice along with our rationale for it. We trust they explicate each other. (And if you think the details of practice in these first pages rudely inclusive, you will be cheered to find the net of rationale knotted no less fine and cast to no less a depth. We have exacted explanations of ourselves, hoping to write the kind of book we have wanted to read — full and ready. We intend to capture not just the notes for a lecture at a professional conference but the germinal part of such meetings, the queries and answers after speeches, the exchanges and arguments over lunch and dinner.)

The two orally developed structures we always use are the fable and the parable. We have found them efficient — that is, they do many useful things at once. On the first or second day the class meets, we introduce the fable. Samples of fables are among the earliest and most widespread products of imagination, and even the oldest of them exhibit great literary sophistication. But once again, it is not to the rich literature of fables that we go with our students; later for that. To start, it is we who teach who benefit from being possessed of experience with that literature. Nor do we draw directly on this experience to describe or announce the structure to our students. Instead, we use it to induce in them the little labor of composing a fable. We start where they are able, though probably not conscious of ability. We know that they already contain the shapes and elements of fables. They are plainly visible, not only in literature but no further off than our human minds.

The fable is a two-part structure, of which each part is itself a literary structure. The first part is concrete, a dramatic dialogue; its other function is to demonstrate the second part. The second part is abstract, an aphorism; its other function is to sharpen the focus of the dialogue, making by analogy a memorable statement about it.

Through experience in writing and listening to their colleagues' fables, students can expect to recognize and use these literary and rhetorical elements: the fable; the concrete; the abstract; plot; dialogue; aphorism; conclusion. (Like all literary forms, the fable offers material which can be classified in many and mixed ways.)

But we have said that, as a matter of principle, we want to keep such nomenclature out of sight in our own teacherly minds where it belongs, until writers have enjoyed the discovery of structures in their own work. This is how the structures are submerged, so that a sense of the structures of the whole and of the parts may emerge unannounced from the reading of a classful of various embodiments:

We begin eliciting the fable by a diversionary tactic. We give a lesson in punctuation, in how to employ the standard graphic signs — quotation marks, commas, and paragraphing — used in punctuating dialogue. Few students are certain of how to do this; it must be learned by rote. So this small lesson has a usefulness of its own. The class session is still very young when we have decorated the blackboard with models of where to put graphic symbols in direct quotation.

We then say that we'll practice using the graphic signals by writing a few paragraphs of imaginary dialogue. "Imagine," we say, "that, in the world of the imagination, it is the middle of the night in the middle of the countryside through which a road runs. A horse is coming down the road, and he meets a bear. For your first paragraph, write what the horse says to the bear."

After writing (and we too write, as always, what we ask students to write in class) we say, "Now for paragraph two, write what the bear says to the horse."

That done, we say, "In paragraph three, write what the horse says to the bear."

We then say, "All of a sudden a storm breaks out — lightning, thunder, rain. Write a sentence or two about that for paragraph four."

We write, then say, "Now what does the bear say to the horse? Make that paragraph five."

Having written, we say, "For one last paragraph, paragraph six, write what the horse says to the bear."

Finally, we ask them to read over to themselves what they have written. Then we say, "Now skip a couple of lines, and write, 'The moral of this fable is:'. Take a few minutes to think it over, and write a moral."

We usually put "The moral of this fable is:" on the board, because we don't expect them to know why a colon is useful here — but using it helps unobtrusively to show its function.

As they work on a final sentence, a sense of the accomplished structure begins to dawn in the group. We do not discuss it further until all the fables have been read and listened to.

It's noteworthy that we have never had a class in which more than one or two people did not know what "the moral of this fable" ought to be like. And those two people are usually habitual question-askers whether of the anxious, the time-consuming, or the attention-getting kind. Sometimes students will ask if they may change or add something to the story to make it more apt or finished; of course they may.

At this point, students know they have really written something. A few are looking eager to show someone else what they have done. Since we will need energetic attention if we are to deduce and absorb principles of langugage from their virtual life in fable, we welcome this surge of energy from within. We ask someone to read her piece to us.

In hearing each other's fables, we take our time. We don't stop for comments on this first set of readings; we just sit in a circle and listen to stories like ancient kings and queens.

We try to have a first reading from everyone during that very first session and ask everyone to hold onto her fable for further exploration in later sessions.

Before we begin to talk together about each story, we talk, or write non-stop, briefly, about what it has been like to write them. Indeed, it would often be hard to avoid such talk, which springs up among students who have experienced, memorably, that first pleasure of structure, the sense of closure, with which we recognize the completion of a whole. Even while some will not be certain they have done what the instructor wanted, or done it well, they will be quite certain they have done something.

Usually one or two will say, when it is their turn to read, that they have not been able to find a moral that truly fits their stories, or that their stories are incoherent and go nowhere. Even so, they won't doubt that they have discovered in trying to write it the shape of a fable; that fact is revealed, of course, by their ability to compare what they see on their page with a mental model of what they should see there. They know how the dialogue should be shaped, and can bring it into conformity with their mental model. They know how the aphorism should work, even though they can't come up with a really good one.

As we read, in turn, listeners compare what they hear with what they have produced. Without being asked, they compare their own with the readers' solutions of the problems: getting character into dialogue; using dialogue to establish the level of satire and to set tone; deciding how the characters interact; taking advantage of stereotypical characters; managing the leap from story to moral. They have a personal basis for being more concerned listeners, colleagues really, engaged with similar experiences in similar enterprises with no loss of individual difference.

There are also the pleasures, then, of listening — as they recognize the accomplishments of each other's shapely little sets of sentences, and as they behold how different, how individual, how clothed in as many ways as there are writers each fable is; as they sense through its various incarnations the same structure repeated over and over, all but it changing each time. These are the pleasures that expand above that pleasure we all take in being told stories.

The fable by its very design calls out for attention to the language that implements it. Fables produced from the initial paragraph-by-paragraph submerged structure do not, usually, display the fable at its full brightness. But completed, they afford a shock of recognition or discovery which for most writers imprints the nature of a fable and exhibits the two interrelating essential parts so clearly that they can go on working confidently. They can, for instance, rewrite their first effort. Better, we can ask them to use the same formula, of dialogue between two animals interrupted by a minor cataclysm, to write new fables on their own; indeed, it is a rare class of twenty in which one or two do not spontaneously go home and write more fables without being asked to. That's because they have newly acquired control of the sturdy basic structure; because that structure makes evident its correspondence to the mind's first and commonest move in understanding what it perceives, moving from concrete to abstract; because the very smallness of the structure works, and works in a literary way, to enable them to produce a satisfying, recognizable whole and produce it quickly, its few elements simultaneously present in the mind.

If we look without disparagement at a student's first raw incarnation of a fable, we see many things to do with it which will better the fable itself, confirm the writer's sense of structure, and add specific new patches to the area of writing under the writer's control.

Take the aphorism itself. By its concluding place in the structure, and by its nature as the smaller unit, it speaks loudly to everyone's artistic sense of completion, asking to be made as strong, as elegant, and as fit a capstone as the writer can devise. It is the easier of the two parts to perfect in itself, though it is the harder of the two to manage, not in itself, but in the way it fits to the whole dialogue.

Trying always to begin where our writers are most able, we leave the question of fit for later. We examine the aphorism and observe that it is in the shape of a sentence. No teacher of writing will at this point think, "Ho-hum, a sentence. . . ." The sentence is a block many new writers stumble over, many climb stifflegged in fear of error, and many travel round by way of one safe, tiresome (subject, predicate, period) rut. In its proper place, the sentence is the keystone from which all the arches of literature spring. And the rules and game-ground of the fable present the sentence in just the way we want to see it, as a literary form, with the need for its dense and enclosed interplay plainly exposed and ready to work on.

Here are two fables, the first by Philip Vitale written in class (an advanced class in writing nonfiction prose). They are chosen not as best or worst but as typical examples of this form everyone can compose.

"Oh my God it's a bear! You are a bear, aren't you?" said the horse.

"I'm a bear. And I know who you are; you're my dinner," said the bear.

"Don't eat me! I'm old and skinny. There's a big fat pig just around that curve back down the road. You should call him, and have him for your dinner," the horse said.

All of a sudden it was thundering and raining.

"Will he hear me?" asked the bear. "I do like bacon."

"Sure, you just have to throw back your head and yell louder than the thunder," said the horse. "You can do it. All you bears have great voices."

So the bear threw back his head and yelled, and the horse picked up his heels and galloped away.

The moral of this fable is: "Fools and their dinner are soon parted," or, "It is better for the bear to be hoarse than the horse to be bear."

The second is by Barbara Cross, written at home after two sessions of work on horse/bear fables in class (a most basic writing class, prefatory to freshman composition):

Alice Hen looked at the rooster passing the hen-house and said, "Just look at that rooster of mine. Isn't he the handsomest thing this morning?"

"What do you mean, your rooster? He's mine, and you had better keep off him if you want to stay lucky," said Sandy Hen.

"You better keep off him yourself. You don't, and you'll be hopping around on crutches — until I break your arms!"

Alice and Sandy were still wild and screaming over who the rooster belonged to when Farmer Jones came into the barnyard and chopped off his head so he'd be ready for Sunday dinner.

The moral of this fable is: "Don't waste time trying to determine if something belongs to you. Some things belong to nobody."

Before the reading of the second round of fables begins, we ask that the class listen carefully so they will be able to write freely for a minute or two, and then tell each reader what they have noticed about her work. We say that all responses are valuable but that the ones to sort out and express first are those that tell the writer what she has said and how she has said it. They readily acknowledge that a writer's first need is to know whether what she said has been heard as she intended. Further along in the sessions of readings and responses, we may suggest the same thing in other terms, asking that expressions of the audience's opinion — that is, inferences — be saved for later, after all the observations we can make have been made. Their expression creates a context for inference, we say, which helps us stick to the subject.

We have already said something of the sort when talking about ways to respond to prolific writing. (See Chapter 4.) Each time the work of the semester brings forth another round of readings, we recall and extend our emphasis on plentiful observation prior to expression of inferences. (See Chapter 5.)

One step in affording a more ample understanding of the terms is taken while we work on the fable. Once we have talked about the difference in how the dramatic dialogue and the aphorism work and have thereby set up the crucial notions of concrete and abstract, we like to take both terms a step further, suggesting that observations are to inferences as concreteness is to abstraction. We use expressions that underline this, e.g., "John, can you come up with another concrete observation about what Barbara read?"

We do this at the start of the semester, for many reasons, particularly because, although the fable well shows concrete and abstract as usable words for ideas, we do not want to restrict our students' view of them to dialogues and sententia. Turning them to account in a new way, almost at once, makes them still more useful and accessible.

True, we do not expect of everyone an immediate grasp of them in all their complexity. A student who has by the end of the semester a good working appreciation of their ramifications in her writing has done well for herself. We reinforce and escalate our use of their implications all semester.

Before Barbara read her fable, she declared that she had had trouble in writing the aphorism. She knew what she wanted it to say, but could find no phrasing that she did not deem awkward.

After hearing it, people found it easy to make observations on the dialogue; almost everyone could tell the story in its entirety, with especial relish for the retort about the crutches and the broken arms. Yet since hardly anyone could recall the moral, even make an assertion about what it had said, we inferred that her evaluation of the moral as weak was correct. We did not spend much time on it that day, but went on as other readers took their turns.

During the next class session, we asked who remembered Barbara's fable. Everyone did. She read it again, to build momentum by making present the vivid language of her vivid narrative. Then we asked everyone, including Barbara, to write a few morals in search of one that would really fit her story. There was plenty of head-scratching, but ten minutes later we were able to go round the circle, reading them.

Reading aphorisms aloud gives us another opportunity to put the brevity of the form to good use. Now and then, after a sentence is read and people are making observations about it, we write it on the board and say, very briefly and matter-of-factly, something about the grammar behind the graphics of punctuation. (E.g., "Since this is a sentence — here's the subject; here's the verb — it deserves a period at the end;" or, "I put a comma here because the conjunction, *and*, is coordinating two equal parts, and both parts could be sentences on their own; the reader needs to know that to read the second half right the first time.") We are not teaching here, what a sentence is in some definitive way (we do not know how to do that in a fashion that improves writing). We are reaffirming the shape of the sentence and the readers' marks which clarify it; these are phenomena to which students have been exposed all their lives. From this exposure to the underpinnings of the accomplished sentence, we are sure that at least the author learns something, and learns it better than she would in any less emphatic and personal way. We avoid "teaching" grammar by penalizing for errors; we try to teach it by confirming and extending what students already partly know, before calling formulae or rules into play.

Here are some of the results of our search for an aphorism to fit Barbara's story:

"If you fight with your friends, you will have no one for consolation" (an implication of one theme in the story).

"Jealousy is wrong. Sooner or later your lover will leave you anyway when he dies."

"Women should help each other instead of fighting, so they won't make silly mistakes" (good advice, drawn from the theme of the story).

"Beware of anyone who wants to sell you the Long Island Expressway" (a long mental jump from an idea about the story's theme to a witty equivalent for it).

We wrote these one by one on the board to demonstrate the correct graphics; and each time, after some comments had come from the group, asked if anyone could find still more elegant versions of them. The second was revised to, "Jealousy is a waste of time. Sooner or later your lover will leave you for death," (grimmer, more effective because more accurate in the first part and in the second, more elegant, especially in cadence). The third was revised to, "People who fight can lose the chance to be right," using the mnemonic and didactic finality of rhyme to phrase an abstract assertion; using wit to modulate the tone of the original good advice.

After that, it was Matthew's turn to read. He glanced up and said, "I don't know if this is right."

We said, "It can't be wrong. Read it and see."

He read, "To possess is not to own, and to enslave is not to master."

A splendid sentence! a leap of abstraction, with the second half still further abstracted not so much from the story as from the first half. We record it here not only to show what good things are possible but how fruitful such native eloquence can be for the class and as an opportunity for the teacher. (We know that most first efforts at aphorism are like Barbara's, but only some second efforts are as good as Matthew's.)

Borne up by the immediate murmurings of "Wow!" and Barbara's dreamy, "That's it!" and by our own exultation unconcealed, we put the sentence on the board, rapidly scribbled signals to show the balancing of its parallel structures, said a word in praise of its coordinating parts, and left off, so the other hearers could have their say. It was a cheering moment — that gorgeous sentence, and with it the obvious unanimity of recognition of its quality by the rest of the group. We have met those who are puzzled by our sense that the dazzle of literature can be produced and understood by people — any people — who are paying attention; this was one of the moments of confirmation.

It was also an irresistible chance to teach parallel structure, that most serviceable device, a kind of classifying of coordinate elements not beyond the reach of new writers or beneath the notice of experts. It is worth remarking whenever it appears. With an indigenous model of such quality, that class was perfectly ready to learn about parallel structure. Matthew's sentence taught it for us. It graced and braced many of their future papers.

Barbara's story differs from most students' early fables in the complexity of its implications, which prevented the production of aphorisms that were old saws. But clichés do turn up often. We usually ask, for every fable after the first, for as many morals as writers have time to invent — at least three. This helps students who are happy to establish the righteousness of their stories with morals that are either clichés or lifeless advice, since it gives us a chance to welcome what is useful in their impulse toward advice and clichés. We are genuinely glad to see them because they show the writer is on the right track. If she has found a cliché, it is because she has reached for the memorable, definite shape a fable needs for its aphorism — and clichés are so memorable they have died of it. We need only suggest that she go on to invent something memorable of her own, either making it more concrete by linking it more closely to her story (as Phil Vitale did, with his witty pun) or making it more abstract and less limited to her story, perhaps by deriving it from consideration of the true sense of the cliché. If she has found advice ("Women should help each other instead of fighting"), she shows she sees that the narrative is, indeed, exemplary; she needs only distance to avoid nagging and achieve analogy in her moral. Writing several versions gives distance from which she can see and express her sense of the story by using her mind in a different way. One sentence may advise or nag, but another express a cooler view of that very advice. In fable literature, the relation of aphorism to tale is an ironic one, by way of analogy; La Fontaine is by no means the only fabulist to multiply aphorisms to achieve increasingly witty levels of irony.

Fortunately, the desire for wit is catching; students can learn from their peers that one way to a good aphorism is through well-devised play with words.

The aphorism, its literary integrity displayed by its place in fable, repays the attention we pay it. It is so engaging we can spend several class hours working on it without boredom, fatigue, or other signs of anxiety.

The first result is that students write and rewrite until they know they have produced some good sentences. Real writing is always rewriting — a simple truism few new writers know. The aphorism helps them to learn it.

Play (in Huizinga's sense, of a game as ruled interaction on a given ground) with language is characteristic of what real writers do. New writers don't yet recognize the playing field though they stand in it. The aphorism, even more plainly limited than the whole fable, is a ground new writers can feel confident of at once. It is so small that the writer becomes a rewriter quickly; she sets down one version, and a few minutes later has finished a second and is at work on a third, practicing rewriting all the time. Working with an aphorism in close conjunction with fable, rather than with just any sentence, is desirable because it keeps the sentence alive instead of plucking it from its context, and because it calls clearly for some special qualities: close reading, concision, aptness, memorability, a certain imaginative reach, neat wit.

The aphorism in its smallness not only limits the game ground, it permits mental replay. Experienced readers like to savor language slowly, repeatedly, so they do not miss anything. Though we can't videotape what happens on the internal field where writing is played, the aphorism allows the writer to run the whole game carefully through her mind, slowing down the interaction, stopping it to catch and confirm effective moments. Spending a long, unwearied time on a small thing, she tries the tactics of verbal, mental, and rewritten rephrasing to achieve the sentence that will stand the most firm. She is practising the moves a good writer needs as she holds her set of words in mind and tries to find among the thousand alternative ways to say it a more excellent way.

The aphorism also, therefore, acts to break down that treacherous bar to decent writing, which is a simplistic sense that *quod scripsi, scripsi*. What they have written, some new writers cannot imagine changing. Perhaps through confusion over what their early training in writing was intended to teach, they treat their writing as an assignment to engage briefly in a continuous process — but a process which stops dead when the last assigned line is written. They then see it as a firmly finished piece, and they do not think or know how to alter it. Some even feel — perhaps prompted unawares by their inability to make changes — that to rewrite or review is dishonest, or disloyal to their impulse while writing. They are stuck, like Midas, with the useless fixity of what they have touched. Completion of a process has taken the results out of their reach and made them into an independent and irremediable product..

Writing is both process and product, of course, despite some offset from the vocabulary of other disciplines — psychology, linguistics, communications theory — which implies that writing is pure process. To teach writing, it is more useful and more consonant with experience to consider how a writer regards her work. She sees it alternately as process and product. "Process" and "product" are identifiable as views, neither definitive, that a writer takes of what she does.

Some contributory confusion comes from failure to separate writing, as in "writing it down," the process of putting marks on paper, from writing, as in "Joyce's later writings," where product is meant, from writing, as in *The Art of Writing Well,* where both process and product are included. We have, in this book, used all three meanings, taking care that the contexts suggest which sense we intend.

Writers at work shift constantly between sensing their words as process and checking them out provisionally as product. When they pause to go back, sound out, and evaluate a phrase or a chapter just written, they must see it fixed and stable as if it were a final product so they may decide whether to move it, cross it out, or let it stand; when they move forward again, carrying out their decision, they again treat the passage as part of a process. For instance, nonstop writing is almost pure process, yet in editing it or reviewing it as a resource we see it as product; writing the aphorism calls for exceptionally rapid shift of attention between process and product, and for strong emphasis on a product with a fine high finish. The ultimate revision of a piece of writing is a product, reviewed and confirmed as a product by the author's best judgment. To limit what a writer must do to the claims of process may be to exempt her from the privilege of standing responsible for her work.

Given the limits of a class session, the aphorism is a practical form with which to emulate these writerly steps. It demonstrates how many good ways there can be to say anything. From the liveliness of the demonstration, some students will deduce that most of writing is rewriting. This wisdom offers advantage and pleasure they can adapt to any sentence they will ever put down.

There is a remarkable fact which we have noted about even beginning writers of aphorisms that are developed as the second part of the structure of a fable: they almost never produce fragments or run-ons. The fable has proposed the aphorism in response to a strong demand for verbal as well as intellectual closure; writers reach in their minds for models of abstract thought enclosed in statement, and naturally come up with sentences. When they do so, we may seize the moment to applaud the energy-retaining power of syntax, rapidly pointing out the ways in which particular subjects and predicates confirm each other. No grammar text or teaching will work in isolation. Grammar should be shown first and last as something anyone can observe in the language she has, and not as something other people have put into a text for us to check our words against. Grammar cannot be taught so as to strengthen writing — or even to make it correct — unless it is learned in the context of writing within which we can at appropriate moments show it to act usefully and beautifully. While we are thus teaching it, students who see they want knowledge of one of the abstract schemes describing syntax and serving graphics can profit or at least not suffer from a good grammar book, even one with exercises.

To start the semester with the fable and extended inspection of the aphorism gives students something useful and enjoyable — rather than merely error-haunted — to look for when considering, with or without a text in grammar, the structures and punctuation of sentences. Whether to coordinate or subordinate, and how to do so, are — for instance — ways of dealing with mental constructs that are vital to sentences, essays, thought itself. A classful of aphorisms will offer many good chances for us to call attention to the advantages and techniques of both. We were able to discuss, in the session that produced Matthew's aphorism, several matters we would continue to encounter: coordination, subordination, verbs as substantives, parallel structure, something about linking verbs. We were thereafter entitled to use these words where fitting, both in class and in written comments on papers.

We need to be aware of our use of such special language. We use it when helpful, along with an appositive reminder of what we mean by it. To some classes we like to say that we use it for convenience, not hermetically or proscriptively, and we ask our hearers to stop us for explanation any time they are unsure of our terms.

In classes of expert writers, too, we practice this habit of naming the grammatical or rhetorical events we notice in what they have written. Good writers profit from the increased conscious control that comes with identifying (in the terms of one or another system of rhetoric or of grammar) material they can produce but have not yet identified as part of their *batterie de cuisine*. It seems that the good writer selects, quickly, from among many possible versions of it, what she will say; a conscious grasp of others' systematic names for what she may choose from does not diminish and may add to her speed and range.

After several weeks' attention to other matters, we return to the aphorism and spend another class session on it, for two reasons.

First is to underscore its memorability. We ask if anyone remembers the sentences we composed; we quote them to each other; we speculate once again on what qualities make some more memorable than others. We notice that these memorable sentences stand in a metaphoric or an analogous relation to the dialogue, reverting upon each other, as much by difference as by similarity.

By the time we are thus looking backwards, we have done enough other work to be ready to suggest another suitable spot for the carefully achieved expressiveness of aphorisms. We are preparing to write essays; naturally we talk about the fables' beginnings and endings, how they should sound, and what they should do. Since we know people in the class are able to rewrite for aphoristic elegance, we will be able to ask them to work on this or that sentence in their essays, particularly those at key points. Both opening and ending statements may profit especially from such consideration. What some instructional methods call a "topic" or a "thesis" sentence is, in fact, a hypothesis, expressed in a sentence which encodes, renews, vivifies the whole essay much as the moral does the fable.

Having begun with the whole fable and continued with close consideration of the aphorism, the next structure we examine closely is the dialogue. Everyone in the group has written, read aloud, and written and read observations about several fables. We have observed in them what features fable-dramas have: brevity, briskness, stereotyping of animals or of roles — the Butcher, the Little Girl — setting as a function of plot, all plot and no action, and whatever other inferences grounded on plentiful observation the class has come up with.

So we do not spend much time on rewriting fable dialogues. Instead we move on to another classic shape. We look for one where we found the fable, that is, where students are already able to write. We find it alive in the oral tradition of today.

3 | The Parable

It is supposed, we think mistakenly, that print has eliminated the practice of oral composition. We find it alive if unrecognized and unrecorded in many places, even in our print-and-picture urbanizing culture. We may safely call on it to generate writing that exhibits its forms and information.

One form in which this tradition flourishes is in the telling of family stories, the informal recounting aloud of how grandmother raised the boys alone, how great-uncle Mike ran away at sixteen and walked from Connecticut to North Dakota; how Dad made his first boss laugh; what happened the day mother and father met: memorable events, worn smooth in memory and retelling. By such tales adults convey to the next generation something of their sense of value and identity. The tales are sometimes cautionary, sometimes stimulating, always in a concealed analogic relation to some value — conforming to or defying conventional morality — which the teller offers the young he cares for as a key, drawn from his past to unlock their future. These family tales are, of course, a domestic variety of that most noble species, the parable.

Just as we had our students produce fables before we described them, so we have them write family stories while keeping submerged our own perception of them as parables. Until writers have produced it, contemplation of the nature of a parable and of its rich history is for the instructor, to ready him to read well the literature his students will offer.

So we step back a little, choosing among personal family stories those closest to the writer himself. We ask for the story of something in their very early lives, something that will perhaps become the kind of story they will use to convey values to their own grandchildren. We offer them choices, for we all choose differently in deciding out of which events to create the myths of ourselves. Besides, we know we must avoid even the appearance of assigning subjects for writing.

We ask them to write in class, as informally as if free writing, for twenty minutes — about three pages in ordinary handwriting — about their favorite special place when they were little, or about the earliest

27

memory they have of seeing their own faces, or about how they learned to write their name or memorize their address or read from a printed book or tie their own shoelaces or whistle.

We read the results aloud for the rest of the hour. Then we ask them to go home and write about one or two more of these experiences.

Once again, we go slowly when listening to the reading of this work. People have the right to expect that what they write will have an immediate and respectful hearing; with short pieces like these, that hearing comes best from the group of peers. Quite often, someone will ask if the reader will reread his work. This is usually a good sign and well worth the time it takes. If we are to respond to what we hear as we would to established works of literature, we know that understanding takes time. We also know how essential it is to make plenty of observations about the work, so each reader receives an observation from each of us. Almost always, we write freely about what we have noticed, taking two or three minutes to do so, then reading these notes. This ensures that everyone will have something ready to say, as we go round the room. It's true that all this takes time. But it is this very work for which class time is given us. And we have observed that a packed class session in which everyone is respected for taking an active part in cogent work is attractive to students. They know when they are getting something out of a class and seldom miss those classes in which they feel something happens.

We use the little self-affirming anecdotes from childhood as a first move toward reaching for more significant stories from family history. They are a practical context, because they bridge the jump from the dramatic mode of the fable. The points of view which dialogues express in fable are here, as in parable, embedded in a point of view, which leads to an embedded point rather than an explicit aphorism or moral. As in the fable, much of the material is directed to a practical, common-sensical, more particular kind of awareness, rather than pointed toward the selected and selecting principles of a system of values as in true parable.

The childhood anecdotes give the writer confidence that he can find, among all the data of his experience, data which together reveal more than they state, the data of significant stories. The material is interesting to the writer and his audience; it links them as it shows him to himself in a new way which others can take seriously and find interest in. It gives the group a glimpse of how the person is the style and how self-revelation need not be indiscrete. Besides, what creates community —

which writers need — is the giving of gifts; these anecdotes provide something imaginative for everyone to give.

After the new stories have been read aloud and discussed, we ask for another narrative that has a good chance of showing still better the characteristics of parable. We ask them to recall stories told by their grandparents (or, that failing them, their parents) about some event in their grandparents' lives. Should there be questions about the assignment, we try to avoid proscriptive answers; when asked, "What do you want to know about them?" we may say that we are not looking for just chronology or for plot or anything else topical; we mean them to try to remember stories someone in the family likes to tell about the past — maybe one that the family itself jokes about having heard too often. We think they will find they know such well-used stories — how grandma says grandpa learned to like her way of stuffing a turkey better than his mother's, why grandma decided to stay in school instead of starting to work at eighteen, how great-aunt Minnie liked champagne, why none of his sons would come into great-uncle John's business.

What we know, that our students may not, is that any concrete narrative which survives long in memory is a telling one, and what it tells, by analogy, is something central to the value-system of the rememberer.

We do not like to send students off with only the abstract directions for any assignment. Having given this one, for instance, we talk about it before the class ends. More than that, to make our hopes for it more clear and to forestall anxious questions, we ask everyone to write nonstop for just a few minutes about any family stories that come to mind. Such preparation is especially useful for this assignment, for which we have not a paradigmatic sentence or nuclear structure; we have given them only a locus in the mind where they can look for the material. It's a place not only in their minds, but in the minds of our culture. Jotting down notes in class focusses their attention on what they want to recall, so that they recall it better and quicker. It gives them something tangible to work from. After two or three minutes of writing, at least a few students will be ready to read their stories.

Sometimes, if there are only a few students with stories to speak of, we take an unusual step, as a way of compensating for the absence of a paradigm. We read what we have written as they were writing, a family story of our own — maybe the one about a turn-of-the-century child at a Christmas dinner who was brought out of dullness when her grandmother showed her how to snuff out a candle by pinching the wick yet not getting burned, how to find an elf-face on the split of a peanut, how to halve an apple the short way to uncover its central star; and told her that boredom visits only the foolish who can't see how entertaining a place their world is. In our house, the teller always ended by saying, "And I never forget it, either." The story is now four generations away from that Christmas child, still unforgotten. Its little parabolic point has gone discretely home, after the manner of parable, time and again. (Of course, the preceding sentence would not be a remark useful to those who have not yet rummanged in their memories and written their own stories. We want them to write for themselves, to discover both how a parable works and how much they already know about how a parable works.)

Having heard some samples, people are reassured that we are asking not for the impossible but for the ordinary. Parables and some other literary structures are like myths in that we are not accustomed to bringing them out into the light; we know them in an intimate way that takes knowing them for granted.

A side effect of this piece of writing often appears in what happens when students go home to do their homework. They ask grandparents to tell a tale over, or ask parents to help them recall half-heard stories. Then they listen well, having a structure for listening while they may to those who have much to say to them. Their sense of a writer's community is enlarged to include their own earliest listeners, too; for those at home whose stories are being written down may actively express, for the first time in years, their wish to read the finished versions. Every writer profits from an audience which invites him to show his work.

When the stories are brought in, we read them aloud, round the room, as we do with most of the writing the class produces. It's a great advantage for us to have the substructure presented in as many full-dress versions as there are writers. The awareness of a point or turning point that the writer of each story may have felt will have hinted to him that this is indeed a structured kind of writing; hearing the likeness amid variety of many parables quickly attunes his ear to what the structure is.

Having provided these experiences, we have done most of what we can. Students have given each other repeated opportunities to feel the way a parable turns back upon itself. They will have felt, a couple of dozen times in an hour, how a parable is a story that makes a point. They will also have felt how the point goes by analogy toward a value-system in which the other term of the analogy is located.

In making observations on the stories they read to each other, students will this time begin on grounds made familiar by work with the fable. The presence of concrete narration and the absence of an isolated, abstract moral are usually inferred first, the fable having established the vocabulary and shown that such matters are germane to the course. Then they may note memorable details and phrasing, characterizing action, or the dramatic moment in which the point of view, that produces a special perception of the event narrated, makes all the difference.

The point in a parable is a point of view, a perception enunciated by one of its characters. That character has authority because of where he stands. What he does or says shows that he is able to see the event differently, see what the other characters have not seen. What he says or does puts the event in the light of a new context, in which the connection of the event to a larger system of values is clearly shown, to the reader's surprise. One reward of the work on parables is this focussing on the point. Ability to imagine, discern, and clarify the point of what writers experience and write is another important writerly skill.

As the parable makes its point, it works analogically. Leo Rockas[3] tells us that analogy is a special form of comparison and contrast. This fine perception (so right that once he has said it we might think we always knew it, so well does it match what we do know) locates the parable within expository methods as one of the definitive ways of illustrating a statement or thesis.

We had used the parable both to get our students a logical step closer to writing straight exposition and to keep them conscious of how what composition classes call exposition (that complex, mixed, literary johnny-come-lately) is really real writing which they are able to do at will; but it took Rockas' insight for us to perceive the network which relates parable to exposition.

Some years ago, in earlier days of our search for ways to incorporate the energies born of doing real writing into the prescribed notions of freshman writing, we had used a simple and not unsuccessful method. We had students practice writing narratives based on personal experience, which we then showed them how to use as the middle, illustrative part of an expository essay. This method will get students to write, readily, well-organized samples of one kind of exposition. It shows them how to produce a simple abstract thesis which relation of a personal experience correctly and concretely demonstrates. The mode is definition, in which a narrative is serving as illustration. The discovery of an abstract set of sentences to express the theme of the anecdote gives the student his introductory paragraph. It also plainly gives the instructor an answer to the common query of those who consider personal writing somehow alien and inferior to exposition: "It's all very well to let them ('let' 'them') write about themselves, but how do you turn that kind of thing into exposition?"

The method works, especially if it follows practice with the fable and the aphorism, so that people have some idea of how to compose a few elegant sentences which express a thesis. It begins where students are able to do something, with autobiographic material for which the student is the best authority. It demonstrates, also, that a concrete event can exemplify an abstract (or perhaps general) thesis to produce a sensible little essay.

Its defects as a starting place are that it gives the student no help in selecting a suitably telling incident, or in shaping the order of the parts of his anecdote, or — especially — in seeing what about the anecdote makes it fit to generate or illustrate a thesis. It may produce impersonal personal essays, sometimes simplistic, banal, or unconvincingly insincere. It is a tour of perhaps excessive force. It may also produce, among many decent essays, too many papers tiresome in their generality, sameness, or triviality. (The first law of survival for teachers of writing is to give no assignment which evokes, for their close reading, set after set of tedious papers.)

The parable does not have these defects. Use of a narrative that is a parable has several advantages:

It comes, and it is obvious to the writer that it comes, from the writer's own mind, from what he already knows, from material over which his authority is patent.

It has a point.

It is ordered economically, telling just enough to make its point.

The point fits, and the rest of the story is in proportion.

It is discrete in what it attempts; the very shape of a parable is a parable that teaches how to limit a subject, how to assert modestly what an essay may modestly demonstrate.

It will help the writer to revise for the best expression of his material when it opens up a new and extracurricular audience for his writing: his present family may wish to read it; he can readily credit that it is work worth saving for his own grandchildren to read, so he rewrites for permanence rather than dashing off something to fulfill an assignment.

It meets our important criterion for all writing assignments in that it is exciting to work on, a pleasure to write and to read, a gesture in the forum of literature.

These are the reasons we follow the writing and inspection of fables and aphorisms with the writing and inspection of parables.

Of all the structures we want to fish for and identify in students' minds, so that their writing may be thereby informed, the parable is the one that most tempts the teacher to spoil its effectiveness by preliminary overdescription or too much literary talk after the event. At either moment, teacherly definition may imply "rules" and kinds of correctness irrelevant to the production or the enjoyment of writing. (There are plenty of rules within writing, but none of these external ones is any of them.) The temptation may well rise as a way to fill what may seem a vacuum in the suggestions for how to assign parabolic stories. The suggestions may seem vague enough to make a teacher apprehensive, and therefore ready to substitute literary or rhetorical rules and information for the absent definitiveness. We would hope that such a teacher would try what we suggest, as boldly as possible. We are not sure why, but eliciting parables as we have described it calls for a confident air — which we had at first to assume without quite believing students would indeed write what we hoped for. Yet time and again, they did; they do; it does work.

It is interesting that very many of our students' parables, especially those drawn from their elders' stories, are written not as straight monologues but as monologues enclosed in a context — of setting, situation, or character — which the student has sensed does not belong inside the monologue yet is gratifying to readers' pleasure and comprehension. The rightness of this literary decision — which we need not mention in assigning the work — we take to be confirmation of our sense that writers know a great deal about good literary conduct before they come to us. They also have a human concern with order and ordering, and an experiential knowledge (named and conscious, or not) of structures.

Plentiful writing of fables, aphorisms, and parables stimulates awareness of structure. By the random frequency of structures within free writing, free writing in an obverse way heightens awareness of structure, too. Students begin to see what kinds of question it might be satisfying to ask about what they read — how does it work? what are its parts? what structure holds them? How can I take this germ of an idea in my free writing and develop it until I have said something else, just as personal but more public, more alive independent of me? Will

Paul, or Linda, get the point? How can I structure it so they will both see what I mean?

Awareness that language is permeated by structures they know and can recognize and can employ at will is a priceless asset in a writing class. It is a consciousness shared by the members of the class, including the teacher, so it gives rise to a shared system of references and meaningful language that make each successive assignment easier to express. It is a literary consciousness and is suited to the work of the group as producers of literature, which is best read as a literary effort.

In that it is a special kind of sensitizing, sensitizing to the satisfactions of structure, it may correspond to the strong and structural element present in education from the earliest English prose through the 19th century, when the greatest part of schooling was in translation and composition in Latin, according to powerful conventions of form and meter.

For a view of how we now move from parables to expository essays, see Chapter 15.

4 | Prolific Writing

Prolific writing — that is, writing uninterruptedly for five or ten minutes to release thoughts and images into visible language, without pausing first to organize them into rational discourse — is a technique so fruitful and flexible that we find occasions for it in all our work.

Those who try it for themselves discover their own sets of reasons for doing it often and ways of turning it to immediate practical and imaginative use. The best way to understand what it can do is to do it. This is not surprising, since it is an approach to writing as a process, and process is notoriously more interesting to do than to hear described.

One of us had, like most writers, during a decade of earning a freelance living, done a kind of prolific writing often. It was called keeping a notebook, or scribbling, or jotting things down. But when I began to teach, I did not look to my experience. Rather, like most beginners, I took my first steps backward, and offered a tottering version of composition as it had been taught me years before. It included conscientiously ingenious assigned subjects; terms and rules of grammar drilled in rule-related exercises; and corrective rule-book abbreviations, ugly, hermetic, and firm, in the margins of students' themes. We rehearsed topic sentences and outlines and separate rhetorical methods of development quite apart from the thoughts in language on which these skills were to be imposed.

The classes were not a total loss. That was due partly to beginner's luck and enthusiasm and mostly to the astonishing willingness of most students to try to learn something from even the most opaque instructor. But most of their papers must have been as dull to write as to read.

Assigned a class in Creative Writing, I sat down to prepare for it and puzzled over the distinction implicit in the title. Remembering what creative energy had carried even the most obedient hack-work, I decided that in my experience all writing is creative, and taught the course on that basis. Those non-academic years as a writer began to seem a resource, a logical place to look for what might, among all the mysterious gestures of writing, be repeatable and therefore teachable experiences.

I knew, for instance, how to get started on writing in the absence of any magical phrase or stunning insight, when faced by the need to produce a piece of work to meet a deadline. I would scribble, scrawl down fragments, force out even the most banal phrasing of an intention, and keep scribbling, until my reluctant mind would rouse and exhibit in words what I had to say.

Such pursuit of thought had always been rewarded, even in the driest mental weather, by some small fresh notion or phrase from which a real beginning would take shape.

So we tried a similar kind of scribbling in the creative writing class. When students liked producing and liked reading aloud what came out of it, we tried it in basic composition classes, now and then.

A year later, I was teaching a basic writing course to a newly matriculated group of adults in Brooklyn. Every street in the neighborhood showed evidence of recent and bitter racial conflict. Martin Luther King was dead. The Black Panther Party was asserting its people's inclusion in the Bill of Rights. The New York City teachers were on strike.

Our class was part of a special two-year program. It met, for four hours one night a week, in a school building that was a locus of confrontation for black community leaders who were keeping their schools open and striking teachers, most of them white, who were picketing to close the schools. Police vans waited beyond the corners of the block; policemen stood on armed guard on the roofs of houses across from the entrance.

The special students were neighborhood people, paraprofessionals engaged by day with the schools, the local board, or the headquarters for community services, after bringing their children through crowds, TV cameras, and pickets, under the guns, to the door of the school.

They were eager students, anxious to master the skills they knew they needed. Political tumult waited outside the doors of our class. Inside, we worked. By November most students could write a fairly articulate brief essay at will.

One woman, however, perhaps the liveliest intelligence and surely the most beautifully commanding presence in the room, could not write at all.

It was not knowledge Ms. Queen lacked, nor language.

For the masterful intelligence of this well-groomed, elegant young grandmother, evidence abounded. On the one night politics cancelled our class, the community was meeting in the auditorium, and we voted to attend after we took our mid-session break. I watched from the inconspicuous seat they found me as some 500 earnest citizens debated with growing anger. Young men in fatigues and berets, arms folded high, stood shoulder to shoulder around the walls, along the back of the stage, ready. I checked the nearest exit.

Then, among confused calls and moves for action, from her place near the rear, Ms. Queen spoke out. Talking steadily she made her way down the long aisle, and confusion dropped away into quiet. She took the stage and spoke with the eloquence of cool reason, summarizing fairly what had been said, and urging everyone to channel the urge to act back into specific ways to ease the lot of the schools' children, in whose behalf the meeting had been called. Her words prevailed.

So, when she wrote a sentence and crossed it out, and wrote another and another and another and crossed each of them out, and never settled on one original written word, it was not because she lacked language. But nothing we tried seemed to remedy her inability.

At mid-semester we discussed the fact that she could not possibly pass a writing course without writing. She took home a random list of some fifty-odd possible subjects for essays, on one of which, every night for a week, she would write, without stopping, 350 words. Even if all 350 words were "the the the the," I wanted them, and not crossed out, either.

The next week she turned in a lot of the's and a precious few paragraphs; she got them back a week later, carefully annotated with pertinent and hopeful comments. She, in the meanwhile, had written seven more sets of 350 words, of course without seeing any of the comments on her previous work. Well, she had done it; she had produced seven free-written papers, two of which were essays on single subjects, rough but readable.

Teacherly comments did not get her to write successfully. Her writing did. Freed, by my willingness to look at even "the the the," of anxiety over correctness, she had been able to put language, enough language to work on, down on the page where she could get at it.

She passed the course honorably, in a flurry of increasingly coherent papers, and went on to get her degree.

Some of the implications for teaching writing are

that the writing teacher's own experience as a writer is an infinite resource;

that although writing and speaking may rise from the same preconscious center of the mind, the paths they travel are separate and must be opened up separately;

and, especially, that for writing, opening up the path begins with pushing a pen.

Trial and error with this "regardless" writing in the classroom led to a further effort to distract writers of early drafts from premature anxiety over results. For students to risk a constant and untamed flow of words, it helped to make a business of timing them for ten minutes, saying "Go" and "Stop," and watching the clock.

When I described these things to Rosemary Deen, whose interest in learning is always both fresh and patient, she introduced me to the work of those who had developed similar methods, and sent me to the library to read the Plowden Report.

The way we use uninterrupted writing now is to ask a class to join us in writing at their best speed, nonstop for ten minutes. We invite them to set down whatever themes or words come to mind. We tell them not to pause to reflect or to correct spelling, syntax, or organization but to keep their pens moving. We say plainly that it is a fishing expedition, that they may be as mild or as wild as they wish — and that last time out, somebody caught a merman. We say that if they get stuck, they are to write "the the the," until they hit on more personal words.

After several such sessions, we assign daily nonstop writing to be done at home, even on holidays. Depending on the course, this assignment may be for two weeks or a month or all semester. We discuss what we think prolific writing does and can do and why, turning to our own work together for instances. Later, we may try many variations, but the simple basic method does not change.

Today, six years later, the use of free, or prolific, writing in composition classes is less rare. It is mentioned here and there by writers or tried by teachers, usually in a limited way dissociated from the serious tasks of a writing class.

Because it is of value, potentially, to writers and writing classes at all levels, it is worth a thorough inspection. What can it do that the teacher of writing wants done? What effect has it

on a writing class?

on each student as a writer?

on the writing that students produce?

Where in the vast and lustrous landscape of literature does it fit?

It affects a writing class by at once establishing a relaxed climate of shared work. A class profits from a pleasant atmosphere — if the pleasure be not idle — since writers work better when they watch not one another out of fear. Prolific writing is pleasant; it threatens no one; it tempers the atmosphere. While writing nonstop, "it is not possible to make a mistake" (as Vonnegut's heroine remarked, defining a paradisical state of human exchange.)

People enjoy producing something of their own, once relieved of the suspicion that they may be doing it the wrong way. When not stammering over spelling or grammar, they enjoy the dynamics of verbal interplay. When not worried lest their data be inadequate or their ideas dull, silly, disorganized, or displeasing to the instructor, they enjoy finding out what they think by seeing what they say.

We can afford to take an interest in the social climate of the class because it is related to what is social about writing. The climate conditions students' willingness to write their pieces, read them to others, respond readily to others' writing, and listen with profit to what others say. As this work in common goes forward, the climate improves. A good climate creates good work, which in turn betters the climate, until the class expects and therefore creates a climate they can work in. Prolific writing is work which can be done by everyone; it starts centrally where everyone is well able to start. It provides a text for all to read, hear, and respond to, ten minutes after the start of the class.

Prolific writing quickly makes familiar faces of the strangers who register at random for most classes. To have a known, receptive audience, willing to talk about her work, is invaluable to any writer. As students write and read a substantial amount of work right away, they develop knowledge of each other. For writing has that power, as teachers of literature know, to tell a truth about who the writer is. Even the least personal writing reveals something of the author's cognitive and verbal style, so that readers ignorant of her life and time yet have insight, true if narrow, which goes directly to the core of the writer's mind. While such insights are not the subjects of the course, they tell those who hear plenty of each others' work that they are acquainted, in the subtle, literary sense according to which the style is the person.

In developing a receptive and willing audience, prolific writing is good material. It allows for active and pertinent discussion with little of the usual fear of what people will think of comments. It is remarkable that students who shy from speech in class or who edit out the most original passages of work they know they will read aloud, often do so not out of fear of instructors but to avoid the scorn of their competing peers. Since it is by definition error-free, prolific writing does away with mere untimely error-catching, that classroom blood sport which kills venturesome writing and response. Students can acknowledge what they write by reading it aloud and be openly interested in improving it, since they are committed to it only as one step in a process. All this helps us maintain a climate which clearly and commonly welcomes risk-taking.

No one will need to strain for something to say, since it's easy to ask the class to respond to nonstop writing by writing and reading aloud, in the same free and immediate way, what they remember of what they just heard. The writer will know by the simplest test of all what parts of her work are the most memorable. And her hearers will listen cheerfully if they expect to participate in discussion.

What we want in a classroom is not a kaffee klatch or a group grope but a roomful of responsible, spontaneous writers and readers. We may not produce Jonson's or Johnson's charmed circles, or the Friday evenings of J.R.R. Tolkien, Charles Williams, C.S. Lewis and friends. We do expect an active audience, ready to talk about what they've heard. It will encourage weak writers to extend themselves and promising writers to take chances with imaginative thinking and expression. Active energy is catching, and comes best not along radii from a single instructional source but from a roomful of writers interested in writing.

On the individual student who is writing nonstop for the first time, the most immediate effect is muscular fatigue. After ten minutes, half the class is flexing or shaking out tired hands, so unlikely is it that our students will have written often enough to have developed the muscles they need to push a pen steadily. Daily prolific writing strengthens the small muscles of arm and hand and, we imagine, establishes fast neurological patterns between brain and hand not unlike those artists develop through practice in one-minute sketching. Physiology is not the heart of our matter, but students physically used to it will be more prompt to write.

Another side effect on the individual writer is evident when, after a few weeks of daily writing, student after student expresses astonishment at having written a big fat manuscript, all by herself. In minutes of nonstop writing, most people will produce an average page and a third. For those unaccustomed to writing anything, a twenty-page manuscript of any kind is impressive. It provides a piece of information the student needs: that she already has in her mind all the syntax, vocabulary, and ideas she needs to create a lot of writing. She learns that for a writing course she has all the raw material at hand, in head. By writing freely she shows herself that she can produce it at will.

A few writers will value nonstop writing enough to do it every day, not for a class but for themselves. Often, for them, one or two lucky hauls — a phrase, an idea, unmistakably their own — have given them a high and addictive expectancy for what the net of writing can catch. Among our students only a small percent will be so fortunate. But in any class of 25, one or two will, four or five years later, still be turning to a notebook for ten minutes every day. Perhaps to provide even two or three students with so happy, cheap, and accessible a habit would justify writing nonstop in class. Yet, from our stance as teachers, this too is a side effect.

We aim beyond the production of strong muscles, bulky manuscripts, and a few cases of addiction. More serious and more general effects of prolific writing derive from the ready way it releases the writer's verbal energy in usable form.

As observers of writers we imagine that the power to use language is rooted in the preconscious life to which we have only limited access, but which is full of the energies of weighted and active words. The free writer earns a greater access to this verbal life. She puts herself in touch with the preconscious mix of memory and desire, fact and idea, which underlie in all mental activity. What she actualizes is a part of that inner self whose liveliness we recognize but for whose life we have a rather feeble vocabulary.

In bearing the subliminal out into the light and air we are fishing — not psychoanalytically, not even separating the psyche from our whole activity — for what we have to say ("Who fished the murex up?" Joyce asks) and we may reasonably hope for surprises. People know vast quantities of things they do not know they know. Prolific writing can be expected to turn up some literary treasure, sardines or Tyrrhinian purple.

And students may find the surge of energy that accompanies treasure-hunting is something worth writing for. One relentlessly rainy November morning a student came into class and said, "I've got to get off my butt and get some energy going. Let's do some free writing right away." No one objected; and, in fact, writing did help dispel the fog.

It takes concentration to reach that energy, and writing nonstop is a way of concentrating. (We might hypothesize that not only Rimbaud but also Pope wrote with preconscious energy at his disposal.) The outer faculties are kept occupied by the act of writing, so that the flow of language can take shape unimpeded. Classic texts in abundance tell us that the scientist, the poet, the stockbroker golfing at 5 pm on Friday, the mystic, and all of us in dream, find that strong insights come when the faculties are otherwise busied. It is then we get glimpses that make us less forlorn. We think that access to the jumbled, junk-and-jewel joke-filled preconscious is easier when recourse to it is regular. Daily prolific writing is a way of distracting the Janus at the attic door so that it stays if not ajar at least unlocked.

In other terms, prolific writers are in prime condition to acquire the habit of writing. The habitual virtue of any writer is to write habitually. "No one who has written a million words writes badly," some one has said.

Our wish is that no student of ours be able ever again to look at a pen without imagining streams of words, her words, flowing from it onto a page. Prolific writing gives such a habit of response, common to those who love to write, to those who would not ordinarily have expected to enjoy writing. Enjoying it, they greatly increase the odds that they will do it enough to do it habitually and well.

We ask students to write freely at home and in class regularly, daily. We do so for many reasons. But chiefly we do so because habits are induced by repeated action, and induced the more rapidly the more agreeable the action proves. In a classroom prolific writing is the most economical and democratic way we know to encourage the habit of writing. We think that habitual writers — like habitual gymnasts, cello players, surgeons — will get better as they go on.

Some students come to us with a crippling background in the arts of language. They expect to fail to write. Prolific writing is, as we have said, helpful in defeating that expectation. It is, of course, not simply unhappy previous education which has left many students with a mistrustful distaste for writing. It is also an aftereffect of life in an often manipulative society. Through misuse of language (along with music and visual art) our world of pervasive salesmanship and cheap entertainment fosters in us passive acceptance of political actions, media stars, wars, and products innumerable. Students are rightly skeptical of what they are thus sold; that skepticism taints their feeling about language. They suspect that active skill in language is for others and is for lying.

We want to restore to them their rightful authority over their own language; we want them to see in it a possible instrument of truth. Writing — and prolific writing as a universal starting place for writers — can return a measure of active autonomy to individual minds. Such autonomy of thought and voice, once roused and affirmed, may well stimulate an appetite for more of the same.

The individual writer, when she can count on a climate of rising expectations lighted by her own and others' reading of well-found and autonomous pieces, will want to show her best work. Wanting to show her best work somehow makes her better able to produce it; this psychological truism is especially noticeable in prolific writing. Prolific writers do catch fire from each other, since competition — which isolates — is eliminated here where each has authority over her work and we meditate on the stages of the process rather than on the product. Ultimately, of course, nonstop writing is academically useful only so far as it serves the product. But the step back to focus on process prevents competition and encourage appreciation — which is what every writer wants and many students seldom get a taste of. The individual writer gets a chance to grow through the satisfying human exchange of defenseless learning with her peers.

That growth shows up in what she writes.

It is on the writing, and what to make of it, that we focus when we teach.

We take a first step in making something of prolific writing when we read it to each other and talk about what we have heard. We take another step, another simple step, when we ask students to mark or recopy what they as writers think the best phrase or sentence in what they have written. We can go on to ask listeners to identify what they liked best in what they have heard. It is informative that time after time people do agree in recognizing the high points.

Here is a moment, with these good sentences before us, at which we who teach can add, out of our larger experience with language, suitable information about the elements of success which will help the writer and hearer to repeat it. We can offer them abstract acquaintance with its parts, rhetorical, syntactic, or logical.

We assume, of course, that all the paradigms of these arts inhere in language and will perforce be produced by those who write. Language comes first; out of plenty of language, rules may be derived and paradigms exhibited. We move from the initial response of pleasure in a satisfying phrasing to a different but sequential response, in which we identify the source of satisfaction so that it can be found again. Nor need we take a stance of unique instructional expertise. The phrase singled out for praise often evokes critical exploration from the class.

Here is an instance of a bit of free writing in which a student first broke free of her cliché-ridden prose:

> Pollution is terrible these days. When we drive our cars we are just adding to the pollution. After a while the city is full of polluted air. Even at sunset the windows have a dimmer shimmer.

The sentences that followed were a return to the safety of derivative ideas — overpopulation, exhaust filters, the price of gas, etc. The class responded by acclaiming the windows, with four people contributing to recall the phrasing exactly. Then:

"It's true, windows at sunset are one of the most gorgeous things in a city."

"The sunset is gorgeous over the 59th Street Bridge, and the way it hits the windows is part of why."

"Yes, but don't forget she's talking about pollution, which is from machines and buildings. And sunset is natural, so it's saying pollution destroys nature."

"Windows aren't natural. But if you have windows, they're supposed to be clean to let the light in. The windows in this room are streaky. So it says people aren't taking care of natural things like sunlight, or of made things like windows."

"That about the light is important but what I like is the way it sounds. Dimmer shimmer. It rhymes, and it sort of fades away."

"You have the same sound in windows, 'windows shimmer.'"

"It sounds all right. You believe it, because it sounds right."

"Not me. I believe it because I've seen the same thing myself. (To the author): Did you see it for yourself? I mean is it something you noticed?"

"Yes, every night after my last class on the way home, and it makes me feel terrible that we don't get rid of pollution."

"I think you practically don't have to say too much about pollution; just that sentence about the windows means there is pollution and it spoils the light and makes us feel guilty. The words didn't have to rhyme, but they did; that's OK; you can tell they passed through your head; they're not just any old words. You say it. I see it. OK."

Alicia never became a verbal free-thinker, but by the end of the semester she rarely wrote a paragraph without including, even if laboriously , something she herself had noticed (often, alas, to demonstrate one more safe thought) and had tried to make sound as though it had "passed through her head." Two months later, in conference, she said that those words had struck her as good advice.

Here's a simpler instance of a comment on prolific writing that confirmed the writer in his ability to produce a rhetorical device, and led him to develop many such structures in his formal writing. Most of the piece was a rather routine telling of the author's leaving home to come to New York. At about halfway he wrote, "In Puerto Rico friends and smiles are plentiful and easy, but miracles and money are scarce and rare." He volunteered that he thought this the best sentence, because there was something he liked about the way it sounded.

The student who often commented on sounds said, "Miracles and scarce and rare all go together with Puerto Rico." Someone added, "It sounds good because you've got "'This and this are this, and that and that are that'."It gave me a chance to talk for a few minutes on the power of parallel structure, that sturdy rhetorical tool, even describing this one (and a few others we put on the board) by naming its paralleled parts of speech.

What we work toward is to elicit from each writer her own voice at its most recognizable; by recognizing it, by showing what we see she has done, we confirm her in the control she needs to be able to do it at will. The rhetorical device, used — perhaps accidentally — and then recognized, moves to the generative level of language rather than remaining a vaguely familiar but inoperative term.

The painter Helen DeMott, describing the most memorable moment of learning in her early art school years, recalls a drawing teacher famous for his way of ignoring work which did not satisfy him. One day, she says, she knew she had drawn well; it was there, in front of her, as she waited for him to reach her easel. He stared over her shoulder for a long minute. Then he stabbed with his finger at the area of the drawing most central to its success, and said, "So! And when you can draw like this every time you want to, you will be able to say you can draw."

When our students can choose a way to write — clearly or allusively or ironically, to invent or persuade or explain — they will be able to say they can write. We advance that hour by recognizing and identifying moments of success in their process. Prolific writing gives us from even the new writer material of her own in which to discern such moments.

Awareness of abstract ideas about language — rhetorical ideas, grammatical ideas — is necessary to the success of more formal writing. We want our students to develop that awareness concretely, through recognition of the paradigms, piece by piece, in their own writing.

Prolific writing also offers an easily amassed collection of raw material, ready to exploit in future, more formal writing. Our flashes of insight or exact language or haunting daydream ordinarily escape us because they are unrecorded. Habitual prolific writing helps us to elicit them in time to save them, and save without petrifying. When we show students that by rereading old prolific writing they can extract seeds which germinate into essays — or stories or scripts — they gain doubly. They have on tap a source of supply of their own subjects. And they have, in using it, begun to teach themselves in an exemplary way the part of writing which is hardest to teach: revision. Prolific writing is unmistakably raw material, unmistakably open to revision. Inexperienced writers usually show an almost magical dread of changing what they have once put on paper. But if it is a page of nonstop writing, it is plain that nothing is locked into place, that all is set lightly and loosely forth. Any part may be taken up and seen again in a new way.

This elementary opportunity to revise is one of the ways in which nonstop writing serves formal rational discourse (or any other form the writer chooses). Another way appears when we use extended prolific writing as a first step in research. To write out about a subject whatever we have in mind — facts, fantasies, queries, feelings, possible sources for more data — is the sensible way to begin research for any essay, personal or academic. The writing may show us that the subject or our approach to it needs revision or refinishing; we may hit on some aspect of the subject in which our interest is genuine and ready. It is a stabilized but not fixed view of our inner resources, and an economical preparation for outside investigating. (In good detective stories, good detectives do it all the time.)

In thinking about prolific writing, it's useful to keep in mind that it is never the sole work of a writing course. Rather it is part of the act of writing, that complex and largely unexamined whole. It is naturally always paralleled in class by separate consideration of other forms and modes and structures.

Clearly, prolific writing is nothing new. It is something real writers do when they really write. What does seem new is its conscious and controlled use in college writing classes. The form in which we use it is slightly stylized, but that does not conceal its correspondence to what writers outside classrooms ordinarily do.

Because of that, it makes the job of teaching writing easier for us to understand and work at. It helps us demythologize our teaching of writing. We see that it is a step in the process which perhaps an older academy could take for granted, as we cannot. Logically, then, we have felt the need to imagine a rationale for it that is not incompatible with those lying behind more traditionally recognized parts of the process (e.g., organization and revision as implied in rhetoric).

As its use spreads, the need to examine how and why it may be useful has been underscored by the comments of those who hesitate to try it or who have tried it with indifferent success, among them teachers of unimpeachable excellence. The commonest is, "I don't see how this can help my students to write better." The preceding pages are intended to suggest some answers to that comment.

Here are some other objections, and our responses to them:

1) "I don't know how to judge nonstop writing. What aspects of it should I evaluate?"

One of the charms of prolific writing is that it does not cry out for judgment. We can without qualms devour the fruit and leave the pudding. We need only be able to discern and extract some of the fruit. The heightened attention we give to analyzing and judging formal or finished writing as an organized whole can be directed instead to finding and identifying well-written elements. Sometimes we select among those which best suit the particular theme of a particular course. Sometimes we select for emphasis what seems nearest the need of the writer.

2) "One of my students writes only about his emotions. But I'm not here for psychotherapy."

We agree in rejecting any psychotherapeutic reading of students' work. It applies to all kinds of student writing, but perhaps most vehemently to nonstop writing which, because it is especially direct and unedited, is especially susceptible to such misuse. Our students may write about chemistry, gossip, politics, personal dilemmas. We who teach writing are qualified to do so by our training in literature, which bids us to mind language in its most inclusive functioning and refuse to substitute anything else for that study. We read our students' works as related to literature and not to case studies in history, moral theology, psychology, alchemy, or any other art or discipline which we have not contracted to teach. What we study with our students, in their writing and in other texts, are literary values and the symbol-systems of literature. We would not neglect the importance of other studies, but we do not pretend to profess them. What is said interests us because of how it is conceived in language. We feel obliged, in fact, to tell our students at the start of the semester what is our concern and what is not. Psychoanalysis is not.

Most of what anyone can write directly about emotion is abstract, ambiguous, and repetitive; the student who keeps mentioning how she feels is likely to get tired of it and reach for more varied kinds of expression. Writing that is indirectly about emotion can be dealt with as we would deal with any writing, as a verbal construct. (And training in literature will have given us plenty of chances to learn how to look at writing indirectly about emotions, in every genre, mode, and period.)

3) "Some of my students write only diaries of the dullest events in their lives. One actually wrote, 'I got up, turned off the alarm, and went to the bathroom. I brushed my teeth. I put the cap back on the toothpaste tube, etc.' for three days running, and never even got as far as breakfast."

Our first hope is that on the fourth day the student, too, got bored and took off on a fancier flight. Another possiblity — remote in all but the most basic composition classes, where it is real — is that the student is, at her own level, venturesome; we imagine ourselves trying to write as well in, say Estonian, or Welsh, which we have not studied.

Yet if several students are clinging to such thin and uncommitted writing, they may learn how to enjoy something riskier by hearing examples. If no member of the class has yet dared beyond the unexceptionable, we might even write something wild and free and read it ourselves. (Though we always write with students, we do not read unless invited, ordinarily.) But almost every class does contain a few who usually provide examples of nonstandard language and idea. We would not condemn the diarist, but would expect the group's and the exemplary author's pleasure in fooling around with language to be infectious.

Sometimes we try deliberately to admit a sense of language-play by asking that everyone begin nonstop writing with "bag beg big bog bug,"or with "Yesterday morning I swallowed a sparrow," or some phrase to point up that we do not look only for formal rational discourse.

In prolific writing, as in all teaching, the teacher's expectations are likely to correlate closely to what she gets. We expect fragments of literary treasure. We do not conceal our enjoyment of reading and writing freely. We advertise our high expectations. And more often than not, they are met.

4) "I see the logic behind this nonstop writing. But I'd feel like a fool saying, 'Write whatever comes into your head.' I'm scared stiff of the whole unpredictable idea."

In a way, it *is* scary. It produces, at best, new ideas, new phrasing, an attitude new to the classroom. The very newness of it, though, keeps the teacher awake and interested; once a door begins to open, it seizes your attention; you can't wait to see how or what comes through. It can help a teacher to listen or read at the very top of her bent. Relax and enjoy it.

5) "My students are bad enough at spelling and sequence of tenses, without my encouraging them to be sloppy. They need more, not less, discipline."

Prolific writing is not a finished effort but a place in which correctness and eloquence can be discovered to their author in memorable ways. It is even a place in which the need for, say, complete sentences or correct tenses will make itself felt if the reader or hearer is attentive. Besides, writing freely goes on in tandem with other kinds of learning the rules. We don't expect to play Bach the first time we see a violin. Writers need to work out mistakes, as well as to work on them.

6) "They enjoy doing it, all right. But now that I've got it, what am I going to do with it?"

We hope that the earlier parts of this chapter reply to this most cogent of questions. We have suggested (to summarize) how prolific writing can be used

1) To establish writers and listeners in a good working climate;
2) to induce in students the energizing habit of writing, the *sine qua non* of good writers;
3) to clarify the way students learn to write by
(a) providing a warehouse of ideas and phrases that function also as an exemplary form of revision;
(b) providing examples in the students' own words for the teacher to identify as paradigms of grammar and rhetoric, as a move toward mastery of style;
(c) providing practice in what is the first step of research.

In these ways, writing nonstop carries what is a usual part of writing over into the classroom, where it belongs if the course is to inform students in orderly fashion of what a writer does.

5 | Working With Writing in Class

Once our students have written a new stage of being a writer emerges: the presentation of their work to others. Reading to others reinforces the act of writing. By itself it may not make a writer better or worse, but it confirms him in writing because as he reads his work to others, he appears as what he is, a writer: a person who writes. When the author reads his own writing, the authority and responsibility of the writing are plainly located.

The kind of class work we set going around student writing and reading is not easy to describe in ordinary classroom terms. Teachers recognize, usually, two kinds of classes: lecture and discussion. Our class work is neither. What we do is fundamental, yet it may strike readers as strange because we work within explicitly defined limits which we require ourselves and our students to take strictly.

We developed this way of working out of impatience with a range of classroom problems: aggressive students who do all the talking, thoughtful students who won't talk at all, irrelevant talk, teacherly tendencies to talk and explain too much, paralyzing, right-answer questions, and the fact that much of the class isn't listening much of the time. Duplicating student essays for discussion didn't help either. Teacher-selected essays set up the same guessing-game as right-answer questions: class members knew that the essays were either "right" or "wrong," and they had to figure out which. It was uncomfortably reminiscent of the classroom scene in *Hard Times*. We never called anyone "Girl Number Twenty," but students signed their student numbers on their papers anyway, just as if they thought we would know them better that way. It seemed sometimes to express their knowledge that they hadn't identified themselves in their writing.

But there has to be talk in class about writing. It ought to be as directly about writing as possible. When we finally devised an economical way of working with writing in class, it transformed all our classes. First, to our surprise, it made our composition classes better than our literature classes. Then we found ways of extending it to our literature classes.

When it is working right, everyone puts a limit on what he is saying. But there's no limit on real perceptions.

We said that we are trying to work within strict limits. We want to discover the minimum: what we can't *not* do, and what can't be done wrong. For us that means that everyone pay attention to all the writing and that everyone make observations about it. This is what we must do. This necessarily eliminates doing other things. For this reason, we don't have to express the negative part of these procedures to students — tell them what they can't do. Here is what we do and what we refrain from doing. (This analysis must be balanced by the description in Chapter 2 of how observations and other work integrate.)

This is what we do:

1) All students read aloud to their colleagues every assignment prepared at home (and almost everything they write in class).

2) Everyone listens to the whole essay.

3) After each essay has been read aloud, we all write observations about it.

4) We write observations nonstop for an interval timed by the teacher.

5) After all the essays have been read, we all read our observations to the authors.

Here is what we refrain from doing:

1) There is no choosing by the teacher or refusing by the author in the reading of the essays. Everyone reads around the room.

2) No essays are reproduced. No one is reading silently (noticing spelling errors) while the author reads. We are learning to listen.

We once felt — and most teachers still do — that we were doing more for our students by giving them reproduced copies of the essays to be read. We didn't think that students could follow an essay read aloud without a written copy of their own to read silently. It's a surprise that students can learn to pay attention better when they don't have a copy to read. They are on their mettle, of course, because they are going to write observations. But it is probably stimulating to listen because listening, more than reading silently, is a communal enterprise.

3) No one takes notes, interrupting attention. We are trying to hear the whole idea of the essay. Listeners need not be anxious; they are not being tested. Anyone may ask for parts or the whole essay to be read again. It will turn out to be important for the author to see just how much of what he has said, his listeners can hear and remember.

It's often a surprise to students that we don't want them to take notes as they listen. None of them seem to have any idea that listening is intensely active work which shouldn't be interrupted or turned off by jotting notes. We usually just say, if anyone wants to know why we object, that note-taking is a way of relieving an anxiety about listening that more experience will soon dispel. There are other problems with note-taking. One is that its product is summary. The other, more serious, is that it binds the listener to the order of what he has heard. We will have more to say later about summaries and ordering.

4) Observations are never made extempore but are always made in writing. Except in the trained literary critic, observations don't just leap to the tongue. They take place, partly in the listening and partly in the memory. Writing down observations opens and holds this place in which listeners complete their attention. When we write, we discover what we hadn't been aware of when we were listening. Many students who have never written except mechanically, experience how writing discovers thought for the first time when they write observations.

When everyone writes, everyone has something to read. No one has an occasion to say, "I didn't really notice anything," or, "I didn't understand it." Students want to do what they are asked to do, especially if it sounds reasonable or fair. Someone may think he doesn't understand a paper. He might *say* that if he were put on the spot by being asked for an observation extempore. But he doesn't write that. If he is asked to write something obvious that he has noticed about a dense essay, he is likely to write, "It had a lot of big words in it."

✓ 5) We do not write opinions, personal reactions, evaluations, or suggestions for improvement. (We say more about observations in the second part of this chapter.) They all invade the authors' right to have the first chance to draw their own inferences from what their audience has noticed. A listener says, "Your essay had a lot of big words in it." The author must make something of this. Maybe he is very proud of these words. Still, he must take account of the fact that most of his colleagues observed the proportion of "big words." He may draw one inference from it at the time and others later on in the semester.

It may seem strange that we ban all adverse criticism. We do so because negative criticism — the emphasis on what is wrong with a piece of writing — makes for competition and stress, conditions which transform writing into work for heroes. But writing is not heroic — it is human and ordinary. The ordinary reaction to being criticized (especially in public) is to defend oneself by justification.

Criticism belongs to the author and to the teacher. Authors draw their own inferences about their own writing from the responses of their colleagues. Teachers give their evaluations in the privacy of a written comment and in conference.

6) We encourage listeners to say what they liked about the essay. To hear, "I loved that part," is helpful, especially when the listener speci- fies the part by an observation. A writer is often as unaware of what he has done beautifully as of what he has done wrong. We have found that everyone in class agrees about the best parts, and these examples of the pleasures of writing put shaped expectations in the writers' minds. No achievement in an essay of Orwell's, however much the teacher admires it, can influence students like the success which they have discovered in a class essay.

But student essays can't compare as literature with Orwell's! Certainly not. But it is not perfection of achievement in another writer that inspires an author as much as the glimpse he catches in it of a possible achievement of his own.

7) We do not need any text for a writing course other than student essays and class observations. Student essays are the "readings" part of a textbook for our writing course. The "instructional" part is the body of observations class members make, and the inferences we all draw from them.

We have been specific about the limits of what we do because our knowledge of limits and the way we keep ourselves and students to these limits frees students for the possibilities limits define.

Students don't notice the restrictions we place on ourselves — which is natural and right. They don't notice that they have been through a 150-minute writing class in which they have done all the reading, writing, and observing, while the teacher has simply directed and timed activities, given approval to accomplishments, and given those literary and critical accomplishments their names ("That was a beautiful parallel structure."). The "restrictions" on students, then, are expressed as ground rules — security, one might almost say — because they enable all of them to work with writing.

"We're doing all the work," one student said, half asking a question. Well, they're doing all the work they can. The teacher's work is submerged in such things as the planning of the assignments and of each class hour. In a classroom a teacher instructs primarily because of what he knows and how that knowledge comes into play: in what he recognizes in student writing and in his own language. The teacher's language gives students the new language they need to develop their power of making observations. We say more about this language in the observation section of this chapter.

These, then, are the limits we keep to in class work on writing, and some of their implications. Now we turn back to consider the activities themselves of listening and paying attention, and of making observations.

I. Listening and Paying Attention

The kind of attention we pay to someone else's writing in class keeps alive all the possibilities for inductive learning. Student essays couldn't even begin to work as texts unless students felt an overwhelming interest in the essays of others as well as in their own. Giving gifts creates community. The way we read and listen to each other constructs the class as a community of writers. But it is also a community of learners; so the way we listen has a certain shape which expresses an idea about study.

We will expand each point of our format to show how it works.

1) All writers read. On the day that an essay is due, we ask students to read, without any choosing by the teacher or refusing by the writers. Writers will read if it is clear that everyone is going to read. (We often hear a brave quaver in the voice of the first reader.) For readings we sit as though at a seminar table, so that no one is gazing at anyone's back.

We expect that there are readers with special problems: speech defects, heavy accents, stage fright that wipes the voice down to a whisper. The cure for all this is simply custom. The author reads, and we hear it as best we can. We know that by the middle of the term we won't any longer hear the problems. It's one of our "professional" skills to grit our teeth and go smilingly past obstacles like this as if they weren't there. My first experience of this was with a student who had a very bad cleft palate. His voice echoed fearfully and unintelligibly in his head, to the dismay of the class. Fortunately for the class, he had been well trained. He knew he had to keep on talking. And little by little we changed. We understood him. By the end of the semester, we forgot there had been any impediment in him or in us.

Students with foreign accents are often especially shy. It is scary enough to read, let alone read in a strange language. But the teacher must try to hear the speaker's syntax and idiom, which may be quite colloquial. There is no sense in letting the writer relinquish his right to his standing as an author by letting someone else read the essay or by reading it ourselves in a moment of panic and assertiveness. Our rule is: all is well; it is not possible to make a mistake.

2) Everyone listens as the author reads. Now the quality of the teacher's listening communicates itself immediately to the class. The first time someone reads, some students watch the teacher to see whether he is really interested. Most teachers are good at paying attention — one of the irresistible ways their training shows itself. The way they can do this consistently and steadily is instructive.

Listening teaches us to pay attention. It is hard to do at first — very hard for some students. But everyone learns it; some astonish themselves by learning it. Learners employ the skill right away in other classes, and that demonstrates its usefulness.

It is important to listen rather than to read for a number of reasons, all based on the fact that the ear hears something other than the eye reads. Hearing is more direct, immediate, more interesting and entertaining than reading. It is also less rational and analytic, part of a pre-critical response. That hearing isn't analytical is appropriate because the essays the class hears are completed but not finished. Their authors may suppose that they are finished, but a writing teacher knows better. Analyzing these first-version essays as if they were finished would harden their shortcomings into obstructions.*

Especially with the early essays, none of us knows what the real problems of a writer are. Some errors and problems are caused by teachers' assignments or the unaccustomed situation of writing. If we set about earnestly correcting errors we ourselves have caused, we are working in an uneconomical way. When the writer has heard how his own writing sounds, has heard the essays of other students, and has been writing about three weeks, some troubles drop away, and the parts of writing that need work are clearer.

Rafferty was a case in point. He was a mature, intelligent student whose first paper was more stuffed with pompous and recirculating jargon than any in recent memory. He read it with evident satisfaction. The class was stunned. Someone asked him to reread the first paragraph, but that didn't help. Everyone wrote observations, but no one

---

*All our assigned essays are to be rewritten. We encourage this by giving the first version a check (✓), check plus (✓+), or check minus (✓−). We ask students to write "To be graded" on the final version.

had many. Several students said that there were many long words in the essay. Others noticed that the essay was shorter than others read. One person thought he noticed three parts. One admiring listener said that the author had a "wonderful vocabulary." Rafferty's second paper was equally short and obtuse, and observations were again sparse. Class members obviously found it easier to make plentiful observations about the work of other writers who had found more human voices. Rafferty's third paper was colloquial, easy, copious, and witty.

All this was instructive to the teacher. Why had such an intelligent student written so badly on his first two assignments? Evidently the fault was not so much in Rafferty's writing as in the teacher's assignments. Had she made the further mistake of busily correcting Rafferty's diction without waiting to see what kind of writer he really was, she would, of course, have been "correcting" her own errors.

When students have a copy of an essay to read, they are apt to pick out faults in spelling and to speculate about faults in punctuation and paragraphing. They know from other classes that these are the important things, or at least (and it amounts to the same thing) they are the things students have language for.

But what the ear hears is the big things: wholes or emphases, such as a memorable sentence, a section of cogent reasoning, some vivid dialogue, a perfect ending, an image. The attraction of the ear for the dominant whole means that those aspects of writing that make for coherence and emphasis will be noticed in class observations and brought into play in future writing.

In fact, hearing is often enhancing. Not for nothing is it the sense of the imagination for Blake and Wordsworth. Even when the essay is not remarkable as a whole, the listener takes some striking or vivid part away as the whole. He forgets, as by a species of forgiveness, the vague and clumsy, and takes the memorable part as standing for the possibilities of the whole. Even one good stroke is suggestive: "Why not have more of that?" we think.

When we take essays home and read them, we may be surprised. Some are not as good as they seemed; some are better. For the weaker essays, our original sense of the possibilities of the essay — what is right about it, how the author does it right — helps us to head the writer toward his next effort more intelligently. What we hear is really a suggestive form that lies embedded in the actual version we are listening to. Hearing the possibilities means hearing the success of the paper, and it is success, however small, that leads all writers on to the effort of more writing.

When we say that hearing is precritical, we mean precritical about the writing of others. It is frequently critical for one's own writing. We can hear several voices at once, of course. So even as we listen to the writing of others, we hear or begin to hear what we have written at the same time. It is an instructive counterpoint: the voice of the essay being read and the voice of our own essay. And the teacher cannot hear it.

Writing and listening to what we write are acts that must eventually go on simultaneously for anyone who wants to get control of his writing. At first the writer simply hears his own essay while he is reading it aloud. Then he hears his own essay as an afterthought while he's listening to someone else read. Finally he hears the voice of his colleagues as he writes hiw own essay, having developed a kind of forethought.

All the listening and hearing is helping the teacher to expand the "time-space" of the class — to create more mental space by changing the timing of the class. We foster activity *and* leisure. We are moving right along because every activity has been timed. But some of those moments are longer than others, when writing and listening take hold. In a classroom charged with listening, students know right away that new forces, new chances are coming into play. There are even new silences that may never have been heard before. People are waking up. They discover that their own attention can be intensified and augmented, not dissipated, by others.

II. Making Observations

Infant, it is enough in life
To speak of what you see. But wait
Until sight wakens the sleepy eye
And pierces the physical fix of things.

WALLACE STEVENS, *The Red Fern*

After a paper has been read, we are ready to write observations. We have told writers before they read that there would be nothing bad said about their work. Now we ask everyone to write for, say, three minutes a list of things they noticed about the essay. We say, "Begin with the obvious. Set aside feelings you get from it. The things you notice can't be too obvious. We'll write for three minutes. Keep on writing even if you think what you're saying is nonsense, until the time is up."

We say no more than this. We do not "introduce" observations, explain their value, or say that this way of studying essays is something new or special. Two things are important here: that we take observations for granted as what they are, an ordinary part of studying anything; and that we get right to work.

We always write along with everyone else. This is important. In the beginning, students are writing because the teacher is doing it too — students can't very well not do it. In a simple way students see how to write and keep on writing because the teacher is writing. But the teacher needs to write, as much as anyone else, because teachers too discover and express observations in the special time and mode of writing.

It's useless to explain what observatons are ahead of time. That encourages more requests for explanation, questions of the sort that become more insistent as the definition becomes more impenetrable. The most important thing is that everyone pay attention and write. The teacher names and praises the observations he hears, and that is how those who haven't caught on yet learn how to do it. The teacher should not comment on observations, make them the springboard for a lecture, or take over the observations by saying more than the students do. A class hour full of observations is exhilarating (the students can't know that ahead of time), and that also teaches students how to make them.

The most helpful thing to say, we have found, is that observations are obvious. This may surprise students, because they think that everyone knows the obvious or that the obvious doesn't have to be expressed. They have yet to learn that the obvious is usually the central thing and is only "obvious" when someone has pointed it out. The most obvious thing about the *Iliad,* for example, is its length. And the interest and problems of its length continue to be discussed after all these centuries, whether scholars are talking about the matter of oral compostion or the matter of structure and organization.

When a student makes a remark and asks, "Is that an observation?" we say, "Check it out. What you notice has to be something everyone would recognize when you point it out." This is the rule that keeps talk about writing from wandering off into bickering or irrelevance. If two people disagree about an "observation," we ask the observer to express it in other terms that will enable the rest of us to recognize what he has seen; for if it is really an observation, there can't be any disagreement about it.

We want to separate observations from inferences. When we get inferences in class, we ask observers to go back and see what more simple facts lie behind those inferences. Failing that, we ask students to put inferences aside till they have more observations to put under them. We say, "It's not really easy to draw inferences from one or two observations, so it's more truthful to wait for more observations."

Here are some examples of the differences between observations, inferences, and evaluations:

A) Evaluation: "The middle part was the best."
   Inference: "The middle part is intense."
   Observation: "The middle part is mostly dialogue."

B) Opinion/Evaluation: "I feel it ended too abruptly."
   Observation: "A new speaker comes in right at the end."

C) This is the way students often move toward observations:
   "It was heavy."
   "Heavy?"
   "I mean it was serious."
   "Serious?"
   "You know what I mean. Wait a minute now. Let me say this again. The words he uses about his disease are scientific words. He says his body doesn't use the trace mineral, copper."
   "There you go!"
   "He uses scientific words. That makes it serious."

D) Here is an observation that made a strong suggestion to the writer:
   "She says she is writing about *envy*. But I notice that the man who envied came up in only one sentence. All the rest was about the injured man."

Students know they need new terms, new concepts to express what they are learning to hear in their essays. They listen to the observations the teacher makes more eagerly than they ever listened to a lecture on *coherence* to find out what sorts of things might be said. The teacher doesn't use inferential terms like *concise, coherent, organized, well-developed, unified.* He uses descriptive terms in observations, like these:

A) The essay begins with the first-person point of view and ends by addressing the reader as *you,* the second-person point of view.
B) The essay is mostly narrative. There were active, past-tense verbs, and connections like *then, after.*
C) The language in the beginning is general: he said *people, many ways.*

We don't offer these as model observations, although they are useful because they describe phenomena common enough in student writing. They suggest the sorts of concepts students need to learn.

Observations are descriptions: public and recognizable. Making them teaches students the language of literary criticism. Like the basic language of any study, this is descriptive, not judgmental. This language is about:

1) *Grammar and syntax.* Listeners notice things like the governing pronoun/point of view, the governing verb/time or aspect. They notice structures like *although . . . nevertheless, if . . . then.* See Chapters 2 (Fable) and 11 (Grammar & Graphics) to see how these terms come early into class work.

2) *Rhetoric* gives us such terms as: *abstract* and *concrete, repetition, balance, parallels, understatement, contrasts,* the *beginning, middle,* and *end.* Here belong the modes of rhetoric: *description, definition, narration, process, drama, dialogue.* The most elegant analysis of these modes that we know is in Leo Rockas' *Modes of Rhetoric.*

3) *Genre* terms. Verse terms would come here if we were studying poetry. Since we are studying the expository essay, the keys terms are *assertion, evidence.*

We do not give a chart of these terms to composition students ahead of time because some students would take it as a grid and force every essay through it till it had been reduced to serviceable bits. All these elements of writing will emerge in observations, probably the rhetorical ones first.

In an advanced writing class or in a literature class, we tell students we are going to use the language of literary description for observations, at least in part. We say that they already know most of these terms (they'll be picking up the genre ones in the course), and, putting the categories on the board, we invite them to supply us with examples of what they understand as *Grammar/Word-Order* and *Rhetoric/Emphasis.*

Sometimes students ask for terms. After one of her colleagues had read a witty passage, one student turned to me and said, "I know that's *some*thing. That must have a name."

"Its name is *irony.* What did you notice about it?"

Sometimes we give students a special term as a little treat. One observer said, "I noticed that she began with spring and ended the first part with winter. Then she began the second part with winter and ended the essay with spring." Everyone in class nodded vigorously.

They had noticed that too. They were interested to know that this too is "something" and has a name: *chiasm,* a very old name which testifies to an ancient pleasure in neatness of connection and closure.

After about three weeks, we ask students to write for ten or fifteen minutes about the experience of reading aloud, listening, and writing observations. We read these passages aloud. We do this two or three more times in the semester. This gives the students a chance to exchange ideas about what they are doing; but even more important, it teaches them to think about thinking, to reflect on their actions, and to make explicit the inferences they have been developing.

What do we do when students don't make observations?

1) *Summaries.* Many students summarize or paraphrase instead of observing. It's natural that they should, for all through their school days they have been asked to summarize in a way that excludes any other sort of study of what they read. Moreover, they have received, instead of instruction, summaries of assigned reading. For these reasons, it's a comfort for them to summarize; it's their way of being "good" students. So it would be wrong for us to reject summaries. Students who summarize are paying attention, and that is what we have been asking them to do. Usually summaries do no harm. We accept summaries, then, but we always *name* them to make the distinction felt: "Yes, that is an accurate summary of what you heard."

The difference between summary and observation becomes more important in a literature class — and crucial in a poetry class. There summaries are harmful, because some students feel they must summarize before they can do anything else. When they can't summarize, they are stymied; when they can, they do so, and then they have often altered the poem beyond hope of learning anything about it. They have extracted a truism from the poem and thrown the poetry away.

It's liberating, therefore, for students to learn that even though they don't "understand" (as they put it) a poem, they can make observations about it. One student, for example, complained anxiously that she couldn't understand "Kubla Khan." But she could observe that the river in the poem is always the "sacred river," and that the dome is always the "pleasure dome." Then she noticed a range of language describing the sacred, from *demon* to *paradise,* and a range of language describing pleasure. Finally she observed that some of the language for pleasure, like *paradise,* coincided with the language for the sacred. Her observations brought her a truer understanding of the poetry than a summary could.

2) *Stock observations.* Sometimes students take refuge in generalized observations. Though we don't give them a grid for observing essays, they figure one out. They "notice" the same things about every essay. This is a loss for the students because observations are stimulating intellectually: they help identify the work we are studying. They are also stimulating personally because they help us identify ourselves. Though observations are public once they are made, they are personal in their origins because they have been made by persons, out of whatever it is that makes us persons. They "deal out that being indoors each one dwells."

If a student can't do this, we don't take notice. We just say, "Thank you — that's right." These students are doing what they can. Whether they lack confidence, experience, or intelligence, we don't know, and it doesn't matter. They are willing to do what we ask, and we welcome that. They are the very students who would be out of it entirely in a "discussion" or "lecture" class.

3) *Aggressive* students who insist on opinionating, judging, talking about themselves, etc. We usually ask them, "What did you notice that we can all see?" Or we say more directly, "Hold off those inferences for now until you have more support for them." When monologue threatens, it is useful to say, "Let's all *write* about that for five minutes." (The teacher is frequently the monologuist, and that remedy works for the teacher too.) We won't give anyone the floor, but we'll give everyone a pencil and a piece of paper.

Aggressive students are better at catching teachers and involving them than diffident students, but they may be suffering from the same disabilities. If they are not encouraged to misbehave by getting a stimulating reaction from the teacher, they usually calm down and learn something, or give up and go away.

Every young teacher has had problems with aggressive students. Twenty-five years ago, when a friend of ours was at a university in Chicago, she taught in a junior college on the south side. In one remedial reading course, four young men set out to entertain themselves as best they could by talking and joking across the aisles. She took counsel with a more experienced colleague:

"I've got to toss those four guys out. They're ruining the class."

"How are they ruining it?"

"Well, we can't work. I can't control the class."

"Why do you have to control it?"

"If I don't, it will be chaos!"

"How do you know that?"

"Well, of course it will be chaos!"

"But how do you know that?"

Our friend had a great respect for her colleague's intelligence and experience. She knew too that if she tossed out the bad guys, it would sour the rest of the class.

She decided to work as hard as she could with the workers of the class and ignore the disrupters. That didn't stop them, but the workers began to consolidate. They moved away from the noisy young men so that they could hear each other better, and that left the young men isolated in a play without spectators. After about six weeks, one of the players dropped out, and the rest started coming in with the homework. Looking back now, she can see they were really more like great playful puppies than the ogres they seemed then. But they almost scared her out of being what she was supposed to be, the teacher.

The point, we think, is that a working class in which everyone has a share cannot be disrupted. There are occasionally unsubduable members. Even when they can't learn, however, their persistence in error demonstrates to the rest of the class that responding to writing by antagonism or personal associations is self-indulgent, unprofitable, and tedious.

What is important about observations?

A) *For the conduct of the class:*

While everybody is writing, everybody is doing something. It's beautifully simple.

B) *For the students:*

1) Students learn to concentrate — or they learn what concentration is.

2) Making observations is like a test — not teacher-given but self-generated — which demonstrates the way they have paid attention as best they can.

3) Students can learn things from each other that they cannot learn from us. We do not even know what these things are. Here is what one student said when asked how he had done so well writing in a langugage not his own and when he had begun poorly:

"I will tell you how it is. I sit at home and write my essay. I have a good idea and I like what I want to say. Then as I write, I say to myself: If you write that, Jan will say, 'I wonder why you wrote this thing in this place?' Or when I am ready to finish nicely, I think: Now

Tammy will say, 'I noticed you said this thing at first, but you never mentioned it again.' So I change it."

4) Everything we are doing is fostering the possibility of the student taking the initiative.

C) *For writing expository essays*:

Inferences shape the assertion part of any essay, and observations are evidence and form a body of support for assertions. Every day in class, then, we are rehearsing what we want students to do when they write exposition: give evidence for what they say, realize their assertions in a way that is publicly recognizable. When they can't point to observations in class, they must suspend their inferences. Then they understand it better when the teacher says about the assertions of their essays, "If you can't support this, you can't say it."

D) *Intellectually*:

1) Observations always begin with the part of the essay that has the most verbal energy. This is the chief reason for having essays read aloud: to discourage students from holding on to the sequential order and to encourage them to reorder the essay in their own minds according to the emphases of the essay. The order of emphasis must correspond with the order of significance.

This reordering is the beginning of analysis, the beginning of having an idea about the work we are studying instead of merely summarizing it. We know that as long as students follow the order of what they are writing about — whether it's a poem, play, novel, or intellectual discourse — they will be unable to discover and hold onto the order of their own idea.

2) Making observations creates a body of critical terms and observations as we go along. As students bring these terms into play, it's clear to them that they are learning something. When terms work, they are intellectually validated.

3) Most simply, of course, observations are the first step in every intellectual endeavor. That is why they are potentially so useful.

6 | Transition to Expository Essays: Student Writing as Literature

Our basic assumption is that all the writers we teach in school are creative, though the catalogue description "creative" is often used to distinguish three literary genres from the others. It follows that student writing is literature, that is, free and disinterested, a product of imagination and thought. In our experience and the experience of those we know, there is no essential difference between writing a poem and writing an essay, except, as we must often say, that writing a poem is easier, its conventions being so much clearer and more plentiful.

We are teaching writing as literature because literature is central to writing. You may object that the academic expository essay is instrumental and utilitarian, a specialized form of prose, like the textbooks students have been reading most of their lives. That is the root of the problem. Writing cannot be learned as something specialized, any more than you could learn carpentry by doing repairs or cooking by working in a short-order kitchen. We cannot begin with the peripheral. Except for technical schools, there is no sense in teaching the specialized at all. Competency can refine itself. We must teach the central first. However we define it, the true beginning is the center, because the center is the core or heart, the axis on which the rest turns, the point of concentrated activity or influence, the subject seen in its most direct and simple form, as poetry is the center of literature. Centers are, moreover, the beginnings we never leave behind. We leaf and flower out from them and ripen back to them, returning to them and renewing our sense of them at every stage.

The center of writing is literature. The power is there. We do not intend to teach writing literature, in the basic composition courses, in the forms of poems or stories or plays: that is no different in principle than teaching writing by teaching the research paper. They are highly developed and finished forms of their nuclear structures. The point will be clearer when we notice the two senses of the word *writing*. Writing is always both a process *(poïeta)* and a product *(poïema)* The power of writing, as process, comes from habit and ease — it is a matter of skills. As product, writing comes from the *claritas,* the radiance of its of its idea or image in the imagination. Writing skills we discuss in other chapters. Here we are concerned with internalizing a sense of product, that is, with the image. The presence of the image shows itself in the way a writer takes a form and makes it so much her own that she can produce her own version of it. We can call this imitation, but we ought to understand that the model we imitate is not on the page. There is another step, from what we write, read, or hear read aloud, to our perception of the form or structure within it.

The structure enlightened is the model we imitate. The model is always within. An experienced writer or a writer of genius derives the model within from masterful works of literature because the superb power of structure shows itself there. Something of the *claritas* of the inner image shines in the finished work, and, if it shines for the reader, it may illumine a central form for him. There are advantages of economy in models from less finished writing, however. A student might learn most from reading Milton, but she would have to learn to read him first. The vulgar sense of *ideal* for *model* blurs the important sense of the word *model* for writers. A source that is unfinished or otherwise less than ideal for a model may be more suggestive than one whose completeness or finish veils the possible models or structures within it for the inexperienced writer.

When asked how we teach the academic expository essay, we say we don't teach it. For one thing, we don't fully know what it is, because we don't have any literary models for it in our heads. Many college texts present a three-part schema, recognizable from music, of theme, variations, and recapitulation. Our three-part form is hypothesis, evidence, and thesis. We find both of these forms useful as writing tests.

If we ourselves can teach only from models drawn from literature we know, why not give students the same chance to meet the source of power in writing? Indispensable, we say, but not in a writing class. The first consideration is time. We have about 42 hours to give students basic training in writing. Cruel as these numbers are, they remind us of important limits. We must begin with economy.

Superlative literature has too much power to be subordinated to student writing in class work. The greatest concentration of energy will always absorb attention. The result is that class work based on such literature becomes literary analysis instead of writing. Literary analysis is extremely difficult for beginning students because they cannot quickly assimilate highly organized prose, and they have therefore no basis for analysis. The teacher knows how to analyze, of course, and in the vacuum that presents itself, she does so.

By very easy steps then, what is intended as a writing class becomes a series of exercises in literary analysis. Such classes tempt teachers to spend time with their favorite writers instead of much less lustrous student writing. The intention of such classes is that the student learn to write from the model on the page and from the analysis that goes on in class. We have already talked about the model on the page. If analysis is a model for writing, there is no reason why such classes shouldn't work. The teacher can tell how well they are actually working by the class attendance, by how widespread the interest is in the class (as opposed to front-row interest), and by the writing that emerges. We have never noticed that analysis leads to synthesis, however. Analysis is *of* synthesis, and by loosening an old synthesis, it makes a new synthesis possible. But until we know more about the relation between speech and writing, and between analysis and synthesis, it will be hard to organize assigned writing on the assumption of a direct relation.

We have said that the model we imitate is in the mind. We have said much and will say more about how the student abstracts structures or models from what she writes, reads, and hears read in the class. But we needn't assume that literature as a model works only in the mind of the student. It works powerfully on students' writing while it is in the mind of the teacher.

We can easily see how the absence of literature in the mind of the teacher affects student writing in the products students turn out when they are taught by a technician: the products are poor things, scarcely able to breathe outside their special atmosphere. Hard as it is to define it, students' writing reflects the models in the teachers' minds. When they have textbook samples in mind, they get starved bits. When they have Milton and Pope in mind, they get something it is fair to call literature.

Perhaps we can see how this works. Expectations show themselves first in the assignment, which, according to our principles, ought not to be a subject or a topic but a literary structure. As an example, we take the structure of parallel balance. If we are thinking in terms of expository purpose only, we could identify this form as comparison/contrast, for parallel balance is the nuclear structure of successful comparison and contrast. But if we want to see its power with real clarity, we consider the poetry of Pope:

Know, Nature's creatures all divide her care;
The fur that warms a monarch, warmed a bear.

We see it there; we don't expect our students to do that. We present the structure as an assignment (in ways which we develop elsewhere). When the writers come in and read their essays to each other and to the teacher, the presence of the literature in the teacher's mind makes itself felt again.

We begin by naming and by praising the literature that we find in the writing. We encourage students to notice and to name what works. Whatever the writer's colleagues remember, what they notice, what moved them, we can be sure that that is literature. It is not the technical names that are important — students often invent very apt terms for an effect they notice — but the naming.

It's not possible to overestimate the importance of this. When we name and praise the literature in a student's writing, she sees, sometimes for the first time, what she has done. Then she sees that what she has originated is not peculiar to her but is a part of her culture:

> The solitary hired man on a farm in the outskirts of Concord, who has had his second birth and peculiar religious experience, and is driven as he believes into silent gravity and exclusiveness by his faith, may think it is not true; but Zoroaster, thousands of years ago, travelled the same road and had the same experience; and he, being wise, knew it to be universal, and treated his neighbors accordingly. . . .

In the teacher's recognition of the literature in her writing, the author gets a glimpse of the power of literature, a power which constitutes cultures. In just the way Thoreau describes, students can discover in college that many of the experiences which they had thought private are in fact universal and will make a difference in their relation to their neighbors. They discover this when they find they have expressed them, by a literary instinct, in universal forms.

When we say that the student originates the literary elements of her writing, we don't mean that she invents them, but that their source in their present form is her own mind. In themselves they are the nuclear structures of all literature. We think of the strong structure of Milton's ode, "On the Morning of Christ's Nativity," for example, with its great trope, the moment of silence or poise, when time and the world pause, and, in the expanding liberty of vision of that moment, the speaker looks backward to the age of gold and forward to the return of perfect truth, until he sees them both together in a redeemed form, the future balancing the past in this present nativity. Only another great writer can equal that. But the strong, fulcrum structure occurs frequently in students' essays when we assign our first essay, built on the structure of parallel balance, which is presented in the formula, "Once I was . . ./ now I am. . . ."

Here is an example in an essay by Alice Gibson, a student in our most basic writing course.

Once I was a Negro, a young, proud, Negro American. To me the red, white, and blue meant freedom and justice for all. If anyone called me black, I was insulted. If anyone called me African, then it was time to fight. After all, I'm not a monkey swinging in trees. Everybody knows that's what an African is. I was so ashamed to know that my great-great-great grandparents were slaves. But that was long, long ago, and if I keep pushing it out of my mind, maybe it'll go away, just as if it never happened.

One morning I woke up to hear my mother talking about a young Negro boy in Mississippi who was taken from his grandparents' house and killed. He was there visiting them for the summer vacation, and in the middle of the night some men came and took him away. They said he made a fresh remark to a white lady. Was that any reason to kill a boy? Well, they caught the man who did it. His name was Ku Klux Klan. That sure was a funny name. I was glad they caught him because then he would go on trial and be found guilty and thrown in jail or electrocuted.

I really couldn't understand why Mr. Ku Klux Klan was found not guilty. My mother said it was because Negroes didn't have equal justice.

Now I am Black, a young, proud, Black American. The freedom and justice that the red, white and blue represent, I now take with a grain of salt. Call me Negro and I'm insulted. Call me African and my soul sings. Yes, I am African. In fact, I've been to Africa, and the people there greeted me and said, "Welcome home, Sister." How grand I felt. Slavery? Yes, my great-great-great grandparents were slaves, and I'm not ashamed. Let the shame be on the ones who enslaved them.

This paper has an opening description, matched point by point by a closing description. Between these parts is a narrative told from a child's point of view. The narrative acts as a fulcrum: it turns the paper from part to counterpart, and it creates the poise or point of balance in the paper. It is a development of the same nuclear structure one sees in Milton's Nativity Ode. And it is not an accident that Alice Gibson's paper has the same structure as Milton's poem. They are both writing about the same thing: justice. They have both originated a trope that embodies their theme: the balance. The similarity goes further. The center of the balance is the same for both: the child. For both, it is the image of an innocent human ideal that makes the balance come right. The *claritas* of this idea in the Milton poem helps the reader of Alice Gibson's paper to identify for Alice what she has done and in this way helps her consolidate it so that she can do it again.

There are other ways in which seeing Milton in Alice Gibson's paper helps her. It helps her first because it makes the reader's attention to her paper more central and more just. It keeps the reception of the paper from being a matter merely of the reader's liking or disliking, and makes it a matter of recognition. The reader leaves the provinces of taste, where they murmur, "We don't like this sort of thing." If a student is writing Kinnell, the teacher can't say, "But I prefer Virgil." Or not if she considers herself a member of a university.

When the teacher reads the paper as literature, she reads it with an attention enriched by Milton, by literary tradition, the kind of attention that says to students: This is an important thing to do.

We don't think we could evoke this paper by teaching the Milton poem and asking our students to imitate its structure. The improbability suggests what goes wrong with assigning readings and asking students to write something like them. Our students come to us not only with language and personal experience in their heads, but also with the shapes that are the seed forms of literature. When we can find structures that *present* these forms to them, without any name that suggests, quite wrongly, that there is some already existing container for their experience, they will work out the shapes that the structure and their own experience suggest.

When we say our students' writing is literature, we are asked, How do you define literature? Here the definition is simple. What we pay attention to is literature. Our paying attention to it and the kind of attention we pay to it helps to make it literature. The student writes his paper, and the teacher is there, like Thoreau's neighbor Seeley, "to represent spectatordom, and help to make this seemingly insignificant event one with the removal of the gods of Troy."

7 | Two-Part Essay Shapes: Coordinate Structures

Writers who can manage sentence coherence and sentence consequence are ready to practice various ways of organizing the whole essay. We have six essay shapes for them. All are two-part structures. In most, the form of the essay and its idea are contained in the first sentence: the essay develops that form and idea. Essay and key sentence correspond. The dominant sentences are, of course the first one, the last, and (often) the one that makes the "turn" from the first part to the second part. In the first three, presented in this chapter, structures are coordinate. Ideally the second part corresponds or "answers" point by point to the first part: parts one and two are parallel and reinforcing, so that the essay has a clear and memorable shape.

For beginners in the expository essay, our advice would be: Choose a strong shape and make sure that shape is evident.

We present the essay shape in a model which writers imagine in their own versions. (We have described how we abstract that structure from literature in Chapter 1.) The first structure comes from Thoreau's account of his former life as "reporter," keeper of the town's "wild stock," and his present life of "business" enterprise at Walden. The model sentence is, Once I was _____; now I am _____. Writers supply the predicates and imagine how a sentence of their own might be the seed of an essay. One student wrote: "Once I was a Negro; now I am Black." The completed form of that sentence is the essay we quote in Chapter 6.

A two-part, coordinate form is obviously a beginning and an end. When we work with such a form, we lead writers to concentrate first on beginning and end and how they correspond. It's the simplest, unified form of an idea we want writers to start with so that they can run the whole idea through their heads beforehand, making a rough or intuitive check on consistency. The seed sentence is a way of using sentence coordination to do this.

The coordination of parts means that writers don't have to explain or account for the change or turn from first to second part. The two parts are correspondences or alternatives or oppositions. The parallel descriptions, the answering or opposed voices present the idea (often ironically) in prolepsis, in dialectic, or in dialogue. In fact, the more nearly both halves of the essay match, the less need there is for the writer to explain or analyze connections. In general, the stronger or more overt the shape of a piece of writing, the less the writer has to say about how the parts fit.

A two-part structure is useful because it gives writers a strong, simple frame on which to sustain an idea so that they can see it as a whole and see how parts might fit.

These are the possibilities of the structures. Essays that don't do this are not wrong. When we say that writers transform the model into an image of their own, we agree that how a writer sees it can't be wrong. The structures are partly ways of helping writers organize what they know, and partly ways of evoking experiences, as the sonnet form both calls out experience we were not quite aware of before and structures the experience it is bringing into existence.

Some writers ignore the two-part structure altogether and write a straight narrative, that being what they are ready to write first or how they are used to thinking about what they know. When they hear how other writers work out their ideas, narrators will try other ways if, or as soon as they can.* I assign the first two structures twice. That encourages writers who try a narrative for the first Once/Now to try parallel structure for the second essay.

As the reader knows by now, we don't explain any of this to writers ahead of time, give directions, or bring in other writing (even student writing) as samples. We tell writers the model sentence, read some sample sentences, and then ask them to write some sentences of their own.

Here is our format. I allow about half an hour for this at the end of the class period. I say, "Take five minutes and write as many sentences as you can on this model, 'Once I was (you fill in this part); now I am (and this part).' Here are some sample sentences for ideas:

Once I was shy; now I am mellow.

Once I was fat and hated myself; now I am slender and happy.

Once I cursed the day I was married; now I am a happily married man.

Once I was a grass-green country boy; now I survive in the Bronx.

*We can promote this by asking writers, for their second Once/Now essays, to reverse the order of the model and begin with *Now*.

Once I played soccer as if a fire were in me; now I study and smoke two packs a day.

Notice, by the way, that none of the sentences has a negative half. The writer doesn't say, 'Once I was shy but now I'm no longer shy.'"

Students write for five minutes. (I write too.) When time is up, all the writers read their sentences. (I don't read unless someone asks me to read.) As everyone reads, we enjoy the ideas and possibilities of the sentences. Some writers may have a new idea after listening to others. We take another minute or two to write more.

I say, "You're going to take these home and use one of them as the first sentence of an essay. If you think of a better sentence at home, use that. If you're not happy with any you have now, take ten minutes and write more sentences nonstop. Let them be as wild as you like if that gets you to a good idea.

"There are only two rules for the essay. Put all the *Once* in one part of the essay and all the *Now* in another part. Begin with *Now* if that looks more interesting to you (it often is!), but keep all of *Now* together and all of *Once* together. The other rule is: Make sure both parts of the first sentence are positive. You won't be able to say much about what you're *not*."

If there is time, we each choose one of the sentences and write nonstop for a few minutes to finish off the class.

The "rule" about going through the whole structure once only (keeping *Once* and *Now* separate) gives writers a chance to try the two-part form and see how points in the first part select the points in the second part.

This is all we have to do. We don't "cook" the assignment ahead of time by suggesting possibilities. We don't bring in sample essays. (I remember James writing that he wished people who told him stories would stop after the first sentence.) And we don't suggest to ourselves how the essays will turn out. We might expect, for example, that essays will be divided evenly between *Once* and *Now,* but the symmetrical essays aren't better than the asymmetrical ones. In fact, it's interesting how one time often implies the other: the past anticipates the present; the present reflects the past:

We would punch and hit our way to the back of the bus where no one else dared to sit.

I was going to college because I didn't have a car to get to work, and rural Hunterdon didn't have public transportation.

How could we have children? We were still children ourselves.

Every day I worried and hoped to remain in the good graces of those who controlled me.

Alice Gibson's essay (in Chapter 6) shows how successful the first assignment usually is. (I don't know what she would have written if I had asked her to write on "Prejudice," or to write a comparison/contrast essay.) We begin with this essay shape because it starts writers off with success.

The second form is the Essay of the Opposing Voice: "They say

_____, but my experience tells me_____." Here are some samples:

They say, "You're in therapy? You don't look sick!" And I'm not — therapy is for people well enough to ask for it and use it.

We all know what Italians are like: dark, overweight, undereducated. But my friend's Italian mother is a trim, blonde, former school teacher who is always correcting my English.

They say, "You're from New York? I bet you see all your trees on TV." Well, friend, let me tell you something about New York's parks.

This essay form is the simplest version we know of argument. In it the writer does not have to construct his own argument for or against something. All he has to do is correct a misconception or nail a stereotype with firsthand knowledge. In a way, it's an "argument" by definition. It makes the opposing voice articulate its misinformation, its stereotype, its provincialism. Then the writer defines what the thing is in his experience of it. Sometimes the writer admits the type and denies the way "they" misprize it.

The key to the success of this essay, we tell writers, is to give the opposing voice enough to say — enough rope, really.

Here are two examples of this structure. One is a first-draft essay by an inexperienced writer. The other is a rewritten essay by a student who is better educated, but whose native language is not English. In both examples we see structure lending strength to writers working under disability.

COUNTRY GIRL

Have you ever milked a cow or picked peas or collard greens? Well, don't knock it until you try it. Ever since I was ten, I have always enjoyed working on a farm. During the summer months I used to visit my grandparents on their farm. It was so hot during the mid-summer months, I used to burn up. The sun used to roast my face while I was working in the field. Sweat was pouring from my body, but I loved it. Once or maybe twice, it rains during the summer, but when it did, I used to enjoy listening to the morning rain. It was gently playing rhythms on my window pane. Have you ever sat down on grass in the pasture and talked to yourself? I have. It is like having a talk with God. You will hear echoes from the north, south, east, and west. You can feel the vibrations through your body. I had so many different things to do. My grandfather had a horse named Fred. I used to ride him every day. Later on during the day, friends and relatives used to come over to play. We used to go swimming in the creek and go chasing chickens around the house. This was without my grandfather knowing anything about it. We had lots of chances to go to the theater, but we were just happy staying around the farm. I wish those days would come back, and I hated it that those days had to go.

Once I was at a party among strange faces. I didn't know anybody, so I decided to make friends. I went over to two ladies who were talking about their dogs. I didn't like talking about that. So I went toward one group of ladies talking about the economy and politics, which seemed like a nice, interesting conversation. They asked me my name and other, nosey questions, just like any New Yorker would ask. They noticed my accent, so they asked me, "Where are you from?" and I told them, "I am from Florida." One lady said, "I knew a person from Alabama, and she is so country." I asked her why she called her "country." She said, "Because all country girls milk cows and pick peas or stay in the house all day, and they are not liberated like we are. They don't even know how to play bridge. I have been playing bridge ever since I was fourteen years old." I said, "Oh, I have been playing bridge since I was ten." I was only fooling myself. It was killing me because I wanted to tell her off. I left the party early and went home.

Country life is the best life anybody would enjoy. People that live on a farm, they live peaceful. I loved it.

HAROLYN ANDREWS

Mrs. Andrews begins not with her opponent's view, but with a broad picture of the country as she experienced it as a child. The shift in the second part to the opponent's voice is also a change of focus: a specific, city scene and a brief dialogue. She ends, without answering this attack on country persons directly, but with a brief reassertion of her preference and with an identification, the name of the quality she values most in country life, its peace. That is the term that she has already "defined" concretely in the first half of her essay.

After we have read the city dialogue, we can see that the details of the opponent's definition match or parallel the details Mrs. Andrews selected to present in her first paragraph. There *were* cows and peas in the country, but the writer shows that the work they represented gave her claim to her country experience. The children did not go to the theater; they preferred swimming, chasing chickens, riding Fred, playing with neighbors. She did not play bridge as a child, but sets against that the childhood experience of one's self as the center of a landscape filled with gentle rhythms or vibrating with divine vastness. This picture, along with the simple diction and syntax, establish a peaceful innocence. The woman at the party is damned out of her own mouth in the funny scene that ends in the retreat — and triumph — of our country girl.

WHY DO THEY THINK WE ALL MUST BE ALIKE?

When other people try to guess what European country I come from, they often say, "You must be Hungarian, with your light coloring and small features." But my experience tells me that there are people in Hungary with black eyes and dark hair, as well as people in Spain with blond or brown hair and green or blue eyes.

I am a Spaniard, and contrary to what many people think, we do not all have black hair and black eyes. When I say I am Spanish, and somebody tells me that I don't look like one, my first thought is, "Why is it that they think we all must be alike?" In my own family I have brothers whose hair and eyes are black, and I have other brothers whose hair is almost white and who have blue eyes. If within a family people can be so different, how can we think the people of a country are all alike? Of course, people from a given country have certain characteristics because they have the same culture and live in the same climate, which influences the way they act and live as well as their customs.

When I was a little girl living in the country, I thought all Americans were tall, blond, and thin. I had similar ideas of how other people from other countries were. Coming to New York taught me to forget all the ideas I had of different people, for I find New York to be the place where one can learn more about people than any other place. When I first came to New York, my favorite pastime was to look at people. I was like a child in an amusement park to whom everything is new and wonderful.

I remember in those first days in New York I wished I were a photographer. I thought, "If I could have a little camera to take pictures of people without their knowledge, I would be all my life doing it and never get bored or tired." There were so many different people, and what I found more important, they all had different expresssions regardless of what they looked like. Those expressions were what I wanted to take pictures of, for they were what make people what they are, human beings. I remember seeing a little boy in a wheelchair. He couldn't move his body, but his eyes were so bright, curious, and full of life that I thought, How can I classify this boy? He doesn't look Spanish or Scandanavian or American. His expression is saying, "I am me, and I am living regardless of what people think I am."

This association of people with looks makes me think how we classify people; it shows how we have a pre-formed opinion of how people from other countries should look, and it comes to us as a surprise when we see that we are many, that in any given country people can look as different from each other as the moon differs from the sun.

OLGA HUERTA

Miss Huerta's paper seems at first glance not to be following out our idea of a pretty full presentation of the opponent's point of view. But the class noticed that she had in fact presented two opposing points of view. One of the points of view is a development or extension of the first and, very tellingly, it is her own former point of view. When she internalizes the opponent, she has taken the necessary and intelligent step to universalizing and extending the debate.

Her former point of view is put at the right distance from the views in the second half of the paper because it is in the past. That view is quietly placed or defined for the reader by the unobtrusive phrases, *little girl* and *living in the country*. We may suppose that sort of view is like a child's or like that of a person with a limited range of experience. The class noticed that Miss Huerta does not try to show that the opposing view is ridiculous, but uses it to get at an underlying question: Why do we think other people all look alike? She can get to this question more easily, they said, just because she has associated herself with that attitude.

The stereotype of Spaniards is answered by a reference to her own family. The larger question, raised by her own former assumptions, is developed by a larger experience, the experience of living in New York. Here she works out the distinction she had begun before between the similarities that culture and climate may give, and the differences that individual human experience makes. The camera suggests a less prejudiced or more public point of view.

The class praised the essay's ending. One person said that "we are many" showed him for the first time the power of very simple words: "Does anybody here want my thesaurus?" Everyone was surprised and delighted by the appearance of the sun and moon. One student tried to say why he thought that was effective: "The sun and moon are universal. They get us off the earth and away from our own, small points of view."

What goes wrong in most essays of argument, in our experience, is that the arguer is writing a list of reasons for or against something. An inexperienced writer thinks that the more reasons there are, the stronger the argument will be. Just the opposite is true. An argument is one line of reasoning resting on a single base. In school debates, a speaker tries to overwhelm and confuse the opposition with mountains of "arguments," but that won't do in writing where the arguments can be examined. The base of the argument is the assumption the reasoner has to be granted to begin with. But each of the reasons on a list of reasons rests on a different base, and each asks the reader to accept a different assumption as its starting point. The more the hapless writer adds reasons, the more the argument becomes a tissue of assumptions and the more insubstantial it becomes.

To construct a consistent line of reasoning is not easy, but it is not hard to correct a careless view with our own experience. It certainly is a service to do so. I never hear a set of sentences from a class without feeling surprised in some prejudice I didn't know I was harboring.

When the first Opposing Voice essay comes in, it's the third essay and the fourth week of class. It's time to encourage writers to extend their ideas and make them more explicit.

In small groups we read the Opposing Voice essay, write observations, and read them to each other. We regroup as one class, and someone rereads her essay. We ask everyone to write for ten minutes on the questions. How did the firsthand experience define the error? What *was* the error? When the time is up, everyone reads what she has written. The author rereads her essay with one of these as the new final paragraph. The assignment for next time is: Write another Opposing Voice essay. When you have completed it, write a final paragraph in which you show the effect of the experience on the way we see the error. When the first Opposing Voice essay is returned, it will be rewritten with the addition of such a final paragraph.

The third structure is the Two Voices, the essay of the Answering Voice. In the second essay, one voice is ignorant; one is experienced. In this essay both voices know. Though they disagree, each is a view that makes sense in its own context. Ideally they complete each other; ideally they will always disagree. The high-minded essays are Mental Fight, "Platonic Tolerance"; the lighthearted ones are Comic Liberty. The model sentence is: "You can do it another way, but you can also do it this way." Here are some examples:

In my family there are the late sleepers and the early risers.

My friend is a private-school, private-life, only child. I'm from a large family; I'm never without a buddy and I never had a pair of sox of my own.

She likes to get her work hours all in by noon; I need the quiet of the night to work.

"I travel to know the world." "My neighborhood is where I know myself."

The move that writers are learning to negotiate in this essay is making distinctions.

Of the example essays that follow, the first is a rewritten paper from a student in the regular first-semester composition course, the second an extempore composition by a student in the pre-English 1 class. The second paper began with a quotation from a poem and then moved into the two-voices form.

RICH OR POOR

I've gone to Jamaica twice now, and each time I have been met with the belief that I am rich. No explanation I gave of my status at home could shake this belief.

I stayed at a place in northeastern Jamaica called Strawberry Fields. It is a campsite where you have the choice of a small cottage (one room) or a tent to sleep in. Since the tent was cheaper, that's where I slept.

Strawberry Fields is very quiet and peaceful. If you haven't a car, you are stuck there. The campsite offers fresh air and total relaxation to recuperate from big city blues. My tent was by the ocean, and every night I was lullabied to sleep by the sound of the waves.

Another nice fact about the campsite was that it was cheap, a poor man's vacation. I travelled light with one pair of jeans, one shirt and one bathing suit. Aside from toothpaste and soap, that was all I needed.

The people that lived in the area couldn't think of why anyone would come to that side of the island in the first place. The beaches were small, the roads unpaved, and there were few telephones. They knew that the Playboy Hotel and other hotels offered everything from swimming pools to dress-dinners and dancing under the moonlight. Since almost every American that came to Jamaica stayed at one of these beautiful hotels, they must have been rich. Carrying their own logic one step further, they felt that any American visiting Jamaica, no matter what crazy place they decided to stay at, also must be rich. So the answer to my being at Strawberry Fields had to be that I was an eccentric rich American, who, with nothing better to do, decided to drop in on them.

No matter how shabby my jeans or old my bathing suit, no matter how I counted my Jamaican pennies — I was rich to them. The cook, as well as others at the campsite, nearly everyday asked for a man's wallet; the wash woman requested sneakers, and the fisherman wanted a tape deck. I couldn't answer these requests by saying, "Give me the money and I'll send you what you want." Jamaicans, outside of the cities, earned about two dollars a day for any labor they could find — road-work, washing clothes, selling fruit alongside the roads. The fisherman-farmers in the area had very little cash handy themselves. As far as they were concerned, I was a rich American who wore old clothes and was stingy with her wealth. The attitude of, "You have so much — spread it around" was prevalent.

Sometimes, though, I secretly agreed with their picture of me. Especially when I visited their homes, which were little more than shacks by the sea, or ate their food, which always consisted of breadfruit and fish caught from the sea. On festive occasions goat's head soup was made. It tasted and smelled as bad as it sounded. Then, when I thought of home, I *was* rich. But this state of consciousness disappeared when I returned to New York. At home, I couldn't afford a tape-deck for a car, never mind the car, and the type of sneakers they wanted cost about twenty dollars — I owned a four dollar pair. A man's wallet, leather, wasn't too expensive, but buying three or four at a time would have been half my paycheck. I had a more solid roof over my head and ate more varied fare, but then again, I couldn't grow my own vegetables or catch my own fish. What it came down to was that, relatively speaking, I was almost as poor in New York as they were in Jamaica, only in my case, it took more money to be poor.

RACHEL BRIGHT

This essay is organized around a neat turn in which Miss Bright finally concedes a point of view that, till the last moment, she has apparently been presenting as alien. The neatness is in delaying this concession, while she gives the reader the evidence for it, till the reader is more than ready to make it himself. She begins modestly with the "other" voice ("the belief that I am rich"), and then, instead of meeting it head on, she describes the scene and her belongings and lets that establish her point of view. She returns to the other voice and sketches the "logic" behind it. She doesn't let this lack of logic put us at a distance, however, but brings us closer to this voice. It becomes particularized as "cook," "fisherman," "washwoman." Finally, just before the turning point, she sums up the other voice, but still in her own terms: "I was a rich American who wore old clothes and was stingy with her wealth."

An absurd idea of theirs, of course, but certain uncomfortable details in her description have set up a tension between logic and life: two dollars a day . . . road work . . . washing clothes. We wonder if these details speak to her as they do to us. No writer can afford to be less conscious than his readers. But this writer is true to what she has described, after all, and the turning point of the essay comes when we hear the justice of the other voice.

The argument is not generalized away from the details of its evidence. Nor are the details simply listed. They are *placed,* in the open narrative frame of the essay: "I visited their homes . . . ate their food." Here the speaker's voice merges with the alien voice, and, though it will diverge once more to have the last word, it has yielded to the other voice that voice's authority in its own place. The speaker's own logic becomes explicit only when she returns to her own place.

The identification of a line of reasoning with consciousness of place — point of view in the literal sense — is persuasive in the modesty of its claim. There has been a question of wealth — perhaps of giving. But these terms have expanded as the essay has developed: the writer is a poor student, but not poor-spirited.

The essay is in many ways a model of economy. It lets the mental point of view take rise from the literal point of view. It gets progressively closer to the other voice and then lets it speak most convincingly. It builds its argument on the details that have appeared previously in the narrative: tape-deck, sneakers, wallet, wages.

THE COBWEBS OF MY MIND

"Don't worry, spiders. I keep house casually." But should I get out the broom, watch out! The house I refer to is the cavern between my ears and the broom, my conscience. My mind is like an erector set, the parts mechanically pieced together, functioning with computer-like logic until a web of logic in which to trap my thoughts is created. In my sober state I am incapable of assaulting this web. It seems that as long as I am sober, my mind spins its web so cleverly that neither I nor my conscience can escape. The secret for me is to put myself in a situation where my logical processes cease to function. The web is weakened and then broken, and my conscience is free to speak its piece.

It was a hot, lazy August evening the last time my conscience spoke. I was drunk, and all traces of logic and left my thinking apparatus. So there I sat as my conscience conversed with two old friends of mine, Joseph and Junior. Joseph and Junior don't have anything in common except me. So when we get together, I try not to bring up anything too controversial that might end in a fight I would have to referee. But my conscience was calling the shots tonight, so I knew it was only a matter of time before I was doomed.

Before I get carried away, let me introduce you to my friends. Joseph is a red-necked country boy. He grew up in a segregated backwoods section of New Jersey. By the time Joseph entered school, there wasn't a racial slur he didn't know, and his attendance in segregated schools only served to expand his bigotry. I wasn't comfortable with Joseph's bigotry, but I rationalized that it was a bigotry born of ignorance, not maliciousness. If Joseph is the north pole, then Junior is the south pole. Junior grew up on the racially-mixed streets of the Bronx. Junior claimed to have many friends from the Black, Hispanic, and Oriental communities, and was very proud of his liberal racial views. I was more comfortable with Junior, but when he said, "Some of my best friends are Black," his liberalism didn't ring true.

At first, my conscience was content to sit and observe as Joseph, Junior and I discussed baseball, but then it too became involved and brought up the Barbara Jordan keynote speech at the recent Democratic Party convention. Joseph had followed the speech on radio and was unaware that the only speech that had made any sense to him had been made by a Black. Therefore he offered praise. Junior offered the speech as proof that Blacks could "amount to something." In his state of confusion, Joseph could offer no reply. They turned to me for an answer.

The answer hit me like a ton of bricks. Joseph was wrong in ignorant bigotry, but correct when he offered praise when in ignorance of a person's race. Junior was right in his views on racial equality, but wrong when he saw the race before the person.

I turned to respond and in shame realized that I was alone. My conscience had spoken. The only Joseph and Junior with me were the Joseph and Junior in Carl Joseph Shaunessy Junior. The web of prejudice I had so logically and carefully constructed in my mind had been shaken off its foundation, swept clean by the broom of my conscience.

CARL JOSEPH SHAUNESSY, JR.

Carl Joseph Shaunessy, Jr. was known to the class by his full cognomen. With this knowledge and even though he had given all the clues to his ironic scene in his essay, no one in class caught on till the last paragraph. Probably the confusing imagery in the first paragraph threw the listeners off. Perhaps few people can so clearly locate two voices within themselves. Both voices seem wrong. The turn of the essay, in paragraph five, is the definition of how each voice is wrong *and* right.

This thoughtful paragraph that sorts out and defines the terms of the dialogue is one of the shortest in the essay. Twice the class asked that it be reread. When Mr. Shaunessy asked whether the class thought the paragraph should be rewritten and expanded, the immediate response was, No. Class members said that they would "get" it better reading it, and that they would enjoy rereading it. He later tried expanding it, but wasn't satisfied with that version. When he tried it on his original hearers, they protested the loss of pithiness. "It's like explaining a joke," someone said.

The response to the essay was interesting because it suggested an essentially "written" quality, that the essay had to be read and reread to be properly taken in. And this reminds us that we sometimes confuse good writing with finish or a polished style. Blake complained that Reynolds praised the "finish" of works that "are not Even Begun." Mr. Shaunessy's essay is complete, but not finished. Its completeness shows most clearly in its passages of greatest brevity and economy. "Joseph and Junior don't have anything in common except me" had class members shaking their heads in admiration of its wit.

The reasoning is complete in paragraph five. Mr. Shaunessy can easily add more bulk to this paragraph but not easily more weight. An authoritative reader like a teacher must be careful about the authority of the author in reading an essay like this. Rather than make the fifth paragraph fatter, it might be better that the author make the whole essay leaner — take his own strength as a model. Certainly, before he changes the fifth paragraph, he ought to reread the first paragraph and the rest of his essay in its light.

For this essay too we write a new final paragraph in class by writing for ten or fifteen minutes on the question, "What was the issue — the point on which the two voices took their stand?"

This is how we see the usefulness of these coordinate structures for essays:

The parallel structure helps writers keep their essays consistent from beginning to end across the two parts of the structure. The first thing we look for in the thinking of a paper is internal consistency.

Beginning with a simple two-part structure helps writers to hold their idea in mind while they consider what kind of development it needs.

The parallel, two-part essay is economical. The first part is really more than half the whole, because it anticipates the other half. And because the beginning is proleptic, everything the writer says counts twice.

CODA: Lists

We have been identifying lists as what goes wrong with most attempts at composition. Certainly it is easy to recognize the rag-bag essay ("There are many interesting/important/significant things about this subject.") and the list (of what is in the bag) as primitive attempts at composition. They are the unconsidered measures of the inexperienced writer. In our classes, lists are part of the preparatory, running-writing students do to sort out or identify their thoughts. Students soon learn the secret that every writer knows: you get your best ideas near the bottom of the page or when you have just about run out of paper or time.

But literature reminds us that we can't always rule out the list as the form for a good piece of writing. The list or catalogue, which is so simple that a child can produce one, is so important that it forms a large part of oral literature. In its concrete, exhaustive form it is either heroic or satiric. Grand and heroic, it is the Catalogue of Ships, the epic geography of *Prometheus Bound*, the misdeeds one swears not to have done in *The Book of the Dead*, the commandments of *Deuteronomy*, the catalogue of tongues in *Acts 2*. These parts call to mind the mighty whole: the completeness of the heroic enterprise, the whole mortal world suspended between tyrant and savior, the restraints that compose righteousness, the catholicity of the descending spirit.

In its prophetic or satiric form, anatomy, the catalogue exposes the shallowness or absurdity of a pretence to integrity. We see it in the prophetic tirade:

You steal, you murder, you commit adultery and perjury, you burn sacrifices to Baal, you run after other gods whom you have not known;
then you come and stand before me in this house, which bears my name,
and say, "We are delivered!" (*Jeremiah* 7:9-10)

And in Swift's dissections:

. . . lords, fiddlers, judges or dancing masters.

Even the most artless of lists, if it is exhaustive and honest enough,
begins to suggest more than the sum of its parts. Here is a naive catalogue of oaths, by a ten-year-old, in the original orthography, contrib-
uted to our files by a retiring fifth-grade teacher:

1. I must pay attention to the teacher.
2. I must not try to make every body laugh
3. I must not leap like a gazzle.
4. I must not fool around in the closet.
5. I must not stick signs in the window.
6. I must get right to work.
7. I must not get sent out of the room.
8. I must not chew gum at school.
9. I must not play with things at school.
10. I must not swing on things.
11. I must not stick my head in the closet.
12. I must not run up to the teacher.
13. I must not get out of my seat every five minutes.
14. I must not speak out.
15. I must not stand up in my chair.
16. I must not play with my friends in class.
17. I must not carry my chair around.
18. I must not pretend to be a lion tamer.
19. I must not talk in class or in special period.
20. I must not fool around on line.
21. I must not distract the ball player at punchball.
22. I must not jump around in the hall.
23. I must not get sent into other teachers rooms.
24. I must not lie on my "chairs"
25. I must not sit on my table.

Readers will have their own comments on this, but it is interesting how
the very exhaustiveness of the list turns it ironically against the law
that brought it forth.

Here is a first-draft essay using lists strategically, in response to the two assignments we have been discussing. If there is a form in which one voice is wrong and the other right, and a form in which both voices are right, it is inevitable that someone will write an essay in which both (or all) voices are wrong. If we get a rhetorical essay and a philosophical essay, we are bound to get a satiric one.

SILLY STEREOTYPES

Stereotyping is a thing for joking; it is not to be taken seriously. Everyone does stereotyping. Sometimes it is a correct assessment, but most times it is not. That is why it is an invalid way of judging people. I do stereotype people, but only for the effect of causing some conversation or for laughter. I have been stereotyped by a lot of other people who didn't even know me. Almost every time, I have proved other people's beliefs about me mistaken. A few experiences will show how silly stereotyping is.

Almost every time I walk near a senior citizen, weird things happen. I usually see them go into a shell, into a space where I won't go. They grasp with strength their pocketbooks and wallets. Well, I guess they are worried because of the high crime rate on them. Every time they get past me, they feel alive again. I never bother them, but the fear of the young is strong with them. Sometimes it bugs me when the old react to me like this. I like to have some fun when I see them stereotype me. If they go into their fear routine, I sometimes say *Boo* in a deep voice.

I have been stereotyped in sports a lot. Last week I went to a night center for the first time to play basketball. There were a lot of people there, most of them over six feet tall. When they chose the teams, I wasn't picked. They saw me, at five feet ten and one half inches and thought they should forget me. I waited for the next game with a burning desire to do these guys in. In the end my team lost, but I scored seven of our nine points and woke those guys up. They started picking me to play all night long.

Do I look like a criminal? Well, every time I go into a store I attract detectives like a crumb attracts ants. They watch every move I make. I often offer to carry them around on my back so they can watch me better. I know they are paid to be suspicious, but they seem to concentrate on teenagers. When I go into a store with my father, the detective relaxes. When I go into a store alone, I see the "detecto" (that's my name for them) light up. His face is on fire. While he is on fire with me in his sight, any middle-aged person can have a picnic robbing the store. When I leave the store with a receipt on my package, I see the "detecto" almost ready to cry.

A stereotype I don't care for is the hippie stereotype. Every time I meet a new person, I get a weird session of handshakes. I try to laugh at these people. My uncles and some friends go through the series of handshakes too. I really get tired. I really don't know all these handshakes. The other person usually has to drag my hand through this routine. These handshakes are strenuous and tire me out. Why can't they just shake my hand in the conventional way? I guess they want me to feel right at home with another hippie. About three months ago I met a black teammate of mine at a football game. He went through the series of handshakes. He saw that I was an amateur. He offered me lessons on the proper soul-hippie-young people's handshake. Now I know how to do it.

All of these experiences are times when people stereotyped me. Most of the times they were wrong. From my looks, age, and background, they took me for what they imagine everyone in my class is like. I enjoy it sometimes and even laugh at it. Other people should not take their stereotypes too seriously.

MARTIN IGLESIAS

Martin Iglesias makes his fun, as the class noticed when he read his essay, by placing himself at the center of contradictory stereotypes. For old folks and store detectives, he is potentially dangerous; for tall athletes, he is no threat. For senior citizens, detectives, and athletes, he is an outsider; but for the well-disposed, he appears to be one of the young and cool. And they are all wrong.

His paper is a good example of how choosing his own subject gives the writer a chance to use his own langauge to his best advantage. As in Mrs. Andrews' essay, Mr. Iglesias' diction and syntax characterize the speaker of the essay: the well-meaning, uncomplicated person, trying to pick his or her way through the incomprehensible, but apparently inevitable obstacles to the simple life: "These handshakes are strenuous and tire me out. Why can't they just shake my hand in the conventional way?" The character is comical. But, even though the speaker's language supports the characterization ("Well, I guess they are worried because of the high crime rate on them."), the construction of the essay shows that the characterization is ironic. The young man who claims that elaborate handshakes wear him out can play strenuous basketball. And among the dramatically serviceable simple sentences and young people's expressions, Mr. Iglesias turned out several sentences and phrases that everyone in class remembered after hearing them once: "They grasp with strength their pocketbooks and wallets," "but the fear of the young is strong with them," and, at the climax of the paper, the wonderful name: "soul-hippie-young people's hand-shake." Here the two-part shape has been dismissed in favor of the satiric anatomy.

8 | Two-Part Essay Shapes: Structures of Subordination

The assignments in our second series take the writer closer to the structure of analysis, though the essays are still largely personal and concrete. All of them are concerned with consequences: looking back to define how they have come out of the past; looking forward, as a weighing of choices; and looking within for that special form of the present we make by analyzing and solving problems. Each is again a two-part structure, but now the relations between the parts are explicit — are the subject of thought.

Thinking about the difference between a coordinate sentence and a sentence with subordination shows differences between the first and second series of assignments. The relationship in a coordinate sentence seems fairly obvious. A coordinate conjunction may be omitted altogether, and a mark of punctuation substituted, because we sense the connection very readily. But we cannot omit a subordinate conjunction. It makes a difference whether the connection is *although* or *because,* whether it is *if* or *when.*

That difference is what the writers of the second series are writing about. There is a turning point in each of the essay types: one thing in the past accounted for a present state; one thing tipped the balance toward a choice; one thing addressed a problem and negotiated it. This turn or relationship needs to be explained in these essays because the two sides of the essay are either not in balance, or the balance is a hidden one.

The first essay is the Essay of Hindsight. Its model sentence is: That _____ is the way it was, and that made this _____ difference. These are the sample sentences:

> When I found out the power I had for harming others, I became a careful driver.

> It wasn't till I celebrated my independence by leaving home that I found out how dependent I was on my mother and father.

> Because my father was an optimist who loved adventure, I grew up learning to trust myself.

I'm going back to college now — though I'm 20 years late — because my father thought no one could be happy for long without an education.

Because the American colonists did not punish the British Loyalists after the Revolutionary war, the country started out with the idea that unity could tolerate dissent.

The essay of Hindsight is the form of the historical essay. The image of having taken a way that made all the difference goes back to Hesiod's *Works and Days* (I, 287ff). When Herodotus' Croesus was about to be burned after the defeat of his city, he understood what Solon had told him about happiness and the end. With a slight change of emphasis, this form becomes the elegy: "That was part of my life, a thing I took for granted at the time. Now I see its value." This is perfectly expressed in a line from Jonson's poem for his dead friend:

> Now I conceive him by my loss.
> ("AN EPITAPH ON MASTER VINCENT CORBETT")

When we look back, we see patterns which seem to us now as our lot. The two parts of the essay are the Way and the Difference. What was the way it was? What difference did it make?

CARELESS TO CAUTIOUS

One of the things I always wanted to do when I was growing up was to drive a car. My parents, however, did not own a car and could not afford to send me to driving school. As soon as we got married, my husband and I bought a car. This was a good opportunity to learn how to drive. Determined to get a driver's license as soon as possible, I paid great attention to my instructor. After 10 driving lessons and some practice, I earned my driving license.

I had tremendous confidence in myself when I drove my car, but it often led to carelessness. I used to drive very fast and not let any other driver come into my traffic lane.

One morning during rush hour I was driving on a busy street. After waiting for a red light to turn green, I made a left turn at an intersection without bothering to watch for cars coming from the other direction. I hit another car. The other driver was not hurt, but I had to be rushed to the hospital for cuts and bruises. I was in my third month of pregnancy. On the way to the hospital, all I could think about was my baby. I was shaking like a leaf while the doctor examined me. After a few tests had been taken, I was told that I was in fine condition. I was very relieved and happy to hear the news.

A few hours after the accident I started bleeding. I knew it was a bad sign. I was examined again and was told to remain in bed for at least a month. The doctor could not promise me a normal pregnancy and delivery. I was determined to do everything in my power to save the baby. I stayed in bed 24 hours a day and obeyed all my doctor's orders. I was very depressed. I kept blaming myself for risking the baby's life because of my carelessness.

A month passed by after the accident, and then one wonderful morning I felt the baby move. I was very happy. I was allowed to lead a normal life from that day. For the rest of the months of pregnancy, I did not dare drive. When my husband drove, I used to tell him to be careful and to drive slowly.

After delivering a healthy, beautiful child, I have become a "perfect" driver. I not only obey all the traffic signs and laws, but also am generous and careful with other drivers. This is one of the lessons I learned the hard way.

BAT-SHEVA RICHMAN

Mrs. Richman's impromptu essay has the recoil-structure essays on this model frequently take: the overreaching/the compensating withdrawal. The turning point is, of course, the realization of a norm: her sense of normal life stirring in the baby and the consequent granting of a "normal life" for the mother "from that day." The compensation at first spills over a bit; the converted sinner has her eyes sharpened to the sins of others; "I used to tell him to be careful and to drive slowly." But the compensation is rightly located by the end. The sense of norm, the balance of the whole essay is recapitulated in the brief coda and manifested as Law: we go from the "bad sign" in the middle of the essay to "obey all traffic signs and laws" at the end. But the balance is not so stern as that sentence might imply. Joy finds expression in generosity: she has received what she has not deserved; she will be generous to others. Cause and effect repeated in a finer tone.

The author of this paper is not a native English speaker. What is missing in the paper, doubtless as a consequence of this, are the abstractions that would enable her to develop the implications of the essay. It is interesting that the abstractions are present and ready to emerge in some of the terms the author is using conventionally or concretely: *normal, sign, law.* These abstractions emerged in the class observations of the paper. As her colleagues used the language of her paper to discuss it, the author began to see the abstract capacity of her language.

EARNING ENJOYMENT

My father's philosophy in life was that we should enjoy whatever we had and not be made unhappy by what we didn't have. He valued enjoyment for its own sake. This philosophy sounded absurd to me. When I was a child, whatever my parents said sounded absurd. But my father tried to make me realize the importance of this philosophy. When I got upset at some hard lesson, he would say that it was only for my own good.

One day I made a comment that I would commit suicide if I didn't have money or if I had a job that required serving others. This remark caused me to earn my allowance. I had to help our cook for a whole week. At the end of the week, I was told that it is necessary to climb from the bottom of the hill in order to get to the top. This experience taught me a lesson, and that was to respect people for what they did. The lesson didn't last me for long, because I made another remark about other people, their clothing and their possessions. These remarks made my father change his mind about my school. The next semester he registered me in a public school instead of a private school. My life changed because I learned so much from others. I saw how people struggled. I saw how poor students were satisfied with what they had, which was practically nothing. I would get embarrassed because I had everything and I was not thankful. I started to value things that I had and I was satisfied with the smallest things I got.

This is the way my childhood was. The way my parents brought me up has made a great deal of difference in my perspective on life. When I started to live alone, especially when I came to America, I had a great deal of hardship. In order to survive, I accepted jobs which I would never have dreamed of doing before. This did not bother me because I had had a taste of this experience before. I always remember that it is necessary to start from the bottom in order to be able to climb to the top of the hill. Today, if I have the best, I will enjoy it, and if I don't have the best, I will still enjoy what I have. Everything is to be enjoyed for itself. Because of my past experiences, now I am not dominated by material things. I think we should appreciate and value what we have.

If it wasn't for my past experiences, I don't think I would be able to enjoy and be happy with what I have. After all, my parents were right when they said that what they did was for my own good.

GAYANA GASHIAN

This essay shows an alternate form: the way has been determined by something out of one's own power or by someone else. The class noticed the balances working here: this is the lesson I learned; the same lesson was later required of me. The lesson, "to respect others for what they did," later yields self-respect for whatever one does honestly. A youthful intemperance ("I would commit suicide if I didn't have money or if I had a job that required serving others") gives place to a more mature equanimity: "a great deal of hardship . . . did not bother me."

This is an impromptu essay. The narrative here is clearly subordinated to explanation, as one can see in the omission of engrossing narrative detail. There are four or five "lessons," as the class observed, and some hesitation about which is the most important. The author might use the strength of structure here simply by sorting out and balancing the lessons.

The essay of Hindsight combines narrative (or process) and analysis: the way — the difference. They are intimately related, which gives us the wholeness we need for good analysis. We cannot understand what the *way* was until we have become aware of the difference; nor can we define the difference until we can characterize the way. The writers of all three sample essays found that comparison/contrast was necessary to the structure: without change we cannot know *same*.

For this assignment we work on two new final paragraphs in answer to two questions: What was the way, then? What is the difference?

The second essay shape in this series is the Essay of Foresight. The model sentence is: "When I saw that fork in the road just ahead in my life, I chose this_____ instead of that _____." Examples:

When I thought about the next four years, I decided to sweat it out in school instead of in a short-order kitchen.

"At nineteen I did not throw myself into the struggle for life, I threw my mother." (Shaw)

I wanted the most boring, routine job I could get that summer. I was preparing for my second chance.

The last essay looked backward; this looks forward, and presents the writer with the grounds of choice. Practical choice depends on foresight, interest, or self-interest, and this essay shapes the choice for the short term ahead that we can foresee. Its prototype is in the large body of traditional Wisdom literature, especially in proverbs: "He that gathers in the harvest is a wise son; but he that snorteth in the summer is the son of confusion." The way practical choice is always tied to a special context or time is expressed in the traditional sense that "there is a time for all things under heaven." It is in Adonis' answer to Venus' proposal to love: "Before I know myself, seek not to know me."

THE DECISION TO ATTEND COLLEGE

The decision to attend college or to stay at home and do nothing of importance confronted me in the summer of 1976. It was during this time when I was at home doing nothing, that my wife asked me about re-entering college and finishing my education. I had been in college twice before, and I was a "drop out" both times. When I had dropped out, I did so because of personal problems both times. But now things were different. I was happy at home with my wife and kids. I was not doing anything about my future. I had never thought about it seriously and was now confronted with the choice of being at home or going to college. I had to decide.

I went to the park alone that day. I sat and watched the birds and squirrels, and then I started thinking about my problem. I knew what I was going to miss. I was enjoying myself by going to parties, get-togethers, bus outings, and movies. I loved going to parties. I loved going to the movies. This I did most of the time after work. I would see a movie during the week, and usually on weekends my wife and I would go to parties or to visit a friend. When I was not at the movies I would sit and watch all the top programs on television. I was really happy. I would take my kids to the park and play ball with them. Or I would take them to an amusement park to enjoy themselves. I love being with them, and I always try to make them happy. If a trip came up unexpectedly, I did not have to worry. I would take my family along without concerning myself about anything else. But then I seriously asked myself these questions. What will I be doing ten years from now? How will I be able to send my kids to school without a good income? Will my wife still be happy to know that I am still a college "drop out"? And most of all, will I be happier as a waiter for the rest of my life or to be able to fulfill my wish of being a lawyer?

To do something that is quite opposite to what I was doing was hard. I knew what it would be like in school. I would have to study regularly; I would have to study on weekends; I would miss many parties and movies; I would not be able to play ball with my kids. I would not see my wife often while I am in school. I would have to change my whole life style.

After considering all of these questions and all of the things I would miss, I told myself that I have to make sacrifices to better myself. I would have to give up parties, parks, movies, and lying around the apartment looking at television. I had to decide.

Now I am in college. I miss going to parties, movies, or the park. I miss many things, but now I am happy to know that I am on my way to being a better person. I have made my choice and I will stay with it until the end.

COMPTON SOOKRA

Frequently these essays of choice begin by putting the choice obliquely. It is as if choice hardly exists at first or only comes into existence as the choice is being made. Von Rad notes something similar when he says, "Experiences without preparation do not exist. Man creates experiences which he expects and for which he is ready." In Mr. Sookra's essay, "to attend college" is definite, but to "do nothing of importance" seems not much of a decision. But that "nothing" is what the essay really defines: it turns out to be the negative choice that is important.

The class noted with approval that the decision is not "made in the air," as one student put it, but located — made in the park. And the park is one of the things the speaker will have to give up. The class relished this irony: "It's in the park he decides to give up the park," was one comment. Another: "It was that life that gave him the time to decide to give up that life."

The future here is counted out as a definite interval: ten years. The possibilities that ten years represent are ticked off, coming down finally to "waiter" or "lawyer." *Waiter,* someone remarked, describes more than his job.

One of the author's colleagues noticed how often the word *happy* came up in the essay and said it was a new idea to him that a decision to change one's life could come, not out of discontent, but even out of happiness with the way things are.

The most interesting thing about the essay of Foresight is how often it is based on a sorting-out, reducing, discarding action. Traditional wisdom supports this: "In knowledge," Hsün Tzu says, "nothing is more important than discarding what is doubtful." This sort of choice is emergent; what do we do or say when the time is here? Not the ideal thing, but the necessary thing. The writer throws away all the possibilities except the last two. Then, often, he decides not which one of these he wants more but which one he wants less, and discards that. This is a useful mental strategy for times when we are writing for an unknown or extremely diverse audience and must find a specific thing on which they can all agree — at least as a beginning.

To extend the essay, we ask students to write on this question: How did the choice you made define the interest you were serving?

The last structure in this series is the shape of the Essay of Insight. The model sentence is: "In this dilemma or crisis, I turned to this tradition or principle." Examples:

I was scared to death — but my mother's voice kept coming back to me from my childhood, "Tell the truth and you won't get hurt."

I said, "But I can't go back to school now. I'll be 35 before I get my degree." She said, "You're going to be 35 anyway. You might as well be 35 and have a degree."

Someone asked the man who had fallen down the stairs, "Shall we call an ambulance? Are you hurt?" But my friend said, "We don't ask *him* if he's hurt. We ask a doctor."

I didn't know whether to leave or stay, but my friend said, "You ought to keep your promise."

Once I did it, I'd never know whether it was right or wrong. My aunt said, "Well, the world isn't going to send you a telegram about what to do. You can trust what you *want* to do, as long as it doesn't hurt anyone else."

The choice of foresight is good for the short term ahead, the foreseeable future. But when the future looks murky, and choice is a dilemma, insight in the form of tradition, principle, or promise comes into play. We often speak of "exercising" foresight, which suggests the effort of doing something in fair weather when we'd rather not think about winter coming. But when we're right in the midst of problems, we look inside for some way of continuing that might have a blessing or a safe conduct on it. The way of conscience, tradition, principle is the way of the prophets who remind their hearers of Covenant, Nature, or Human Nature: law and its balancing action:

You have stripped the vineyards, and the spoils of the poor are in your houses. Therefore I will strip you of every prop and stay, warrior and soldier, priest and prophet.

(Isaiah)

You have kept from the underworld the child who belongs there, and you have put into the dark the child who belongs to the light.

(Antigone)

The babe that weeps the rod beneath
Writes revenge in realms of death.

(Auguries of Innocence)

Not every day do we have to look past ordinary matters of prudence to a larger good. When we do, when writers do, they are in the position of the lawyer or judge who asks, How does the principle of the law fit this case?

ANSWERING THE QUESTION

I had to choose between the comfort and safety of a sun-baked beach and the chance of answering a question. I chose to answer the question because the chance of a truthful answer arose.

As a young teenager, I had the good fortune to spend the best part of the summer at a town called Long Beach. The streets were named after the streets of the U.S. and the months of the year. I only remember three main avenues — there might have been four — but then the Atlantic Ocean ended the naming of them on one side, and the bay did the same on the other.

Most of my days were spent on the beach and in that never-ending mystifying body of water. At times it resembled a large, peaceful lake, and at other times, the meanest, angriest, most brutal place my young mind could imagine. I was fascinated by it, I loved it, I feared it, but as a youth I had fun in it. The beach was almost as vast. Looking to the right or left, you couldn't see the ending of the long, sandy beach. Although it appeared as vast as the ocean, that didn't matter. All you had to do once you reached it was collapse, relax, wiggle a little and you would be caressed by sun and sand. The beach had as many faces as the ocean, but it seemed much safer. We played all sorts of games, like football, volleyball, and games that have no names.

It was easy for me to meet kids my age, younger and older. The guys I met had similar backgrounds. They were from some part of the city, here for the summer or staying with relatives for some part of it.

After a full day of sun and surf, we'd all go home for supper. Then we'd meet each other on the boardwalk and decide what to do. Some nights we would walk down the boardwalk to the amusement area. It was about a two mile walk and well worth it just to hear the tall tales we youths could spin with such inaccurate detail. Each one knew that the other was lying, but who cared as long as his tale was accepted as well as that of the last guy? By the time we reached the amusement area, each one of us was equal to William the Conquerer, Attila the Hun, Tarzan, and Mickey Mantle.

There was one question we asked each other, the question that couldn't possibly escape us. We all had been exposed to it as spectators by spending a good deal of time at the beach. Our daily watching of the professional life-guards also made us aware of the true danger involved and the possibility of it becoming a reality. We didn't all answer it the same way. We all did our best to answer honestly because, knowing the truth of what happens when a person is drowning, we knew it was no disgrace to say, "Hell, I'm not going to let someone drown me!" I answered as honestly as I could, and said I really didn't know but that I thought I would try to save someone who is drowning.

Four years later I was once again out at Long Beach staying with with relatives. This time was different from the early years I spent there. For one thing I was older. Another was I hadn't been there for years and none of the guys I spent the previous summers with were there either. Most of all I was there, at a place that held for me nothing but memories of good times growing up, against my will. My parents had forced me to come because I was getting into "city trouble."

I had been there two days. The weekend was just beginning, and my aunt was having some of her friends out for a barbeque. I found out that they had a daughter around my age and a son older than me. When I thought of the possibilities, I put back the train fare I had secretly borrowed from the cookie jar. If she wasn't friendly, maybe he would buy a few beers. At any rate, I had found the cookie jar and could leave anytime.

It was early afternoon when they arrived. She was friendly, but friendly like one of the guys, which was OK because she looked like one of the guys. At least it was someone to talk to. Her brother was not so talkative. He was about a foot and a half taller than me and looked the type that waited for the draft board to send him his card, so I didn't bother about the beers.

As soon as it was suggested that we go ahead to the beach, I felt better. Although I had been there two days, I hadn't gone for a good swim yet. I had just gone down to the beach to look around and feel the wind and listen to my ocean. It was strange, but I think I wanted to let it know it was me before I went in. Now the three of us were on the beach. After I secured the blanket, I dove right in. Ah, I was in love again. I swam out to catch a good wave to ride in on. I hadn't forgotten how to pick a wave nor how to ride it in. Body surfing — it gave me great satisfaction. When brother and sister asked how it was done, I just said, "You see a rolling wave and swim with it."

After a while they came in to join the fun on the ocean. I was enjoying the spotlight so much I wasn't paying attention to what was happening until it was too late. The three of us were walking out farther and farther until only big brother was able to touch bottom. Then I saw the playful smile on little sister's face slowly change to fear. Big brother wasn't holding on to her, and she was moving out against her will. In the seconds it took big brother to reach her, I took a quick look around and saw we were way out past the end of the jetty, which meant dangerous cross-currents and a powerful undertow. They drifted past me about ten yards to my left. I saw panic begin to show on her face. The current wasn't pulling me out. I was safe.

I made my choice. It only took three or four strokes before I felt the strength of the current that they were caught in. My presence seemed to diminish the panicked expression on little sister's face. I said, "Don't be afraid. We'll all keep our heads above water, and in a few minutes some handsome life guard will have you in his arms." I filled my lungs with air and yelled as loud as I could, and with my free arm started to splash the water for some more attention from shore. Big brother, who up to now had been silent and trying his best to keep his sister afloat, followed my lead. The splashing caught the life guard's attention.

I heard the whistles and saw the guys in orange hit the surf. I saw the tow line and buoys along with the lead man moving toward us fast. My act worked. I kept panic from reaching us before the life guards. I placed little sister in his arms, and he put the tow line around her and big brother. As soon as each had a buoy under their arms, I put my all into it and headed toward shore. No sooner did I begin to swim in when I felt that familiar feeling of catching a big wave. It lifted me up and with little help from me carried me all the way to shore.

I walked past the gazing crowd, hardly noticed. The blanket was my destination. I reached it, stood still for a split second. Then I collapsed, relaxed, wriggled a little and let sun and sand do the rest. About ten minutes later, brother and sister disturbed my weary body with thanks and hand shakes and all.

It made me feel especially good that I was there, because my character was in question. Actually I was thankful. I had answered that question the way I had hoped I would several years ago.

MICHAEL PELLITIER

Mr. Pellitier's paper is an essay of testing. Probably the most remarkable thing about it is its tact, the modesty which we notice first in the tone and then in the structure. The narrative frame enables and impels the writer to sustain his essay. Even more important, it meets his need to circumstance his decision rather than boast of it.

Everyone in class noticed something about how the setting worked. The places of the past and the people of the past are, oddly, both vast and small. The vast ocean and beach, and the small town, of whose streets "the Atlantic Ocean ended the naming of them." The little boys made themselves big with brags, but were honest about real choices. The question, brought in very obliquely, is localized and seen only through the boys' perspective. Though it is a big question, it is kept quietly in hand. The decision, when it comes, is not played up by being dramatized, but reported, as past: "I made my choice." The seascape/

landscape description, as usual, gives the writer the chance to express his attitudes indirectly. All the scenes are contained within a doubled or ironic perspective of a past within a past.

Out of this distance the decision comes. The turning point comes when, "'Hell, I'm not going to let someone drown me!'" — a fully respectable thing to say — is balanced against, "I saw panic begin to show on her face. The current wasn't pulling me out. I was safe." But there is no moral drama directly expressed. The author uses the narrative to transfer the drama to visible action: "I heard the whistles and saw the guys in orange hit the surf." His part was simply, "My *act* worked."

In the end we know a good deal about the decision described so discreetly: how it comes out of a good past, the fear and love of the ocean, youthful versions of heroism; and out of a present when one's character is in question. The principle is not defined explicitly. Like some of the games the small boys played, it has no name. But that fits the old literature. The prophets are explicit about failure, when they speak to those whose hearts are fat, whose ears are heavy, and whose eyes are shut. Although the principle this essay evokes has not been defined, it has been described so generously that it is recognizable.

So recognizable, in fact, that the next move after a writer reads such an essay, is to ask the whole class to write about what the principle or promise is — to give it a name. It is good to think about values, but apart from their bracing situations, they decline easily into clichés or truisms. If we want writers to define value, we ask them to abstract the definition from the experience. The two questions that extend this essay shape for two more paragraphs are: What is the value at stake here? How did the predicament test the value or bring it to life? (Or, how did the principle solve or dissolve the dilemma?)

All six assignments are based on these assumptions about expository essays:

> An expository essay is one that supports what it asserts. What students are learning at all levels in college or university is that the work they do must meet tests of truth: Is it accurate? Is it verifiable either in fact, in evidence, or by a consistent line of reasoning?
>
> A good essay is neither a summary nor a list.
>
> As a practical matter in the first drafts, a writer begins best with the center. (It is practical because the heart of the matter is energizing, motivating.) These essay shapes are ways of making

that center appear right from the start as clear and self-consistent so that, right from the start, the writer is working to define it, to assert it, and to support it.

An Overview of the Six Essay Shapes

1) *Once/Now:* Once I was ____; now I am ____. Simple parallel, juxtaposition, comparison/contrast, ironic prolepsis.

2) *The Opposing Voice:* They say ____, but my experience tells me ____. Correcting a misapprehension, stereotype, provincialism. Simple argument.

3) *Two Voices:* You can do it another way ____, but you can also do it this way. Mental Fight, Platonic Tolerance, Comic Liberty: Making a distinction.

4) *Hindsight:* That is the way it was, and that made this difference. History, elegy, ironic realization.

5) *Foresight:* When I saw that fork in the road just ahead in my life, I chose this ____ instead of this ____. Prudence, practical choice, interest, self-interest.

6) *Insight:* In this dilemma or crisis, I turned to this tradition or principle. Tradition, principle, promise: Problem-solving and the Law within.

The assignments are two-part forms or structures. In most, the form of the essay and its idea are contained in the first sentence: the essay develops that form and idea. Essay and key sentence correspond.

In the first set of "coordinate" structures, the second part often corresponds or answers point by point to the first part. The correspondences and parallels clarify the relations between the two parts.

In the second set of "subordinate" structures, the relations between the two parts become explicit, the subject of thought. There is a turning-point sentence in each of these essays which becomes the point to develop or analyze.

Here are some questions we have been asked about these essay shapes.

1) How can I provoke writing like this when I don't know what is in the writer's experience?

No one can know that, of course, not even the writers themselves before they begin to write. It's not what the teachers know about the students that provokes writing, but what they know about literature. The structures draw the experience out of a mass of living into some sort of conventional shape so that first the writer and then the readers can see it. The teacher recognizes, names, and praises the literature in the students' writing. That teaches writers what literature is in an irresistible way.

2) Where can I find such structures?

We ourselves find them in oral literature and in very early literature. Most of them, of course, we stumbled on by a gradual process of recognizing what sort of essays were always successful. When we saw the traditional forms submerged in them, we worked to define the shapes and develop suggestive model sentences. Back of this is the idea that the form of a whole essay could be built in the same way that sentences are structured: coordinately and subordinately, by parataxis and hypotaxis.

We can think of other or more complex structures, but our principle is that we'll concern ourselves with the elemental and leave development to the writers. We want shapes simple enough to repeat with increments, a practice that steadies and strengthens writers. When we use these structures in advanced classes in writing, we do get more complex writing than the samples we have given here, which are all from freshman or pre-freshman classes. Stronger writers, as you would expect, use the structures to sustain more complex thinking.

As we see it, the real problem is not finding more structures, but designing a coherent course of writing where each assignment is a development of what went before and can itself be developed in the next assignment. We don't want gimmicks.

3) How many structured assignments must I give before I can count on student writing to produce ideas with the whole structures they need?

We use all six shapes in one course, with the first two structures repeated. (See the sample syllabus in Chapter 15.) A good course in writing has to find the balance between instinct and cultivation:

The splashing of the ink around the brush comes by instinct, while the manipulation of the ink by the brush depends on spiritual energy. Without cultivation, the ink-splashing will not be instinctive, and without experiencing life, the brush cannot possess spiritual energy.

The Wilderness Colors of Tao-chi,
quoted by Marilyn Fu and Wen Fong
from Tao-chi's treatise. Metropolitan
Museum of Art. Plate 9.

4) But don't these structures subordinate material to imposed form?

From the teacher's point of view, they do. They seem to leave the material out of consideration. But we are really leaving the material to the consideration of the writer. It's not that the material is unimportant, but that it belongs to the writer, and we want to respect that.

5) Must I not find the material first in the looser embrace of a form that releases thought?

It's always structure or form that releases thought, we believe. We are giving writers the model of a structure, and they are imagining the form. We don't begin by depending on writers' spontaneity. Such writers wouldn't need a writing course.

But, of course, structures are not the only way of finding material. Most writers probably alternate between trying to realize a convention and doing a good deal of prolific writing to get down to the language that is true for them. In the chapter on prolific writing we remind readers that prolific writing alone won't carry writers long without forms. In these chapters on essay shapes we remind readers that structure by itself is not sufficiently nourishing. The Basic Writing Course Syllabus (Chapter 15) shows how we use these two skills together.

6) When do students stop writing autobiography and start on general subjects?

Whenever they are ready with enough verifiable knowledge to support generalizations.We make the next step in writing formal rather than material. Juniors and seniors know more specific subjects and also more of the forms that structure each special study. The next move is to do more prolific writing in class on the writer's chosen subject and look for the form proper to that material and embedded in it. Susanne Langer calls this "the commanding form" and points out that it "guides the artist's judgment," being "a measure of right and wrong, too much or too little, strong and weak."[4] *(Feeling and Form,* 122) Once seen, the commanding form "opens to him and others, a deep mine of . . . resource. For the commanding form is not essentially restrictive, but fecund." (123)

At first we assist this process by pointing to the forms we recognize. Writers might see these as we do; or roused by what we see, they might see something else which comes partly out of material they haven't thought to put down. In this way the developing form elicits more material.

If by *autobiography*, however, we mean the narrative of the events of a life, then we never see students' essays based on personal experience as autobiography. We think all good writing is personal, not because the material is personal but because it bears the marks of having been written by a person. We think too that experience is a matrix. We encourage writers toward Thoreau's way of using his life to connect with or confront the larger culture.

9 | CODA: Analysis

"Insert an instrument that has no thickness into a structure that is amply spaced. . . ."

Analysis is hard to do and impossible to tell someone else how to do. It looks systematic when it is done well. But it can't be done methodically, and attempts to do that end up in illogical tangles or in the bands of tautology. The difficulty of analysis is partly here — that we expect it to be something it is not and go at it in a way that defeats it right from the start.

Analysis depends first on an act of imagination, not on systematic logic. That's how it surprises the inexperienced writer. Imagining is fairly simple; we all do it. Imagination is a kind of perception and works in two ways: we see in wholes and parts, and we see concretely and abstractly. Though we usually identify the imagination with the concrete, the perception of sense, it is always working simultaneously as abstraction, the perception of structure. We can realize this when we think about learning games. When we see a new game played a few times, we intuitively abstract its "rules" — the underlying structure of it, the thing that makes it one game, no matter how many times it is played. We have perceived the rules imaginatively.

Analysis may be difficult for a variety of accidental reasons. For example, the writer may be inexperienced. That means he writes his paper as a chronicle, setting down his thoughts in the order in which they occur to him and reaching his idea at the end. He's still using writing only to help himself *think* and doesn't know how to recast the thought in order to *tell* it to someone else. Or a writer may be trying to analyze unfamiliar material, material that either is or seems to him to be inconsistent and disordered.

What lies beneath such accidental reasons for the difficulty of analysis is one central reason: analysis doesn't exist by itself nor does it come first. It is the second part of a two-part operation. It doesn't exist by itself any more than an answer exists without a question or a response exists without an offer, or solution without problem, or plant without seed or spore.

Analysis depends upon synthesis. A synthesis is not simply a whole thing; it is an ordered thing. That is to say, it is a thing put together in a certain order. We can't analyze disorder or chaos. And this in turn means that not all problems can be analyzed — only those than can be synthesized first. So the experienced writer knows he has to do a certain amount of "thinking-writing" first till he gets his idea. Then he is ready for "telling-writing": he puts his idea up front and describes it as completely as possible. That idea is his synthesis and that is what he is analyzing. The more he has of it to begin with, the more successful his analysis will be.

In every way, then, successful analysis depends on the synthesis which precedes it. The most common sort of analytical writing is probably the problem-solution essay. An inexperienced writer gives the problem a little sketch or brief mention and rushes on to the solution — only to find himself in trouble. Trying to untangle it makes the snarl worse. It will not ordinarily occur to him that the way out of his trouble lies not ahead of him as he heads for the end of the paper, but behind him in the brief nod he gave to the problem in the first paragraph. The experienced writer knows that he can describe the problem so completely that the solution almost writes itself.

Analysis begins with imagining, especially the abstracting power of the imagination to see structures, patterns, shapes; and it begins by abstracting a certain structure from material. Then synthesis presents that structure as a structure, that is, systematically: ordered as a system in which all the parts relate to *one* thing. The beauty of analysis is just this release of one set of relationships, as a chart of the lymph system separates it from the system of veins and arteries, the system of nerves, and the skeletal system. Charted, one system holds and can be examined.

Though the intuitive, imaginative part of analytical writing can't be taught, it can be learned by doing it. The most obvious way of starting imaginatively is to encourage play — freedom and play being what the imagination loves most. We present two ideas for the synthesis part of analytical writing at the end of this chapter. But analysis can be described so that we can identify its characteristics. Then we can at least say to ourselves when we try to write analytically, "Does this have the identifying marks that all analysis has?" What follows is an examination of analysis by means of an analogy. The synthesis with which we begin is a story from Chuang Tsu.

King Hui of Wei had a carver named Ting. When this carver Ting was carving a bull for the king, every touch of the hand, every inclination of the shoulder, every step he trod, every pressure of the knee, while swiftly and lightly he wielded his carving knife, was as carefully timed as the movements of a dancer . . . . "Wonderful," said the king. "I could never have believed that the art of carving could have reached such a point as this."

"I am a lover of Tao," replied Ting, putting away his knife, "and have succeeded in applying it to the art of carving. When I first began to carve, I fixed my gaze on the animal in front of me. After three years, I no longer saw it as a whole bull, but as a thing already divided into parts. Nowadays I no longer see it with the eye; I merely apprehend it with the soul. My sense-organs are in abeyance, but my soul still works. Unerringly my knife follows the natural markings, slips into the natural cleavages, finds it ways into the natural cavities. And so by conforming my work to the structure with which I am dealing, I have arrived at a point at which my knife never touches even the smallest ligament or tendon, let alone the main gristle.

". . . Where part meets part there is always space, and a knife-blade has no thickness. Insert an instrument that has no thickness into a structure that is amply spaced, and it surely cannot fail to have plenty of room. That is why I can use a blade for nineteen years, and it still looks as though it were fresh from the forger's mould."

TAKEN FROM ARTHUR WALEY'S *THREE
WAYS OF THOUGHT IN ANCIENT CHINA*
(ANCHOR), P. 47.

As an analogy for analysis, this seems mysterious. One begins by looking until one *sees* the animal already divided into parts. How does that happen? How could one actually carve without touching "even the smallest ligament or tendon"? And finally, where can one find such a marvelous blade and amply-spaced structures? But process is always something that reveals itself in the doing. We can find out what the story has to tell us by doing what it suggests.

First, we fix our gaze on the animal in front of us and attempt to see the divisions and their analogy to analysis. We notice these:

1) Analysis is based on a direct and sustained study.
2) Analysis is a change in the way we see something. The important step is to "apprehend with the soul," that is, to hypothesize the animal, make it a mental thing. Then it becomes a structure, like the intimately-known, carefully-timed pattern of a dance.

3) The change analysis brings about is a reduction: "no longer the whole bull, but a thing already divided into parts."
4) Analysis proceeds by "conforming the work to the structure" with which we are dealing. Analysis is of a structure.
5) Analysis has an instrument that "has no thickness" and works on a structure that is "amply-spaced." The instrument is one with its function.
6) Analysis is like carving.
7) Finally, analysis is an art and is therefore active, designed, purposive.

The first important point is number 6. We notice that Ting is a master-carver, not a butcher as we might at first suppose. The animal he works on is not raw. Something has been done to it before it came into his hands: it has been cooked. The carver has not to separate joint from joint, but only to know where the "natural markings, cleavages, and cavities" are as a guide to his own division into parts. The master-carver, as Ting claims, would remove all the meat, leaving bones, tendons, ligaments, and gristle neatly behind, untouched.

This idea fits what we noticed in parts 2 and 4: the idea of the change that seeing makes and the idea of structure. Not everything is the right object of analysis, which searches out structure. There are, for example, evils — sorrow, parting, death — so random and disordered that they cannot be analyzed. Before analysis can begin, there must be a structure and it must be "cooked" to be ready for carving. That is to say, "apprehending with the soul" changes the object into a coherent mental structure, a synthesis. Analysis is of synthesis.

This suggests that in writing analysis, we must begin by synthesizing what we are about to analyze. We will be analyzing our own synthesis in any case, with or without being aware of it: better if we express it fully ourselves. That is the only way we can hope to conform our work to the structure with which we are dealing.

The dance of analysis suggests a finer action than arbitrary severing and an action fitted to the structure of a particular situation. Of course, the root of the word itself would tell us that. *Lyo* means *loosen, unfasten, untie, slacken,* and is used also of opening the mouth, bending the bow, unyoking horses, and releasing captives on receipt of ransom. The range of meanings here is suggestive. The writing analyzer would do well to think of himself as opening his mouth to communicate, bending his bow to direct and extend his power, unyoking what might work otherwise in other combinations, and releasing what is captive.

Analysis is usually taken as a metaphor from chemistry, another helpful analogy. The whole enlightenment tradition of analysis, culminating in Mill's remarks, tells us that analysis is a dissolving agent.

What does it dissolve? What is dissolved in a chemical solution? Not the atoms themselves but their molecular bonds. If the synthesis we are working on is a problem, then analysis dissolves the bonds of the problem and so dissolves the problem. But not, of course, the raw problem. The problem the writer tackles, it will be recalled, is an order seen or synthesized as a problem. Analyzing a problem of poverty, a problem of taxation, means working on a synthesis that the writer has made; only that problem will be dissolved. This does not mean that analysis is a sham, but only that we must analyze what is fit for analysis. Death and sorrow will not go away because we analyze them, but if what binds us to them can be formulated or synthesized, it will yield to analysis.

After the carver-analyzer has loosened meat from bone, ligament, and tendon, he sets the meat aside to be served, and we are left with a considerable reduction of the animal in front of us. The result of analysis, and one of the most beautiful things about it, is that it reduces a puzzling or swollen issue to the clarity of an alternative, like a stroke of wit. Analysis clears up error or confusion by resolving the terms and reducing them to one, two, or three. But the writer must note again the limits of analysis: it is appropriate for whatever he wants reduced. The beauty and charm of the literature he is writing about are not fit for analysis. But he can release them, by analysis, from the error and misunderstanding that hold them captive.

Mill is very clear about the limits and the powers of analysis, which he laments when it loosens the affective bonds of hope and belief, and praises when it breaks up the constricting and deforming bonds of prejudice and superstition.

By now we can see that when a teacher assigns a paper of analysis, he does not want a pure analysis, for that would be simply a graph, chart, or paradigm. At the least, he is after a synthesis-analysis, and probably he will require a new synthesis after the analysis, the sort of synthesis Ting himself gave us after "putting away his knife."

These characteristics of analysis show how active it is, activated by a purpose so that every touch, inclination, step, and pressure fit as the steps of a dance fit the design and timing of the dance. Analyses must differ, then, according to different purposes; Melville's analysis of a whale differs from that of a whaler. Such a difference appears when we compare the master-carver with the guests at the king's feast. Both take in the meat in some way. We think of the carver as concentrating on the parts, but in fact it is the guests who are interested in the portions, while the carver has his eyes on the cavities and cleavages, the partings, or empty spaces between the parts. And because he sees them with such concentration, they appear "amply-spaced" to him. He has taken the animal into his mind; he is a thinker, a lover of Tao rather than of meat.

Finally there remains the question of the instrument of the carver. The instrument is abstract language. An analysis, we have been saying, is purposive: it is structure-seeking, reductive, and dissolving. All these purposes are accomplished by the qualities of abstract language: 1) it is speculative or hypothetical (unlike general language, which is referential) and so sets fact or actuality aside and puts the "animal in front of us" into the mind, where it is simply the structure of the animal; 2) because it eliminates everything but structure, it reduces to few parts; 3) it dissolves the emotional, associative, or personal connections among parts, everything that makes for emphasis. Nothing itself, it sees "nothing that is not there and the nothing that is." Abstract language is the knife-blade that "has no thickness."

From the guests' point of view, the man who sees cavities sees nothing. What has the carver achieved by his work? The knowledge of an essential structure, to put it abstractly. To put it concretely, we will have to transfer the knife of analysis to another analogy and consider the pruner. Pruning a fruit tree is a kind of analysis. Having said that the strength of analysis is its dissolving power, we start with a problem: our apples have flesh on only one side of the core. The fruit obviously needs more light (where "fruit of sense" abounds there are few leaves). Now we have a purpose for analysis: we must open the center of the tree and get rid of everything but the essential branches and fruiting spurs. We study the tree and abstract from the actual tree its essential structure, for we must conform our work to that structure. Using it as a model, we reduce the tree. By reducing ramifications and letting light into the center, we ensure better fruit. And that is the point of analysis.

Assignments for Analysis

Our two writing assignments rise out of our observation that there are generally two sorts of imagination among class members: the idealizing imagination, like Milton's, and the satiric imagination, like

Swift's. One constructs a model of desire, the other a model of aversion,* as here:

> I call, therefore, a complete and generous education, that which fits a man to perform justly, skillfully, and magnanimously all the offices, both private and public, of peace and war.

> Everyone knew how laborious the usual Method is of attaining to Arts and Sciences; whereas by his Contrivance, the most ignorant Person at a reasonable Charge, and with a little bodily Labor, may write Books in Philosophy, Poetry, Politicks, Law, Mathematicks and Theology, without the least assistance from Genius or Study.

Each assignment has two essays, a synthesis and an analysis. Writers compose the synthesis freely, without regard to any use it may be put to or any questions that may be asked about it. In the second essay, they address themselves to a question.

The Essay of Possibilities:
Imagine yourself five years from now ready for the job of your dreams.

> *Essay I:* Write a description of the job you would most like to do.
> *Essay II:* Write yourself two letters of recommendation for the job.

The Essay of Satire:
Think of a social or moral problem and invent a mechanical "solution" for it.

> *Essay I:* Write a letter in which you describe your invention to someone concerned with the problem.
> *Essay II:* Write an essay in which you expose this pretended solution.

For these essay assignments, more than for most, writers need to be assured that they can't go wrong: "It is not possible to make a mistake." There will doubtless be some adjustment and rewriting after the second essay is written, because the whole shape of the idea will not be worked out till the synthesis-analysis is complete.

---

*An idea developed throughout Frye's work, perhaps most simply in the essay, "The Keys to Dreamland," in *The Educated Imagination*.[5] On page 22 of that book is the neatest definition of imagination: "It's the power of constructing possible models of human experience."

The first set of assignments (invented by our colleague, Martha Winwood England) makes use of one of the most common kinds of analysis, the recommendation. Recommending the self slows the torrent of immoderate modifiers that usually make up a recommendation and gives the writer a chance to see the challenges of the form. When successful, the letters show the marks of analysis clearly. First drafts of the letters themselves give writers interesting problems of analysis.

Forging solutions is frequently a strategy in satire. When Gulliver's Projector describes his contrivance to enable people to write important books "without the least assistance from genius or study," he presents it as a solution, but the rest of us recognize it fairly easily as the problem. The signs of analysis are clear in the essay of exposure, even when writers take the opportunity to double the irony and write this as a satire too. Either assignment gives the writer a chance to produce his own lively model for later more abstract or formal synthesis and analysis.

To sum up what we have said, here are the identifying marks of analysis and synthesis:

Analysis expresses a purpose: it is structure-seeking.

Signs:

1) Conversion of referential terms (whether concrete or general) to abstract terms.
2) Reduction to few parts.
3) A changed order and one that is symmetric (not emphatic). When successful: a whole order.

Synthesis expresses a point of view: what you see from where you are standing.

Signs:

1) Conversion of abstract or general terms to concrete ones.
2) Developing, amplifying connections and associations.
3) An order of emphasis or dominance. When successful: a bright or memorable order.

10 | Rewriting

We have shown how writers, given their own plenteous writing and control of some basic structures, can produce first drafts of essays. The next necessary step, the next pleasure, is rewriting.

We would be less surprised by the many who say they hate to write, were we to realize that they have never done enough of it to know where its best pleasures lie. (I who have never tried it hate to play the trumpet.)

True working pleasure waits, for the experienced, in rewriting, which calls all their skills into play. The inexperienced have no idea that this is true. Nor can we expect it to come to them without instruction. They can imagine neither what rewriting is nor what it is for. The activity is not, for them, conveyed by the name until after they have tried it and found they can, by rewriting, move a written piece toward the state in which it is a coherent, expressive whole.

Once a first draft is down on paper, it is ready to be well worked — by reading, testing, changing, thinking, rereading — into the malleability that allows the writer to pick it all up at once and shape it into its most suitable form. She knows the pleasure of the maker, as she seeks to set it on the way to a virtual life of its own. As she sits, pencil in hand, she absorbs what it says, compares that with what she has in mind to say, and looks to it to see what it has to tell her of what it needs.

We say, "it needs," to underscore that the writer's work, after the first draft, is work in behalf of, sometimes in search of, an understanding of her idea — first, her own understanding, then the language which will open it to the understanding of her readers. The first draft is a whole; rewriting strengthens it part by part with the whole in mind. With the draft before her, she can grasp it as a whole, see where it is strongest, where it is unbalanced, where it provokes further questions or thought. She can cut out repetitions, reduce rough lumps to easy sequence, find more expressive words and syntax. She may find that she knows additional ways to further substantiate the idea; or that she sees contradictions — especially of tone — to resolve; or that — especially for researched writing — she needs to build up thin spots where she has not yet furnished the data the idea demands.

We distinguish four phases in the work the writer does after the first draft. They are rewriting, revision, copy-editing, and proofreading.

In rewriting, the writer rereads and rewrites a draft of the whole, clarifying and extending the fitness of its parts in a whole structure.

In revision, the writer has a new vision of her idea and, to incorporate the vision or put it into perspective, recasts the whole. Such discovery depends on luck and readiness; luck is ungovernable, but rewriting, because it is a state of readiness intensified by slowed pace and close focus, may be the occasion of a new vision. Revision means that the writer has discovered a deeper or more original idea, hidden but implicit between her mind and her writing. Attentive rewriting can find it and bring it out onto the page.

In copyediting, the writer establishes in the final draft of the work correctness of spelling, syntax, and punctuation, including paragraphing.

In proofreading, the writer compares a clean copy of the work, ready to hand in (or publish) with the copyedited final draft from which it was made; she makes sure the copy is faithful.

Of these four, it is revision that can move the work most radically forward, sometimes by changing it profoundly. It is also a step we cannot count on demonstrating or require anyone to take. We can only show how certain kinds of hands-on work with the written page may engender it.

What we can demonstrate and expect is rewriting. Necessary in itself, hopeful for revision, it can be practiced. Writers need active concrete experience of rewriting, so they can abstract their own definition of it and know what to do when their own impulse or another's instruction says, "Rewrite this." We do not need to teach specifically what to do with it in every kind of writing; if we get across the meaning of the word, practically, using the writing they are producing, writers will see for themselves the dozens of ways they can use it. The work we have already described in connection with the aphorism which winds up the fable is, in fact, a first step in basic training. All of the moves economically practiced there are part of all rewriting.

Repeated recasting of the fable's aphorism does two things. First, it establishes how a single sentence relates to a larger whole. The two parts serve the one thought, in radically different ways.

Second, it establishes the sentence as a whole structure susceptible of the greatest elegance and use. The writer learns to produce any number of strong, purposeful shapes; each new aphorism is an alternate or rewritten version of the others composed for that fable. The writer sees in practice that language is ample and her own supply of it plenteous and controlled.

The economy of the fable, with its dozen benefits at once, earns it a place in all our writing classes. It can be counted on to light up the mental stage of operations and make visible some separate elements of the writing process which are too often left in the dark and lost to writers' attention. We assume, in speaking now of further practice in rewriting, that we are able to work in the clarity the fable provides.

Rewriting is as particular to the writer as style. It would not be possible to make of it a flight of steps and teach it as a fixed entity. But climbing can be practiced; for that we need only one step, perhaps two. Those who can climb can climb any flight, all the way. We negotiate rewriting, this necessary step often proposed and seldom taken, by taking it.

We take it frequently. The first time we do so, it is most of a week's class work. After that, it takes up at least fifteen minutes, every time students come in with a new set of first drafts. Just as free writing makes writing habitual, so taking this step often will make rewriting second nature. We want everyone with a first draft to turn as a matter of course to this stressful pleasure.

We begin with the smallest whole structure, the sentence, because it is brief enough to be read, understood, and held in the mind as a whole, in a few minutes. Rewriting a whole paper calls for the same reading, understanding, and holding in mind, but it takes longer.

We begin, naturally, with the writers' own language, of which they are taking charge. Will they rewrite rickety sentences? Yes, certainly, that is one clear responsiblity. Rewrite good sentences? Yes, we think so; that is fruitful work. It is on good sentences that we practice first.

And we begin in class. Like most skills, the skill of rewriting is more readily essayed if learned socially, with the example of willingness to set about it multiplied by the number of persons in the group. One inexperienced writer, told to rewrite on her own at home at her desk, may do no more than stare at her unbudging sentence. In the company of others, all of them rewriting imperfectly — it is an activity of tentatives, of imperfections diminished — she too can read her paper for its active possibilities and her mind for the gesture that will realize them in language. She sees she is not stuck with the words she writes. She may choose them; or she may take them as her given ground and rise from them. Rewriting is refreshing, for here more than perhaps anywhere else in the process of composition the author exercises her full authority.

We begin to practice rewriting on a day when everyone has a first draft of a new piece of writing in hand and we have begun to read to each other.

We choose at random a decent sentence from a paper we have been listening to, and put it on the board. Since the drafts are new to us, this makes visible that we need not hunt for a sentence deserving of rewriting; all sentences are deserving. Usually, we make two kinds of preliminary remark.

One is about the form and its power to contain and mold meaning. Sentence-making is the skill which most empowers human beings, and it is never inappropriate to remind writers that they exercise that power.

The other remark is about a rhetorical or grammatical view of the sentence we have chosen. Usually, though not always, we show how a live sentence can be related to some usable notions of grammar. By pointing out simply that its unsubordinated subject and verb conform to the definition, we demonstrate why it is, indeed, a sentence. This is done quickly, for it is not the principal rewriting task.

That task is for everyone to write three new versions of the sentence. They may change or retain words, word order, or images; they are to take two or three minutes and say the same thing as the sentence, in any three different ways they wish.

While they do so, a working quiet fills the room, easing the work, as it always does when people are writing together free of inappropriate anxiety.

Each person, in turn around the room, then reads three versions. It is unfailingly interesting, even amazing, to watch as a wide array of expressive possibilities springs from the language in our minds. Those new to rewriting are always surprised. Even those who have written a good round of fables need to write and hear these fifty transformations to know that rewriting serves writers of all kinds. The instructor, too, is refreshed by such affirmation of the power of words. From this evidence, students begin to imagine what rewriting is.

If there is time, we repeat the experience before expanding its usefulness further. We choose another sentence from another draft we have heard, put it on the board, and ask everyone to rewrite it in three versions.

This time, when the rewritten sentences are being reread, we write many of them — one or two from each reader — on the board. (It may save time to have two or three recorders.) We group the rewrites, roughly, according to any one set of the possible ways to classify sentences. One set would put simple assertions or questions on one board, coordinate-clause sentences on another, and subordinate-clause ones on a third.

(Another possible set would sort sentences into groups labeled abstract, concrete, general, and mixed abstract/concrete; since the original sentence has been read in its context, these distinctions are possible. Still other sets might be planned to exhibit rhetorical features — say, simple sentences, sentences with extended subjects, sentences with extended predicates; in which case we would talk about the effects of extending by qualifying and by compounding.)

We quickly label the groups on the board, define the labeling words, and point to the qualities of each sentence which have led us to classify it. We count on work like this to show the correct graphics of punctuation, which must be memorized. This is an occasion for reinforcing memory of the conventions. If the group handles basic graphics well, we might instead emphasize the qualities of forcefulness, balance, or focus special to each of the three kinds. From that emphasis emerges a sense of how an essay, like a sentence, can profit from being structured by coordination or subordination.

The proliferation of meaning and language in these sentences confirms that everyone can take this first step at will. We do not, in this exercise, aim directly at rewriting the whole draft from which the sentence was extracted, for we do not stop to consider the relationships and consequences, the rhetorical figures, tone, or rhythm, of the sentences before and after it. We are making conscious a step which, conceivably, might be repeated sentence by sentence, to rewrite the whole.

Few writers would, we suppose, in fact go about rewriting a whole essay sentence by sentence. Yet we know that good writers must test each sentence mentally, rereading it and comparing it to other possible versions. They also rewrite many of their sentences, just as we are doing in this first step. The intellectual and evaluative skills are the same, whether the rewriting be carried out mentally or physically. Doing it physically, in rewriting visibly on the page, is training in both uses of this mental skill essential to good writers.

So we are doing more than showing off the marvelous flexibility of language. Starting with good sentences rather than weak ones helps us here. Even the clichés of a draft can, on examination, inspire good re-writing. A good sentence is likely to pack surprises, and rewriting is a practical way to unpack them. The mind of the writer of the original sentence often grasps further implications which may enable her to ex-pand or alter other parts of her piece of work. Often enough the early version is the one retained for the final draft; even then, more of what the writer can say of her idea may have occurred to her, given the heed rewriting enables her to take.

For the purpose of opening up dense sentences into useful para-graphs, decent sentences are preferable to feeble ones. They are also useful for the purpose of establishing firmly that rewriting is not reme-dial merely, but the natural way to make progress in writing. We think students will write fewer weak sentences, identify the weaknesses more quickly with less dismay, and strengthen them more deftly, if they have first learned rewriting as an art useful in itself.

What we ask for and how we ask for it, once we have selected a sen-tence, may vary. We can just point to our selections and ask people to say the same thing in two or three different ways. When we do so, and especially if we do so soon after work on fable aphorisms, many will abandon the context of the selection. They probably will write distant extensions or redirections of the original.

On another occasion we may ask that people rewrite while keeping the context of the selected sentence in mind and staying close to its lan-guage; then, the rewrites are likely to rework the phrasing rather than re-examine the material. Both approaches are worth taking.

Here is a set of sentences typical of the first approach. The group was asked to write new sentences that would say the same thing, but in other ways. The results show some leaps away from the context of the essay, and a few moments of aphoristic elegance. (We had been re-cently at work on fables.)

The original sentence, taken from an essay using a family parable to exemplify its idea, was:

"Surely and quietly, over the years, we slip into routinization which kills creativity." And these are some of the rewritten versions it occa-sioned:

1) The nick of time makes no sound.
2) The pit viper makes no sound.
3) We acquire steadiness at the price of readiness.
4) Steadiness is next to deadliness.
5) So who wants to gather moss?

6) We think we want a life that is sure, quiet, and regular until we get it and it puts us to sleep.
7) If they are not creative, slow and hasty both get wasted.
8) By the time we know the way home, life is a downhill street.
9) Surely and quietly, over the years, we slip into routinization, and if they are the right routines we'll get a lot done, but if they are not we end up living for the sake of our routines.

The first five rewrites sprang in a rush from the pen of a very bright woman. We see rise in the first two a royal impatience with the sentiment of the original, which she expresses abstractly in three and four, and transforms and rejects in five. Someone in class advised her to consider writing a whole essay, herself, using "We acquire steadiness at the price of readiness," as her hypothesis in paragraph one, and "Steadiness is next to deadliness," as her thesis at the end — if she could find the right material to substantiate the middle. Had she done so, she would have written a revision of the essay (though the original sentence was not hers); she had a new vision of its meaning. Revision by reversal is perhaps the kind of revision most accessible to the imagination.

The seventh afforded us a chance to mention the neatness of the move through abstract qualities to personification. The eighth was, like the first four, greeted with gratifying murmurs of appreciation. I.A. Richards may be right in maintaining that most people in most classes can't tell bad poems from good, but in a class of authors used to their own authority and given these small wholes to contemplate, everyone notices and enjoys good writing.

The ninth version, a careful if pedestrian view of the original, turned out to be useful to the writer of the draft. It gave him a chance to hear and toss out that awful "routinization" and, by distinguishing "right" from other routines, showed the writer of the draft a flaw in his expressed logic. Through rewriting, and after hearing others' rewrites of his words, he was able to strengthen and amplify his conclusions.

And here is a rewriting which clarified the writer's development of her essay. This time the group was taking the second approach; they were asked to convey all the information of the original, keeping the sense of the context in mind. I put this sentence on the board, from the draft of an essay we had just heard:

She worked and struggled for twelve years against the popular trend, on the job and in her personal life, until the coming of the war made personal issues unimportant.

In the final draft of the paper, she turned the one sentence into two: "When the war came twelve years later, she had to forget her personal crusade. But by that time she had already shown her version of the good old ways to whoever she met, wherever she found herself." She was then able to expand her subsequent single paragraph about places into three small paragraphs of lively concrete anecdote.

Even one class session spent doing such rewriting will earn for the instructor the right to assign rewriting of sentences or passages at home. As more class sessions follow, the assignments may reasonably reach further toward the rewriting of the whole.

This class work also gives the instructor the right to include among comments on students' papers the suggestion that a sentence be rewritten, either because it is inadequate or — more usefully — because it is dense with implicit material, not yet freed to run through the course of the paper. Until we teach through experience what "rewrite" means, it is not only unfair of us to ask for it, it is utterly in vain.

After we have rewritten good sentences two or three times in class, we may turn to weak or awkward sentences. Some of them call loudly for rewriting. We do not limit our play with words to the words of acceptable sentences, though we do teach the moves of rewriting through them and spend most of our rewriting time with them in class, for reasons we have given.

Most weakness rises from incoherence, or from a previous sentence that closes the door of further thought, or from ignoring a door some sentence has opened. We therefore practice rewriting poor sentences by working on them in the context they have failed to enhance. When we put them on the board, we put up the sentences before and after them as well. The weak sentence is often hardly there; it is but some words, set down and left to hold the space open, which demand replacement. The failure is one of consequence, through poverty or excessive richness. Good writing is made of consequential sentences. So we ask the group to rewrite the weak sentence in a way that will move the reader easily from fore to aft. Occasionally this means changing proximate language too — perhaps adding subsequent paragraphs to carry the bridging idea the whole way; perhaps simply eliminating the whole problematic passage. (Prolific writers are not afraid to delete. They know there is more language where the inefficient words came from.)

Trial and error, here as ever in real learning, are instructive. For the writer who cannot imagine rewriting, to find she has written ineptly or weakly is depressing. But to make the mistakes that are offshoots of vigorous growth and to be able to prune them away, so that the line of development stands clear, is both satisfying and energizing. "To be an Error & to be Cast out is a part of God's design," Blake says. The writer too makes use of the errors which are part of her trial design and within her power to cast out.

How do we select inadequate sentences for class rewriting? Almost never on our own. Rewriting the unsatisfactory is not uncommon in our classes, and is always initiated at the author's request. Without plenty of practice in rewriting good sentences, such requests would be rare and come from the desperate. Among those who have practiced rewriting, the request has sometimes come for help in improving work we thought quite passable — but the author knew better.

Practice in rewriting the sentence in class will, in itself, afford writers these advantages:

> *sine qua non,* a working understanding of what the proposal "to rewrite" means;
>
> a more conscious control of the essential structure of a sentence, and therefore power to avoid fragments and run-ons;
>
> a conviction they can always rewrite anything, which increases their willingness to take writer's risks and to try untangling even the thickest skeins of language;
>
> a means of narrowing and slowing down their regard for their writing, so that they notice and freshen what they have said, expand what they have to say, or delete what they do not need;
>
> the gratification of good composition, which lends energy to the task of writing;
>
> conscious control of how to take the first and paradigmatic steps in rewriting the whole essay; and, perhaps,
>
> the flash of intuition which makes revision possible, and which most usually occurs to those who know how to prolong their concentration on the work at hand.

Some students are not slow to experiment on their own, rewriting as and what they choose. Their enthusiasm may encourage others to follow their example. We carry our encouragement a further step, toward rewriting the whole essay by expanding our consideration to parts of the whole which are larger than the sentence. In class we look again at the essay in terms of its three most famous components — beginning, middle, and end. We affirm that there are no fast rules for how to structure these parts.

We recall the shape typical of our sub-genre, the academic expository essay, a shape useful to any effort at exposition:

> the first paragraph introduces and formulates a hypothesis (sometimes mistakenly — since prematurely — called a thesis) which proposes the writer's idea about the subject;
>
> the middle paragraphs develop and support the idea concretely (through examples, or contrasting and comparing its parts, or dividing and classifying them, or through analysis/synthesis which presents the whole idea in terms of one set of its parts and/or the set of the parts in terms of the whole);
>
> the final paragraph restates the idea about the subject in the light of the evidence of the middle; if that evidence is adequate, it is earned as a thesis statement.

Though this is not the first time the class will have met this division of the parts of the essay, it serves our purpose to present it again, briefly, at this point.

Of the three parts, the one we choose to rewrite in class is the end. Its rhythm, the rhythm of conclusion, is the easiest to produce. Besides, it sheds the strongest light on the other parts, which can be recast if noticeably in need. It is likely to be the part which the writer has most fully invested with her idea. It is, by its placement, the part readers are most likely to recall, and so is the writer's best chance to bring her idea home. It is also the part writers are readiest to imagine.

This readiness is to the teacher's advantage. For the end is the part whose shape, in a conventional academic essay, we are best able to describe in terms of its function in the whole composition. Students are ready to see, and we can say, what is called for.

We go about it simply. We have a set of first drafts of 500-700 word papers. We ask someone to read her paper to us, omitting the ending. (The author can decide at what point her paper begins to end.) We write five minutes of observations about the beginning and middle we have just heard. We read these aloud. And then we each write an ending.

Just as with other structures when first introduced in class, we listen to all the endings without halting for comments or observations, letting a sense of the form emerge from the many examples. When we've heard them all, we write observations on what they have shown us an ending can do.

Though there are usually interesting surprises, many observations cluster around two ideas. One is awareness of the relationship of the end to the whole of which it is a part: the end reflects the hypothesis of the beginning and the development of that by the middle. The other is reflected in comments on the characteristic sound, rhythm, perhaps tone of the finalizing cadences of definition. In a class which is writing well and is ready for more speculative observation, someone might see if the abstract idea of a hypothesis has become general in expression in the final thesis.

Though it is rarely possible to rewrite endings and review their process for more than two or three draft essays in the fifty minutes of a class hour, or to put class time to this use more than two or three times a semester, we think it an important exercise. It is exemplary. And the value to the writer of the paper is considerable. We know of no more telling way for her to see where her beginning and middle really lead the reader.

For that reason, we sometimes have students bring in their second drafts with the endings on a separate sheet. They exchange papers (beginnings and middles only), go home, write their version of the missing endings, and return them to be used as valuable information for the final rewrite of the whole paper. We always hope — and a note or two from graduates seem to confirm — that people who have found such work a practical way of helping themselves and each other will try it beyond the confines of the class. It is an active way to be a good audience for each other's work.

The reader knows by now that we want to teach the writer from her strengths not her weaknesses. Students are at first surprised by this. It may take a few sessions for them to grasp why we identify correctness and commend them for it, as a way of teaching them control of grammar; they have long endured a climate in which grammar is taught by catching errors, learning rules, and doing exercises from a book. But in our teaching of rewriting, when we look at writers' strengths as their best instruction, they concur at once. They learn this natural post-draft next step rapidly, without worrying that we conceal an answer they must risk guessing at.

In rewriting final paragraphs their native good sense and ingenuity come into play in a particularly nice way. No lectures on closure (concluding, thoroughly closing) are needed. Students can practice rewriting endings with no more preface than the announcement that an essay can be analyzed as having a beginning, middle, and end; and we will work on the end. They know quite a bit about how to have the last word.

Rewriting comprises more than work on isolated sentences and endings, of course, though they are the only steps we practice in class. It is a strong part of the semester; it even suggests, by its interacting community, that there is a rationale for holding composition classes and writing workshops instead of just telling everyone to go away and write. The work with sentences alerts students to what rewriting is, and provides them with the elements of competence. The work with ends exemplifies how to extend the work with sentences.

Once our definitions — of the expository essay which supports the idea it asserts, and of the set which sees the essay as beginning, middle, and end — are plainly in everyone's mind, there is little more that is either general enough or practical enough to do in class to rehearse the rewriting of beginnings and middles. We count on our students to know that since they are composed of sentences they too can be rewritten.

Both are fascinating; in successful writing, both are original. That is, they are invented by the writer and particular to her in ways that do not invite collaboration. The beginning, however objectively phrased, is especially personal; it must establish tone, and it must fairly introduce both an idea about a subject and the stance of the person who is writing the idea. The middle is personal in that it offers evidence chosen from a collection fully accessible to no one but the writer in whose mind it resides. Beginnings and middles are under the author's authority; we can make our observations about them, but we can not improve them by replacing the author's invention with our own.

Structures which elicit the individual's power to imagine and control whole expository structures, including beginnings and middles, will be found in Chapters 7 and 8. We practice rewriting them in relation to the overall structures examined there. We do, in conferences or in written comments on papers where the personal is appropriate, sometimes discuss what we have noticed about one or the other. We know that, given care for particular differences, the skill of rewriting is the same for beginnings and middles as for sentences.

Practicing and extending the usefulness of rewriting is work which anyone who can write a draft can undertake. It is not theoretical but practical, and its practicality is derived from the fact that it is the next logical step for the working writer of a draft to take. We think that it accomplishes with economy what handbooks of composition seek to accomplish with "prewriting" or "prethinking" techniques, which are bits and pieces, and not identical with the writing of a first draft.

They advise the writer to outline, or brainstorm by spinning off whatever comes to mind on a subject, or jot lists of words related to the subject, with the expectation that with this help the first draft will emerge fairly close to where the writer wants it.

There is nothing wrong and much right about these activities. There is good in any painless enterprise which increases the time spent paying attention to writing. We have observed that those who prewrite most successfully have already mastered — that is, learned by heart and understood — some discrete body of information, have developed an idea about it, and are about to write to convey what they think about what they know. This prior understanding is a vital part of their prewriting.

Less skilled writers and writers working outside their special field (and also skilled writers eager to discover new ideas beyond what they know they know) run the risk that prewriting will solidify the material in their grasp, before they have thought it through so thoroughly that they see it all at once and can find in it more of what is original in their idea about the material. These people want a loose first draft, and a method — rewriting — for unfolding its implications into a substantial whole. We encourage them to begin straight off, by writing that draft of the whole; the sooner the playing-field is cleared, the sooner the articulation of the game plan appears. Writers, who by rights choose their game and its rules each time they compose, need to establish their basic field of operations quickly, before the details of their data take over their concern. (To that kind of takeover, in our view, we owe those congested misarrangements of others' data and views that turn up among outlined, card-carrying freshman research papers.)

"Prewriting," because it is proposed in books and classrooms, is a term familiar to many students. But they have not, of course, noticed the absence of further instruction — other than assorted rules for correctness — that would lead them beyond the confines of their first draft. They have not been shown anything to do, after a first draft (dismal or promising) is on paper and before a final draft may be considered ready to copyedit and proofread. They have not even been shown that there is anything to do.

We like, when we think of prewriting, to remind students of its one inescapable form, fortunately in the possession of us all: the sum of our experiences which is ours before we begin to write. Whatever students write is but part of what is already in their heads: syntax, inflection, lexicon, experience, and understanding. Free prolific writing helps them to be certain this is true. They can omit outlines and jot-lists if they wish, and just start writing prolifically in search of their idea about their subject.

In the long run, the only way to get a first draft is to write one. Because the plunge to the page makes some hesitate, devices for prewriting appear in handbooks as help for the reluctant. Reluctance, however, is increased by attention to anything (feelings about self, thoughts of others' judgment, anxiety about getting started) other than the writing. The anxious are anxious because they are looking in the wrong direction, at a crazy mirror rather than at the page. So we do not teach prewriting as a preventative for hesitation. We write our structure-based first drafts, or at least the beginnings of drafts, in class. All plunge at once. The next plunge is also taken together, from the springboard of the draft into rewriting.

It does take time. Those of us who see rewriting as a vital skill will certainly give it time in class and in assignments. Experience will show it as the move which is neat and natural after the raw material is drafted; interesting, necessary, and sometimes intensely rewarding. Those who learn to rewrite are simultaneously learning to read their own — and any other — texts critically. And if they do not know absolutely when a piece is rewritten enough to be called finished — who does? — they will at least know when and where it is not finished and how to set themselves again to their task.

There is yet another way to look at the kind of work this chapter has described. Considered from the point of view of classroom procedure, it is an economical and instantly available way to use class time for the active development of writing. It can take fifteen minutes or fifty or as many as can be spared, and not one second will be wasted or taken away from the activities we are paid to supervise. (Plugging in an improvised discussion of reactions to hastily-read literature is one instance of a wasteful mistake most of us have made at least once.)

The kind of rewriting we propose obeys the injunction: Try the obvious. In a writing class, write. Writing — and reading — of course are not subjects (since they are not objects). They are skills. Skills, to be learned, are to be practiced. In class, we practice them.

CODA: Rewriting As Evaluation

A careful look at rewriting will refine our understanding of the vexed and vexing matter of evaluation. Where, in evaluation, does the writer's authority lie? At the center: for what the writer does in rewriting is to evaluate her work. Among all the possible aims and techniques of evaluation — about which debate is long and intense (and often circuitous) — this owner's evaluation is the only one which properly affects writing.

The writer's real authority is exercised as she decides whether to expand, cut, rephrase, rewrite her work; or to let it stand. It is the only essential evaluation.

To rewrite, writers examine what is written, test it against imagined alternatives, and select the best word, cadence, image they can produce. They can keep doing this until, in their judgment, the piece is finished. The process is one of weighing and judging according to both the models in the mind and the words on the page.

All other kinds of evaluation (of fitness to a publisher's or purchaser's needs, of students as writers, of "progress" in writing, of programs or methods designed to improve writing, of diagnoses of a writer's problems or powers) may serve the editor or the instructor or the institution and so, quite indirectly, serve the writer, and, still more indirectly, the writing itself. They may be mandated, even, by institution or instructor; they may determine grades, curricula, placement in classes, publication, or rejection. Instructors and editors are employed to take them, at least some of them sometimes, seriously.

But the evaluation in rewriting is proper to the writer, a task she must perform in the exercise of her authority over her writing. We avoid interfering with it and try to prevent the writer from confusing any of the standards of secondary evaluations — including her own grades — with the primary evaluation that is her obligation. In that evaluation, we who write do not ask, "Is this an 'A,' or a publishable, paper?" or even, "Is this a good or bad piece of writing?" unless we do so not as writers but as distributors of our writing, and after we have asked, "Have I done everything I can imagine doing to this piece of writing to make sure it asserts my idea and substantiates the assertion well?"

The writer reads and rereads, until she can pose real questions to which she alone can speak:

"What have I said?" (This calls for paraphrasing.)

"What other ways can I say it?" (Here comes some pen-in-hand rewriting of key sentences.)

"Is it what I want to say? Where does it lead? Does it imply trains of thought I should explore? Include?" (These call for comparing and judgment.)

"Do I need to say this? Have I put it where it best articulates the shape of the whole?" (These are two steps in synthesis.)

And then, still evaluating, the writer can fruitfully extend her consideration of her work by comparing it with the overall structures she has in mind. She need never look over her shoulder; she is responsible, at once author, audience, and critic.

When the piece is completed, the writer will have earned, through the pleasure of exercising her proper authority, the pleasure of claiming the piece as her own.

The kind of evaluation that is not the writer's task is evaluation according to those who have authority — but not over the writer or her work. There are responsible readers, critics, and academics, with their standards — carefully evolved to reflect their requirements — over which they do have authority. They are all in a position to compare the writer's work with the standards they have in mind — or in hand as a departmental directive. The student writer knows something of this, and suspects more — the worst.

We hope to forearm her against the stultifying anxiety and misdirected guessing which such knowledge usually occasions. The best shield is the earned sense that she has rewritten and chosen what she puts in her final draft. She will have that sense when she has done everything she can imagine for the integrity and richness of her work. We believe she will, in so doing, present her best aspect fairly to any outside examiners.

A steady grip on her own authority — which we may weaken or strengthen — is the preventative medicine of choice for "writer's block," which may emerge when there is conflict between the writer's primary authority and her imperfectly internalized impressions of what other, secondary authorities might look for. The writer's gaze, deflected from where it belongs, on her writing, to where it does not belong, on her apparent success either private or social, beholds Medusa and she is stone.

Rewriting, then, teaches writers the essential and primary self-evaluation that alone can work changes in their writing. We are confident that it will empower writing acceptable by various secondary evaluators.

As a corollary, it will give us work we can grade and respond to expeditiously. The work will be much closer to the standards of academic acceptability than it would if the writers had kept merely those standards in mind. It will have been worked over, and many of the difficulties we try vainly to point out in hastily-written papers will have vanished before we see them. It both reduces the time it takes to comment on papers and elevates the quality and cogency of our remarks, if the writer and not the teacher does the first evaluation and acts on it by rewriting.

11 | Grammar and Graphics

We meet many, in and out of class, who say they hate to write. Of these, a good number will, if pressed, evidence defiance or shame, which they substantiate by saying, "I hate grammar," or, "I don't really know any grammar" (this, often enough, from fluent speakers who are referring to their native language).

In writing classes, we expect to find that "grammar" is a word loaded with confused anxiety. We also know — first from experience and then from statistics in the copious professional literature — that those taught rules well enough to complete grammatical exercises without error do not therefore write either better or more correctly.

So, while we can't by-pass grammar, which our students in one way and we in another perceive as useful information, we know we can't put our hopes for conveying it on rules taught by textbook exercises.

Yet we do not think handbooks of rhetoric or grammar are useless to teachers of writing who have formulated their thoughts on these matters:

of what whole the handbooks are part;
in what way they are part of it;
what other elements constitute the whole;
what relation handbooks have to the skill and practice of writers; and
what relation their part in the practice of writers has to the work of a writing class.

Ideas or information about these essential matters are not explicit and not always implicit in the many traditional handbooks to which we have had access. Nor, among the many interesting twentieth-century works in linguistics, including grammar, have we found these matters explored for their usefulness to writers or teachers of writing. The first are often remote derivations of nineteenth-century excerpts from Renaissance models; the second are philosophic views of the nature of the mind.

The situation is odd. More and more people reach young adulthood naively ignorant of grammatical systems and nomenclature; more and more sophisticated grammatical systems and philosophies attract the interest of linguistic specialists. The middle ground is fogged. We must, for now, clear ourselves a workspace on that ground. We survey it as writers and teachers of writing. What we see is not final but primary.

Because grammar is a subject about which few people can assume they agree, let us start with some calming definitions. They are well-known to many, but for many more, unexamined assumptions. We set them forth for the part they have played as we have tried to think through our notions about the place of grammar in the way we teach writing.

1) A grammar (like a rhetoric, a poetic, a logic) is a set of abstractions about a language, drawn from observation of many written and spoken examples of that language. The set of statements is drawn from the unity of a language already flourishing. The language, in the verbal acts of its speakers and writers, comes before the grammar. Grammars may be normative or descriptive or historical. Teachers of writing usually observe some version of normative grammar.*

The abstractions of normative grammar make statements — cast as rules and definitions — about syntax, inflection, and lexicon.

A. The rules of syntax show the way words are placed to form sentences.
B. The rules of inflection show the ways the forms of words are changed to exhibit their relation to other words.
C. The lexicon defines the meaning of words and idioms.

All the statements are about what normally occurs in sequences of English sentences. Correctness, in normative grammar, calls for adherence to this norm.

2) The word grammar is also sometimes used to indicate the power of a speaker or writer to produce at will language structured into meaning, in a variety of sentences that have all the attributes grammarians have found in the language and analyzed out into syntax, inflection, and lexicon. Grammar, construed as this prolific power, is not rulebound but the origin of the material from which grammarians draw their rules and classifications.

*This may be traditional grammar. Or it may be a derivation of one of the speculative descriptive grammars of contemporary linguistics; these differ somewhat, in content and nomenclature, both from traditional grammar and among themselves, and some versions appear also to include hypotheses about the neurology and psychology of those who use language. Our nomenclature is drawn from that traditional grammar which is still in the most wide use in print, in and out of the classroom. What we have to say about the relation of grammar to writing will, we trust, have some application to any set of normative grammatical abstractions.

To teach grammar, it is essential to keep in mind these two very different meanings and their implications. The second meaning, of grammar-power, corresponds to a strength our students have. On it we base our teaching.

In either of the two meanings, grammar is clearly not remedial. Like baking powder, it can't be stirred into the cake after the batter has been poured into pans. We can tell students they have all, or almost all, the grammar-power they need in order to write correct English. We can extol the good use they make of it; we can free their appetite by easing their anxiety about it; in the context of their own writing we can clarify their awareness of it. We can offer them a cookbook of healthy things to do with the language they have. We can also scrupulously distinguish their ignorance of someone's set of abstractions or conventions from their authoritative knowledge of grammar in the sense of power to use language.

Fortunately for us, it's not necessary to know the abstractions of any system of grammar to write or speak English well. Students who are native speakers have mastered in practice all but a few minor details of syntax and inflection and a large part of the lexicon. What many have not mastered, and what is usually miscalled grammar, is use of all the graphic signals, or reader's marks, of punctuation with which a writer's mastery of a language can be confirmed in writing for the benefit of the reader. (They did not learn graphics, as they did speech, at their parents' knees — any more than they did spelling.) So we must also distinguish between graphics and grammar-power.

Unfortunately for us, the usual way to teach the graphics competent writers need is by reference to a normative set of rules for grammar, which few students have mastered. Their ignorance is a handicap both for that reason and because they have become persuaded that their ignorance makes them incompetent in grammar and in writing.

It is also unfortunate that few have learned to write a foreign language well, for historically the mastery of a second language has had as one of its benefits a deepened consciousness of the linguistic structures underlying correct English forms and syntax and their evidence in punctuation.*

It is from meeting many embodiments of a structure that we intuit knowledge of that structure. Given such knowledge, rules and definitions may at last show their true usefulness, as handy formulations for what is already known intuitively. This applies to the grammar of a language as well as to the shape of a fable.

So, as we decide what to teach writers, we investigate the structures normative grammar proposes and choose the ones that are essential. It is those structures we write and read in class, in the context of writing our literary structures. We produce and listen to them until we develop an intuitive sense of their workings. By then, it's safe to formulate norms and rules which, rising out of writers' grammar-power, are also located in the body of normative grammar. It in this way that we can mediate in behalf of writers, between their power to generate writing and the demands for control of traditional grammar from other instructors, editors, and the world of business letters, memos, and reports.

To begin with, in class, we try to say a few brief words to confirm our belief in the grammar-power students bring to their writing. Usually, we say something about the order the mind generates through language. Language presents meaning inseparable from structure; that is its property or characteristic quality. When the mind generates its meaning-full structures of language, we may look at the results and perceive, by analysis, elements of a grammar. When the mind uses its imaginative power to generate meaning-full structures of language, we may look at the results and perceive, by analysis, elements of a literature. It is not grammar which is generative, but the mind. What the mind generates is order. The order which the mind generates in language may be discovered, under analysis, as simply grammatical or as at once grammatical and literary. It is with these ideas in mind that we watch for moments in class when we can address ourselves to students' work and, in simple terms, assure them of our confidence in them as potential writers.

*It is bizarre that some people view those whose English is a second language not as gifted but as handicapped by shameful ignorance. Because not all professors of English can write error-free and eloquent papers in Latvian (or Latin) on even the undergraduate level, we admire those few who can. We therefore approach ESL students with the praise due the multilingual. Such respect does not solve, but may keep us from worsening, their problems. It is always inappropriate to assume that others' ignorance is more culpable than our own.

Since ours are courses in writing, not grammar, we limit what we will teach. We have had to decide which elements of syntax, inflection, and lexicon most need to be brought to writers' conscious attention.

We distinguish what we will teach into two parts: one, the conventions of English themselves; the other, the graphics which conventionally convey them in writing.

We teach both together, but make the distinction clear. It's practical, because it's both limited and encouraging. Writers who realize that they have considerable mastery of the hard part are more ready to master the few remaining odds and ends and to learn the graphic system of punctuation according to American conventions. Besides, there are always some who produce graphically correct work before they grasp the abstract rule which governs it.

We want all our students to control all of grammar with authority no less than that of J. Donne, J. Swift, J. Austen, and J. Joyce. That means we must show them how to hold firmly to what they do correctly and to expand their power to do more. As always, we start with what students have shown in writing that they know. We do not teach from rules. We teach from repeated production and enjoyment of whole structures, which students produce, then discern, identify, and define. Correctness is a result of elegance.

Sentences

Since to define something — say, a horse or a house — does not enable anyone to produce it, we can in a writing class stop fretting about the impossibility of defining a sentence. The sentence is to a language what a live myth is to a culture, too pervasively essential at the foundation level to be up for inspection on all sides. A rough, short, working definition will do, for the times when we need it. What we say at those times is that we confirm the presence of a sentence when we see an unsubordinated subject and its verb.

It is as a whole structure that we work on the sentence. At the start of the semester, we announce that since we expect our essays will be written in sentences, we will work toward mastery of that ability to do so which is an exit criterion for our writing course.

We begin paying heed to the whole sentence structure when we are writing aphorisms for fables. We use our recognition-guide phrase, "A sentence needs an unsubordinated subject and its verb," in looking at the aphorisms we have classified on the blackboard. "Hate is heat without light," Angela has written, and read in her turn. We admire it as a metaphoric sentence, and add that we know it for a sentence because it shows a verb — "is" — and its subject — "hate" — with no subordinating word, like "if" or "when" or "because" in front of the subject. Students who have watched us day after day write up their own sentences, underlining subject and verb and putting a caret to show the absence of a subordinator, have taken one step toward conscious control. They have somewhere to look and something to do, to find the identifying marks.

The marks are further affirmed by our rapid sorting, into boardsful of simple sentences and sentences with coordinate and subordinate clauses, of the aphorisms or other sentences students read aloud. To show coordination of clauses, we identify the parts that could be independent sentences according to the definition. To show subordination of clauses, we call attention to the subordinating words in our samples, and demonstrate both the sense and the graphics of connecting the incomplete enclosure of a subordinate clause to the complete enclosure (or main clause) which orders it. With a few subordinated sentences on the board, we can amplify what our little recognition-guide means, by compiling a list of "subordinating words" from examples of clauses on the board.

We start at this basic level of grammar in classes at all levels. If everyone practices and knows the conventions already, so much the better; we can go on more quickly. But since we require papers to be written in sentences, we need to lay the groundwork for understanding that abstract word, sentences, by concrete exemplification.

All of these efforts are repeated biweekly when we rewrite (see Chapter 10). Where we think it suitable, remarks written on papers we are about to return will include pointing out and naming the parts of successful examples of unsubordinated subject and its verb.

We work primarily to show the strength of the sentence. That is the whole structure we want writers to sense, admire, understand, and make prolific. We do not note its identifying marks in a void. We call attention to them in students' good sentences in the context of students' good writing, since we find that the quickest road to correctness is the roundabout one of aiming for literary excellence. Perhaps in some fabled golden age when all college freshmen wrote well, their instructors used literary anthologies to provide plenty of experience of wonderful sentences. Today we start close to home and find — in part by expecting them — wonderful sentences in material students can pay attention to because they have written it.

Given the words of such good sentences, we then look to their graphics. All the graphics of punctuation are intended to enhance the reader's sense of whole structures, sentences as well as essays. Graphics we require writers to use correctly are those which point up the wholeness of sentence structure. They are four. Most writers practice and know the first two:

> begin the sentence with a capital letter;
> end it with a period; and
> coordinate independent clauses either by a semi-colon, or by a
> comma + a conjunction.

We are able to say that, for our course, this comma before the coordinating conjunction is THE comma in American English, since it alone announces a fact about the sentence as a whole; it tells the reader that the syntactic weight of unsubordinated subject and verb is the same on either side of the comma + conjunction. Writers who must learn to observe one use of the comma, and know which one and why, can usually learn it not only as a rule but in practice and in relation to their sense of the whole sentence structure.

This limit on discussion of commas is tactical. It defines one sentence-related use which we know from experience we can expect everyone to grasp by the end of the course. True, we haven't dealt with prepositional phrases or compounded verbs, or with many other pleasures of syntactic analysis. Instead, first and most often, we work on the big thing — sentences, those whole structures which, when informed by imagination, are the breath of literature. Surety about the basic shape of a sentence prevents some lesser error. It also begins to free those writers whose imagination has been stilled by fear of making mistakes.

Governing Pronouns

The next noticeable element of the whole structure of an essay which affects grammatical choice — and which many students have not noticed — has to do with the hierarchy of pronouns, which show who the speaker of the piece is and perhaps show to whom the piece is spoken. We find the parable, which turns on point of view. a good place to look at pronouns and how they shift but remain coherent because one of them governs the writing. In classes which have aims other than composition itself (writing about the law, for instance) we might omit the parable. Working with writers of some experience, we follow the fable, which establishes the essentials of our critical vocabulary, with an essay. We advise them to choose a governing pronoun as they begin the rough draft. This pronoun identifies the stance of the speaker of the piece. We look back to fable aphorisms they have written, to see the effects of the person, sometimes reflected by the presence of a pronoun, in which the sentence is cast.

Then we write nonstop, to discover what we know about the implications of each of the nine possible governing pronouns. Here are some of the implications:

I is a natural in the essay which always expresses what the speaker of the piece has in mind. Some fear it as egotistical, though it is in fact an accurate, and so a modest, limiting of the author's claim to authority. It is proscribed in — almost excised from, by anonymous consent — essays which seek to appear objective or formal. (There is something unsatisfying about this state of affairs; it may be in the process of changing.) "I" is a way of taking direct responsibility for the data and ideas the essay presents. It allows a convenient shift to "we."

We suggests commonality of the speaker with others. It can mean the speaker and the reader, or the speaker and like-minded others (or even the editorial "we," or what our grandmothers called, "we, queens regnant and pregnant"). Where no community exists, it may seem to presume too much. It allows a convenient shift, in the course of the essay, to "I".

You (we have lost "thou" as a practical option in ordinary discourse) advises, admonishes, exhorts, encourages; can produce a nagging tone; implies that the speaker knows the reader or understands his welfare. It occurs often in advertising, propaganda, and sermons, as well as letters.

One has never been fully acclimatized. It is distant, formal, even artificial. Since it is rarely used in conversation, it is awkward and generates error in the work of writers who rely on their "ear" for correctness. Only very experienced writers can sustain it for long without error when a shift is called for, especially in sentences with subordinate clauses.

She/He conveys that the writer has knowledge of others' actions, relationships, or states. "He," once taken for granted as the generic pronoun for person, is now rightly and painfully visible as expressing the dominance of one half the human race over the other. Since the conventions of language do not create but reflect the state of affairs, "he" will probably continue in use as the generic pronoun for human being, for a time at least. Those who prefer to use "she" are welcome to do so. It admits of a convenient shift to "they."

It is properly suited to discussion of objects, ideas, and nonhuman beings. (Its use in the United States to designate non-human creatures has declined; use of gender-specific pronouns not only for domestic animals but for most animals and birds is less neat but rather common. Plants and insects are still usually "it" in the singular.) It is often forced into play to give an air of objectivity; some think it more authoritative to say, "It has often been observed that" instead of, "I think." This abuse often evokes passive verb forms with their veiled subjects. (However, as we remarked about "I," we sense a tendency to change away from the depersonalizing use of "it" toward a willingness to let authors speak more directly, in some nonfiction prose. We think, for example, of New Journalists and of specialists addressing a general public.)

They, like the third person singular, conveys the writer's knowledge of things or others. It implies difference between the speaker and some or all others. It may suggest that the writer is detached from the subject. It shifts readily to the singular. It lends itself to a tone of objectivity. When paired with a speaker "we," it gives the tone of debate or argument.

These perceptions, drawn from many bits of prolific writing done in class, on what pronouns suggest, are summarized in the following little table:

singular conveys:	plural conveys:	for writing about:
1st person expression of personality	assumption of community	attitudes, ideas, and their origins in experience
2nd person invitation to listen	assumption of intimacy with reader	choices, values, and reasons for these
3rd person information	assumption of impersonality	facts about persons, things, and their relationships

Clearly, these distinctions are relative, and no pronoun is in itself either more or less correct or desirable. But since the governing pronoun is the carrier of the very voice of the author, it is worth choosing with care. Such choice organizes the essay in which it operates; it is a literary choice. Having made it consciously, writers can trust to it to help them keep their references and focus clear. It will even give them something practical to check over, to assure coherence and agreement of pronouns, when they copyedit their work.

Governing Tense

The second continuous and sustaining member of the whole structure of an essay is the tense of the verb. We ask writers, when they have chosen a governing pronoun, to choose a governing tense. We remind them that verbs convey not only the action or state of the subject; they have another essential task: verbs tell what time it is. They locate the time within the essay as past, present, or future. Writers will use several tenses in most prose, but of these tenses one or another will indicate the location in time of the speaker of the piece. Consciousness of that time will keep the writer from defusing the essay by inconsistent tenses. Firm choice of, say, a past tense even revives, now and then, in copy-edited versions, that useful though fading stalwart, the pluperfect.

A little stint of running-writing will evoke from students their impressions of the uses or effects of various tenses. We may list on the board forms which are largely self-explaining, to show what the choices are. With more experienced classes, we include subjunctives for the options they offer. When setting forth these paradigms, we mention the least time-limited form, the infinitive. Even today a few students will have had experience with it in foreign language courses or in using the dictionary. It shows, by contrast, what we mean when we say that the verb tells time through its tenses (or times). In many essays, the tense seems almost dictated by the structure; even so, we ask that students be conscious of their choice of tense. We want them not to alter it but to recognize it. Then, if the common time of an essay is the past, and this is expressed by a governing perfect tense, students who recognize it will have one more major structural member of their essay in place. And when they come to proofread, they have a standard time from which to ascertain if all their time-telling verbs are properly regulated.

The idea of attending to a governing pronoun and a governing tense is not ours. We learned it in seventh grade from Mrs. Atkinson, whose battle cry for young writers was: a governing idea, a governing pronoun, a governing tense! It is one of her many usable truths, and we thank her for it. The strength of continuous verb and continuous pronoun supports the continuing idea. Especially in first or early drafts, well-chosen tense and pronoun will — without calling on Roman numerals or otherwise impeding the integrating power of imagination — give the essay coherence of grammar and matter which people call organization. When we write with a grasp of these three elements, and can refer back to them as we go, our first drafts are more intelligible. Many tangles of error in syntax will be avoided. So we teach the battlecry; it names what writers can do — *instead of* making mistakes. Specifying for students a manageable number of things to do, that they can do, expands their repertoire in unpredictable ways. It also prevents many errors we cannot tolerate but are hard put to it to correct in their causes.

The Paragraph

Still another graphic readers' aid, conventionalized in printed works, is the paragraph. Its very name tells us that it is not inherent but external to the composed text. No wonder students "get it wrong" and feel in constant danger of improper paragraphing, for this useful device has no long or definite standing in grammar, rhetoric, or literature. Yet paragraphs are useful. Their strongest use is to point out for the reader the parts of the essay's whole structure. We avoid asking students to write paragraphs when what we mean is to ask them to write briefly. We do ask them to compose paragraphs intended to do what paragraphs can do — serve as definite parts of the whole structure (e.g., beginning, middle, end); or emphasize, by extra visibility, some significant element of the whole. Here again the author's authority gets full play. Only the writer will know which elements should be isolated and which clustered, in paragraphs, to produce the rhythm of the whole structure he has in mind. There is no paragraphing in Herodotus or Cicero, and no common formula for paragraphing in Bacon, Milton, Swift, Wollestonecraft, N.O. Brown — or in the actual practice of some of the very handbooks which teach something called Paragraph Units.

By tending to the shape of the whole, and by describing paragraphs as devices to enhance a reader's grasp of the whole structure, we eliminate a needless fear of error and restore the paragraph to its original useful function. To fault "paragraphing" and "organization" is hopeless; only by insisting on a return to looking at the whole structure can the parts be reordered under the governance of the writer's idea.

Handbooks and Workbooks

Well, we're at the end of what we have to say about teaching grammar in writing classes, and we still haven't said much about using handbooks or workbooks. Here are the uses we've put them to.

Though we depend on bringing to conscious control that sense of grammar which is a power inherent in writers, we think many students can profitably refer to a handbook which depends on stating and exemplifying the rules of normative grammar. Handbooks are dangerous only when people try to use exercises and rule-memorizing as substitutes for writing and for what teachers can teach about writing, or as weapons against those who make mistakes.

Handbooks and workbooks are useful to writers whenever — having produced many concrete pages rich in the varied possibilities of language — they want to turn to a text or two to explore others' abstract systems.

They are useful to writers who have a paper to copyedit before its publication (perhaps to a class or a teacher) and who want a reference book to confirm their notion of, say, the serial comma or the MLA method of entering an article from an encyclopedia in a bibliography.

They are useful to some of the writers we meet who are confused or crippled by previous experience in "getting the grammar wrong." ("I used to like to write," said Marva, "but I can't stand getting the grammar wrong.")

We think their usefulness is greater after we have demystified them by treating them like any other text to come before our writing class. We treat them, that is, exactly as we treat our own written assignments. We choose a chapter or part of one, of an appropriate length (say, of two or three pages, perhaps on pronouns or on indirect objects). We read the pages aloud to each other in class, taking turns paragraph by paragraph, in small groups; we write down our observations; and we read our observations aloud. In other words, we practice together how to read literature — even if it is a grammar handbook.

We want to defuse fear of nomenclature and enable writers to open a text for themselves, at will and unassigned, in order to see if it may serve their needs. We want students to know that because they are intelligent, any book is intelligible and accessible to careful reading. We've learned that (for all but the rare omnilect who trains by reading the backs of medicine bottles and cereal boxes) people do not think of composition handbooks as readable. So, in most writing classes, we read bits of handbooks together, as we've described. We often recommend that writers visit secondhand bookstores, collect some grammar texts of any vintage, and read them.If they know other languages, they can compare texts written for Americans with, for example, texts written for English classes in a French lycée. It's gratifying for native speakers to see how much they know — irregular verbs ! — that others must memorize. It's provocative to learn how much nomenclature was expected of fourth-graders in 1920.

When we assign a common text, we expect it to be used as a reference book and to be as handy as a dictionary. We neither require students to fill in blanks in exercises nor forbid them to do so. They may, when they are ready, find such exercises instructive or at least calming. Any text, including programmed workbooks, can be treated the way we treat our assigned writing, reading and making observations, to make it more helpful.

We want to repeat that we teach grammar every day, but seldom from a text, and always as subordinate to the writing from which grammatical abstractions are drawn.

Two parts of handbooks which interest some students are those presenting items concerning the lexicon, or usage, and tables of inflections, chiefly of pronouns and verbs.

Usage

Most writers are more ready to entertain niceties of usage than of syntax. When they can read handbooks and workbooks without discomfort, they often choose to read about usage first. Since usage is particular — not a whole system, like syntax — it is well suited to voluntary solo reading and study.

Many handbooks are thought unreadable because they in fact contain no sentence anyone would be glad to have written; to propose a contrast, we often suggest that writers read Fowler. *Modern English Usage* is full of splendid sentences. We naturally think people will gain more, in more ways, from Fowler than from other writers on usage, both because he writes lucid explanations and because many of his entries are exemplary brief expository essays. He is prolific of pleasure and instruction. (For a good view of his genius, try the exercise described above, of reading a text aloud and writing observations about it, with both Fowler and any other text dealing with one of his subjects.)

In responding to students' papers, we treat usage as we do spelling, discreetly pencilling in correct forms, so as to offer the writer the visual stimulus of seeing them correctly written.

Inflection

Writers' need for help in developing accurate usage varies unpredictably among them. Usage is as individual as vocabulary, and like it is much improved indirectly by wide reading. Inflection — the ways the forms of words change to exhibit their relation to other words — is another matter. Questions of inflection are few but thorny. For various legitimate reasons of clarity (and perhaps most often for illegitimate causes related to racial or class prejudice) many readers who come upon the two common deviations from standard inflection leap to absurd and fierce conclusions. An "s" missing from a third-person singular verb form in the present tense, and a past participle lacking its final "d," come between such readers and the text before them.

We can warn writers against this handicap. We advise them to copyedit attentively for the "s" and "d" when preparing final drafts, and encourage them to patient persistence in teaching themselves to use the correct forms habitually when writing.

The rules are simple, of course; anyone can learn them in a few minutes. But following them habitually is difficult. Here instructors have something to learn — about what grammar is most teachable. Young adults come by these tiny points of inflection with great difficulty. It's a warning instance of how hard it is to teach a language: It encourages us to be glad our students already speak English all but perfectly, when we realize that this one small aspect of difference — whatever its origins — can be changed to standard form only slowly and with effort on the part of the writer.

Written comments on papers can help sharpen the writers' awareness, if we are careful. Most papers of those who habitually omit the "s" and "d" will occasionally include them. Pointing with praise to correct instances is far more effective and economical than marking and commenting on incorrect ones. Where we find the letters missing, we neither circle them in red nor let them stand. We simply and discreetly add them, as if it were a question of spelling (which, in a sense, it is), then in the margin write again the subject plus the verb, to give the writer one more moment of meeting the standard form.

Some students who need to develop the habit of using the final "s" and "d" will do so before the semester is out; others will take longer to acquire consistent control. We need to remember that spending class weeks on this question alone has been tried and does nothing to speed up a change in habit, though it does tend to teach the writer to write haltingly and hate writing, and to madden those in the group who do not happen to make these errors. Probably the first thing we must do is to identify these tiny bits of language, and show the student what difference they make to the reception of his work. Then we must tell him that though we cannot teach it, he can learn it, not just as a rule but in practice. After that, we can notice his successes.

Here is a summary of the few essential matters of grammar and graphics on which we always work with students:

I. a sense of the whole structure of the sentence
    A. as an unsubordinated subject and its verb;
    B. shown graphically by starting with a capital letter and ending with a period;
    C. as a whole structure including subordinate and ordinate parts;
    D. as a whole structure coordinating two or more parts which might syntactically stand alone as wholes; the parts may be joined either
       1. by a semicolon, or
       2. by a comma plus a coordinating conjunction.
II. what a grammar is and how it relates to the graphics of punctuation.
III. the choice of a governing pronoun and a governing tense as structural members of the whole essay.
IV. the use of paragraphs to punctuate (i.e., point up) the whole

structure of the essay.
V.   the ability to read a reference work useful in copyediting.
VI.   the conventional inflections of the third person singular in the present tense, and of the past participle.

Though in the course of comments in class and on papers we may address other notions of grammar as well, we choose to work consistently on these six carefully limited points. The range of grammar and grammars is vast; time is short; we must focus on what is most necessary. Our students need a place, however small, of sure standing; they need to know both what and that they know.

Always we work from correctness, from strength, from what is well-known or well-done, toward extension of the writer's power. We no longer find time to deliver the session-long lecture on verbals with which we once dazzled students; they loved it, for it was College English undefiled, but it did not effect change in their writing. We have taught a course for those who hope to write professionally, in which a third of the semester was spent mastering the skills of copyediting; in that course those highly motivated students learned to digest and put into practice the fine points of conventions governing grammar and its graphics, all the way down to compounds hyphenated according to position. Even then, with the very bindings of their manuals of style showing the effects of their efforts, their mastery of commas was not a coefficient of their ability to write.

We began this book by avowing that it would discuss the teaching and learning of a universal set of skills necessary to writing. At moments in our long work of identifying that set, we have simply asked others what skills they would nominate. (To many, the question itself was absurd or distressing.) Most of those questioned suggested grammar, meaning a normative grammar, as one of the essentials. None omitted it. Not a few suggested only grammar, or only grammar, spelling, and vocabulary.

It is plain that we do not share their views. Grammar (normative) is not a member of our universal set. The time we give it by itself is short. But it is frequent, and in the context of student writing. The matters we think essential are few.

Yet we praise and value the workings of sentences and the powers of syntax. We recognize, too, that unless inflection and graphics are correctly observed, the writing will often evoke not interest in itself but a rash judgment that the writer is an idiot. We work against that danger as we must. But we save our best time for tasks which forestall error by calling on writers' human capacity to use whole structures, making many levels of intellectual order out of a worldful of random data. Of those levels, one will be grammatical.

12 | Reading Writing

Many students tell us that they've learned, in our writing classes, to read better and pay more attention to what they read. Better writing has, it seems, produced better reading. (We'd always assumed it was the other way around.) To consider the connectedness of writing and reading gives us still another focus for our thinking about the work of a writing class.

A page covered with structured lines of letters is the field where writer and reader are at one. Without writing, there is no reading; but also, without reading what we are writing there is no way to write more than a sentence or two.

Writing comes first, in the plain sense that until something has been written nothing can be read. In our culture, it's conceivable that someone could learn to read who had never learned to write. But it's not conceivable that someone could learn to write without learning to read — if only back to himself — what he had written.

Reading and writing interpenetrate, like breath breathing in and breathing out. So intimate is the connection that a writing teacher, if inadvertently, always teaches reading as well.

Are we suggesting then that writing teachers should return to the practice of twenty or thirty years ago, and reach outside their prescribed curriculum to give students anthologies of Great Essays to study? No; on the contrary. Students should, of course, read literature, and the literature suited to writing classes is the students' own writing. Their writing assignments are all based on literary structures, and our expectations for these assignments are that they will be readable as literature; fully authorized by the authority of the author, fired by ideas original to the author, and informed by the great literary conventions, in prose as elegant as the author can manage, with correctness as a secondary effect.

It's in this way, by doing what we can to make students' essays worthwhile, that our writing courses teach the reading of worthwhile essays. Students' reading of students' writing as literature interacts to improve both, on the levels where we find our students able. When students write the literature the class reads, they bypass economically the deep split between reading and writing which afflicts classrooms from first grade forward.

It's a tribute to the powers of the mind that we can, for example, at twelve years old, shift every forty minutes for six hours from one to the other of, say, algebra, ceramics, Spanish, earth science, lunch, American history, and something called English (which may be anything). We can, without going mad, continue thus for another decade, spending larger bits of time on fewer and more specialized subjects: three weekly hours each of classical French dramatists, general linguistics, elementary Portugese, and Proust. Some minds, eventually, begin to unify the variety and to use the material from one course to understand others; to perceive for themselves, say, the relation of Descartes' philosophy to Proust's image of man.

So the split, begun in the earliest grades, between teaching reading and teaching writing is neither surprising nor quite fatal, though we think it inefficient and unnecessarily drastic. But, as students reach toward mature control, a practical conscious experience of the oneness of reading and writing will increase their power.

At present, numbers of freshmen are aware as they enter that they are short of that reach for control. They are as readers not sufficiently expert to succeed readily in enjoying and understanding courses in the humanities. To help them, reading courses begin to appear in college catalogues. The deadly jargon of remediation in English is heard in the land. But, though daft and contradictory assumptions about what readers and writers need to know are common, the primary question goes unanswered, perhaps because it is not asked. That question is: what do readers and writers need to know to achieve their independence?

A real question, it must be answered, both theoretically and practically.

Basic skills for writers are **not** "grammar, vocabulary, and spelling." Basic skills for readers are **not** "outlining, skimming, and finding the main idea with supporting details." A basic diet is not a caloric chart, a list of local food stores, and a recipe for meringues. Reading and writing are for the sake of ideas and information. Ideas and information are in, and not outside of, language. What is basic is what good readers and writers do.

What we think good writers do, that we can engender in our students, is compressed in the set of five skills we have returned to throughout this book. The same five skills are essential to intelligent reading. Learned by and for writing, they are extended by and for reading at the same time. In a writing class, each writer composes an anthology of essays according to literary structures, and reads not only it but as many embodiments of each structure as there are colleagues. This double usefulness is economical. Here is how we perceive the effect on reading of our writing classes:

Whole structures draw from writers' minds a full and balanced presentation of their ideas. Readers also need — for savoring, for comprehension, and for memory — to sense the ordering of parts into a whole. To recognize readily, and identify, the kinds of order they encounter is to read expertly and reap the expert's rewards. Perception of whole structures is a mental activity; we may discern it under various names throughout intellectual history. (Coleridge relates it to imagination.) The same mental faculty perceives and produces the sets of whole structures named in logic, grammar, and literature. Awareness of any of these structures aids the mind to grasp and keep in memory what the parts say about the whole; and to anticipate and enjoy its completion. How writers divide a subject and classify the parts is often a crucial aspect of their idea. Since exposition, using a mix of literary structures, is the mode in which most textbooks are written, and since students must read textbooks well, students' practice of expository literary structures will help them grasp what they read.

Abstract and **concrete** are polar forms of verbal expression, and the movement between them describes something essential about the activity of all thought. In good writing they are controlled to engage the mind of the reader by involving it progressively with the development of the writer's idea. They are perhaps related to what reading texts propose when they advise, "Find the main idea and the supporting details." (We are dissatisfied with this advice because we have never met any real-life habitual good readers who set themselves this task. Further, "find" is not a telling word for the process of understanding an idea; it does not suggest that ideas are to be imagined, and that the idea we do not imagine we do not retain.) Good readers of good writing can appreciate what is before them in the text and what it occasions in their minds. They notice the play of abstract and concrete expression. They are, for instance, tempted neither to skip the descriptions (which are concrete) nor to duck the opening argument (which may well be abstract). What they have learned to heed as writers, they are able to heed as readers. They know what to pay attention to in the interaction of concrete and abstract, not only in the unfolding of ideas but also in the evaluation of proof and the patterns of analysis.

Distinguishing **observation** and **inference** trains writers to eliminate fruitless opinionating by supplanting it with original perceptions, carefully unfolded and sustained by pertinent evidence. Readers who habitually distinguish them know something about the reliability of a text's inferences and judgments, even as they read. They will locate, in their text, originality by evaluating each inference and reliability by noting the cogency and completeness of observations which justify it. From another vantage point, they will also be able to evaluate the reliability of their own response to what they read, by looking at what they can observe in the text to see if it justifies what they have inferred. The effect of practice in writing and reading observations on our students' power to read accurately is unmistakable. Highly skilled readers, as well as those beginning to acquire expertise, have told us that this practice in particular has made their reading noticeably more productive and memorable, and increased their powers of concentration.

Rewriting is paralleled by rereading. Writers find that rewriting is the way to open out and clarify what is hidden in their idea, to order the parts and put them at the service of the whole structure — and to enjoy the action of their minds engaged in this strenuous exercise. Readers with an appetite for the fullness of understanding that rewriting provides (even of their own words) may expect such gratification from texts other than their own, and reread them in search of it. Recognition of concrete and abstract language and of observations and inferences gives them something to look for attentively as they reread. These skills make their reading more active. They can pursue it longer. Habitual rewriting means that they know how to spend time mulling over a text until they have made it their own. We have noticed that people listening to a colleague's essay prior to writing observations sometimes ask quite intensely that it be read over again; we hope that this wish to understand will transfer to their own silent readings where they can reread to their satisfaction.

These are some of the ways in which we think the universal set of five skills, essential to writers, turns out to be basic to reading too. There is another way of analyzing our work in writing to see how it affects reading. That is, by starting with the dominant rhythm of each class section (exemplified more concretely in the syllabi of Chapter 15).

The rhythm is composed of four alternating elements or stresses:

we write;
we read aloud;
we write observations;
we read them aloud.

It's plain at a glance that half our habitual work in a writing class is reading. True, it's the writers' own work which is the text. This is an asset. Given their own work to read, we can be sure that everyone will be able to read well — and it's our principle to always begin where people are able.

While one person reads, others in the group are listening and getting ready to write observations. This means that we're acting out the two parts of the double act that reading always is.

The first part is an eye-voice translation of printed letters into their sounds as words. The second part is an ear-mind reception of sounds which are transformed into understanding. Even when we read silently, there are (Ong and McLuhan explain) flickers of neural response and muscle involvement in our throats. Medieval readers, even when alone, would read audibly; we have silenced that voice by internalizing it. The ability to "hear" or take in the sense of our silent reading voice is essential. Many readers, nervous or unskilled, show evidence of an odd state, in which they do not heed what is contained in the words they can translate into articulate sound. It's as if they cannot hear themselves or cannot decipher what they hear. A considerable number of those whose reading test scores are low seem unable to recall what they have just read to themselves or even read, correctly, aloud. They seem to process their reading automatically, eye to voice, rather as a fast typist may wish to process a manuscript eye to fingers, shorting the ear-mind circuit which would open the language to comprehension, so that they take nothing replicable from the reading their eyes have done.

Understanding depends on the mind "hearing" or grasping what the voice says or the eyes transpose into mental echoes of words. The rhythm of our classes brings this step out into the visible and audible world, where it can be reinforced at need. Listening to the work of colleagues, or reading their own, with a communal expectation of writing down observations about what they have heard, locates the step. It may ease the transfer they need to make, from listening to a reading voice and making the results visible as written data, to "hearing" their own voices and remembering what they are saying, when they themselves read, silently or aloud. That the classroom gives them the company and example of other readers' voices is also helpful. If they cannot "hear" what they are saying, they will have colleagues who can reflect back to them, through written observations, what they have said.

The effect of colleagues' observations on good readers is equally striking, for it reveals to them what they have actually said — a revelation even the experienced must strain to achieve in reading their own work. It is, in fact, an act of analysis which would otherwise be added to the tasks of the instructor as reader of students' papers.

Another point about the class rhythm is that it is an active one. Students are always either reading and preparing to write, or writing and preparing to read. The inner dynamic of motion between abstract and concrete is constantly at play. It enables readers to improve their power to read by working only indirectly on reading, while giving direct attention to writing. We need not spend time trying to effect a transfer of writing skills to reading, for the two are intimately one. Given the more active, physical, and limited work of writing, followed by reading what they have written, they learn to listen actively too, as they prepare to write their observations. Listening is, as it were, the primal form of reading: taking in another's words. We note that many of those who have told us their skill in reading was increased in our writing classes have been initially very competent readers; they are surprised to notice how they benefit from the quickness of apprehension and the accuracy of retention which listening followed by writing provides. It gives readers something effective to do, to fine-tune and focus their skills toward better retention of any text.

The class rhythm, shifting as it does from taking in a text to putting out in other words something of what it contains, is a comfortably expanded, forward-moving structure for paying attention to written material. It is, among other things, practice in setting the right pace. To be able to set and vary the pace is essential to intelligent readers. It's not slow reading or speed reading that matter, but how close the time spent reading brings us to the text. If we go slowly with densely written material (dense in its literary complexity or dense in its ordering of data), the slowness should reflect presence of mind, not absent-mindedness. If we go quickly, our speed should correspond to the speed with which we assimilate the material. To read well, we deal with the text at a speed which lets us apprehend, distinguish, and savor what is there. Practice of the five skills which establish the rhythm of the class should give students enough to do to make their reading rich and full, without the strained attention or the anxiety which frustrate pleasure and beget impatience or boredom.

We offer these remarks on reading though we are self-trained and have no special expertise in measuring what happens when people read. We do so because we have noticed that students at all points on the academic spectrum can improve their control of reading in our classes. People with low reading scores may begin to read on their own for pleasure for the first time. People who are lifelong habitual readers find that to practice, as we do, the working parts of reading — a voice speaks; a mind takes in, considers, and sets forth what it hears — produces remarkably accurate and thoughtful readings of texts. We trust that our awareness of the inseparability of reading and writing will guide us to getting the most good for readers out of what we know is good for writers.

13 | Writing About Literature

I: Reading and Making Observations

I am reading a paper for a seventeenth-century English literature class by a serious and intelligent student. His paper, on Bunyan and Hawthorne, reflects his interest in American literature. He has found two striking passages to compare, and I begin reading eagerly. Now I come to the statement of his main idea: "Bunyan is didactic and religious, but Hawthorne is psychological and profound." I put down the paper in dismay.

The problem of the paper can be seen in two lights. From the reader's point of view, such papers fail because they stand between the work of literature and the reader. You *can* do something for me, said Diogenes to Alexander: Stand out of my light; do not, at least, take away from me what you cannot give me. Perhaps we have all read pronouncements that sound like the one in this paper by critics of genius. The student is probably imitating the tone of such criticism without realizing that he has omitted the substance, the knowledge of the work that the critic has passed on along with his opinion.

It takes a critic of genius to sum up an idea in such a way that the key observation in the idea can easily be separated from the implied judgment of the pronouncement. "Spenser writ no language," Jonson said. Whatever the judgment implied in this, the observation is central to an understanding of poetic diction, especially in the epic tradition. The sentence might be said of Homer; certainly twentieth-century studies of Homer's language show the literary implications of Jonson's observation in a way that could not have been realized in Jonson's time. "When once you have thought of big men and little men, it is very easy to do all the rest." Boswell took this as a signal to defend Swift, but, again, the observation has far more importance than the implied evaluation. Johnson has signaled out one observation about *Gulliver's Travels:* that Book I concerns little men, and Book II concerns big men. (A good example of the importance of noticing the obvious.) Then he has made a crucial inference: that Books I and II are a unit with a single ironic key. To express this fittingly, Johnson has

154

wittily emulated Swift's own ironic style and put the important thing, Swift's genius, in the subordinate clause.

Each of these pronouncements contains one, selected, and therefore crucially important, observation about the work, which the reader can take away with him to consider on his own, an observation that is separable from judgments and evaluations. In contrast, the problem sentence we began with contains no observation about the works, no knowledge for the reader to take away. We would conclude that any literary paper we taught students to write must contain in the central assertion of the author's idea, some demonstrable knowledge, some observation about the work to be reviewed.

If we consider the problem from the other point of view, the writer's, is it a reading problem or a writing problem? It seems to be a writing problem; the author demonstrated an ability to read, a genuine literary perception, when he found the two passages on which his paper was based. There is clearly a writing problem. But we think there is a reading problem too. He can read well, but not with control, not consistently, not with the sort of consciousness that can draw on reading whenever he needs it. His reading is an undeveloped literary instinct, not yet a ready instrument of perception and analysis.

From the point of view of this book, then, from the writer's point of view, the writer has turned toward his weakness, away from his strength — his knowledge of literature and his literary perceptions — because he cannot use his literary instincts. He draws instead on his stock of unexamined opinions, confounding description and evaluation. This results in the crippling loss of descriptive terms, such as *didactic, religious,* and the collapse of the possibility of sustaining judgments. The painful antitheses of the sentence show the writer's predicament clearly. Is the *Divine Comedy,* one wonders, didactic or profound?

We have been talking in this book so far about writing courses for which there is no text outside the students' writing. Now we consider how we adapt the skills we have been teaching when the author must write not simply about the experiences that have come to him, but about those experiences, already formed by abstractions, that he must acquire deliberately. We will posit a course, Writing About Literature, which will still be emphatically a writing course, but which will be, almost as emphatically, a reading course. How will we get to the writing of a good literary essay?

What kind of literary essay? There are many possible kinds, of course, but if we consider the principle we have been following with the academic expository essay, we realize that we cannot teach the specialized, only the central. Because there is no time to teach a variety of critical approaches to literature, we must teach a basic way to write about literature. How do we know what is basic or central? By thinking of the sort of requirements a writer must meet. Much student writing is done in situations the student has chosen, one governed by a favorite teacher or a favorite literary genre or period. He may prefer a teacher whose approach to literature is metaphoric, that is, using the terms of another study, such as psychology, economics, or sociology, as metaphors for the experience of literature. And as he takes individual courses, he learns what individual teachers have to teach. But there comes a time, writing not for an individual teacher, but for a department test, a qualifying test, an essay written for honors, for scholarship, or for admission, when he must write in a truly public way: show how well he can read a piece of literature and how well he can meet a question set him concerning what he reads.

In addition to being a test of reading — of the ability to find out what one needs to know — such a task requires that the student write a good expository essay: one that begins with an idea warranted by the work at hand, supported by an analysis of the evidence, the whole essay set forth in its proper order — the order of the writer's idea — and written in a selection of language really used by men. The sort of essay we are calling central is one that would meet a general test.

The two requirements for a good literary essay then can be partly met by the sort of work we have been doing in writing from the start. The requirement for a good expository essay — that an author support what he asserts — does not faze the writer who knows how to begin with the whole structure of his idea. And the requirement to read literature and make observations and inferences about it in the language of literary description is already familiar to writers who have learned to pay attention to their own writing and that of their colleagues, and to treat it as literature by describing its literary elements.

There will be differences. First, a new emphasis on reading. We have emphasized listening, getting the big structure of the work and its main emphases. Now we add to that, reading work that is finished as well as complete, work of such power and concentration that it can support the analytical possibilities of reading.

All along, our authors have been learning to read their own writing — one of the best ways of learning to read. Reading is essentially an act of attention to something continuous, and a coordinating of several activities which go on simultaneously and which exchange dominance and subordination. So far it is not very different from listening. But reading is capable of a special activity: analysis, or the development of ideas by a process that opens up — an activity that loosens one order without destroying it and permits a synthesis of a variety of coexisting new orders. Analytical reading differs from ordinary reading because it is purposive, reductive, and it alters what it reads. A little practice in analytical reading usually makes ordinary reading more enjoyable and more varied: richer or brisker.

For the experienced reader, then, reading is partly response and partly analysis. Our writers have been learning this by reading their own writing, by making observations about the writing of their colleagues, by drawing inferences from these observations, and by rewriting. They have begun to hear and to internalize the voices of their audience — that is, the social or public aspects of language. But now it is as if they must learn to read new languages. Each piece of new literature is a complete system and self-contained world, and because it is a literary world, each system or world is a language.

In common with other writing classes, however, the main business of our Writing About Literature class will be writing. This means that the literature we study must be brief, chosen not because it is easy but because it is exemplary and powerful. As in all writing classes, work is based on the principle that writing comes from what is in the writer's head. Practice in reading follows from this; no one can write about literature without first putting it in his head.

Our class work toward the writing of papers goes on in three stages:

1) *Learning to read the language of the work.*
Work at this stage is reading the work and making observations. By the end of this stage, the work *takes place* in the imagination of the reader. The imaginative synthesis that is the work has been re-synthesized by the reader, a synthesis of the poem and his response to it. The emphasis at this stage is on the personal.

2) *Learning the language of literary description.*
Work at this stage is expressing observations as description, setting them down in the order of the observer's attention, and selecting the big or dominant observations. The activity is the beginning of analysis. Its purpose is to formulate an assertion about what pattern the reader noticed in the work. By the end of this stage, the author

has an idea, expressed as a hypothesis. The emphasis now is on the public.
3) *Learning to "speak" the language of the poem and the language of literary analysis.*
Work at this stage is drafting the paper. This is another stage of synthesis, for the paper is a synthesis of the language of the work and the language of literary description — the language of response and the language of analysis. The essay will be both personal and public.

We begin the first stage by reading, let us say, something like the 23rd Psalm, a poem with which most people are vaguely familiar, which no one in class has paid any real attention to, and about which there exists no body of high-powered literary criticism which the teacher is in possession of and considers the "right" way of reading the poem. The ideal way of reading poetry would be to memorize it. But short of the ideal, we can put a brief poem on the board and ask students to write it out in a notebook. When we copy something, we pay attention to it in a special way. At this point we are trying to slow the usual skimming (students skim poetry and read secondary texts very slowly — a reversal of the reading each sort of work calls for). We all read the poem silently and then have two or three oral readings.

What we are encouraging is what Frye calls the precritical, "participating response" ("The Road of Excess," in *The Stubborn Structure*, 160-174). It is the instinctive response to the impulse of the lines, the burst of image or its widening circles, the perfect falling into place of phrase, syllable, and rime, the suspense of narrative, the ironic overview of dramatic action. Like all instinct, the primary response to literature carries a charge of energy that goes beyond its first essentially wordless expression and can be turned to intellectual uses.

Its first use is that it keeps the reader engaged, keeps the eye going eagerly down the page or the ear tuned to the singer's voice. Participation is the beginning of paying attention — the pleasure of paying attention, in fact. All learning depends first on the sustaining of attention, and then on the quality of attention. We do everything we can to promote the first so that we can help to develop the second.

Two things are important at this point, one because it is happening and one because it is not happening. Students need the "negative capability" to hold off criticism and free them to see what is actually before them. The application of pre-formed ideas is apt to be deforming. I recall a highly rational paper based on a statement that a satirist ought to do justice to the system of ideas he is satirizing. It sounded right to the student, who had read very few satires. But a theory that will not fit Aristophanes' treatment of Socrates, nor Voltaire'sview of Leibnitz, nor Swift's sketch of scientific experiment — to name the first examples that come to mind — will have to be put aside. We encourage and sustain the primary response in students, as in ourselves, because it forestalls false judgments.

Primary response permits literature to take place in the imagination. And when the primary response puts the poem within, the later observations we make about it are acts of recognition. The satisfactions of the primary response ought to be so firmly established that no subsequent analysis removes them. In fact, when you want to study literature, the pleasure feeds the study, gives it life and power to generate its own continued work. That first knowledge gives you something to keep going back to when developing an idea, something to keep checking the idea against. It keeps you from exaggerating "insignificant" features:

> The chopper who works in the woods all day for many weeks or months at a time, becomes intimately acquainted with them in his own way. He is more open, in many respects, to the impressions they are fitted to make than the naturalist who goes to see them. He is not liable to exaggerate insignificant phenomena and events. Not so the naturalist; enough of his unconscious life does not pass there.
>
> (Thoreau, *Journal,* November 18, 1851)

This chance for his unconscious life to pass in the presence of what he wants to know is the main chance for a writer. Because it is wordless, this acquaintance will not by itself lead to writing. But because it is imaginative identification with what we read, we can't form ideas without it.

This time of reading is difficult to describe and difficult to carry on in a classroom, mainly because the teacher is in a hurry to get the reading of a poem over with (he has already read it and studied it) and start discussing it. In another sort of class, the work would have been assigned and read at home. But the discussion in this class will be less important than reading and making observations, because the aim is not to teach students some body of knowledge about the work, but how to read and study the work. Students need a model for the sort of reading we expect. They often think that a very deliberate reading and re-reading before any attempt at analysis is the sign of a "slow reader" and therefore a "slow learner." Their model now is the teacher's confident, leisurely reading.

We call this stage "learning to read the langugage of the work." It seems to students that the work they read, especially poetry, presents itself in a foreign language — an impression that has a good deal of useful truth in it. A man visiting a foreign country whose language is unknown to him and where his language is not spoken needs an interpreter. Though he goes through the country very attentively, he goes through it at a remove. He knows it would be better if he understood the language of that country directly, and better still if he could speak it. Then he would have no need of interpretation.

Students often accept the apparent foreignness of a work of literature too easily. They consider that they have an interpreter at hand, the teacher, and that supplemental interpreters are ready, waiting in the library. But for them as for our imaginary traveler, it would be better to understand the language of the country directly and speak it themselves. The interpretation that they crave gives them the "meaning" of the work, which is often merely the gist of it. So much the worse if it *is* meaning. Here more than ever, "meaning" overbalances or pre-empts the "truth" of the work. Our first concern, and in class our mutual concern, is the "truth" of the poem, that is, what we can all see, all name — whatever is not false or doubtful.

In our class work, we reject all "interpretation," because it makes permanent the condition of being a stranger in a foreign country. Students grasp at interpretations and are overwhelmed, because they are afraid they cannot learn the language. But they can. They will find that reading and speaking the language of the poem is a lot easier than trying to interpret it. When they have learned to speak the language themselves, they will be better able to interpret it in their own essays, insofar as they need to, and not as though to other barbarians either. Reading allegory with students quickly reveals the reader whose primary responses have been spoiled and who has given up hope of reading the language of the poem. He tells us what Duessa "means" but he did not notice the color of her dress. He has picked the meaning from the note at the bottom of the page and thrown the poetry away.

The crucial turn in writing about literature is the turn from the poem to write about it — the turn away from the poem on the page to the poem in the mind. What we write first are observations, which are not so much notes about the work as they are notes about as much of the work as we have got in our minds when we write. We turn back to the work for renewed periods of study, but this is the first check on how much we have learned so far.

This secondary response moves from participation to recognition of pattern in what we are reading. At this point, as Frye says, the sequential order of the work, the linear order of words or images or sounds subsides, and a simultaneous order emerges in our mind: what we recognize as the fundamental action or plot, the turn or trope or poise of the poem. After we have moved, for example, through the brilliant, mocking, interlocking shifts of "A Valediction: Forbidding Mourning," we recognize that we have met, though not until the end, its center; that the "plot" of the poem is its changing feeling into understanding acceptance or intelligence, and that it has been doing that from the beginning.

Of course, this doesn't happen all at once. But observations are the beginning of it. Because they are, they are free — undirected by the teacher. Observation, like the literature it is directed toward, is both a personal experience and a public and social one. It is personal because the power of observation is a primal and identifying power, beyond the reach of teaching. *I* see *this* because of who I am: "What I do is me." In identifying some aspect of the work, an observation identifies the observer and the work — or makes that identification conscious — and releases for the observer some of the energy of the literature so that he does not need the prodding of what the teacher thinks he ought to observe.

The students' freedom of observation does not mean that the teacher is dispensable, of course. He has established the deductive framework of the class. Once he has thought of that, it is very easy to do all the rest. His knowledge of the literature is the context which controls pointless excursions and corrects errors. But he is not teaching that knowledge in this sort of class. Free observation means that the teacher does not knock out every hope of inductive learning by asking directive questions ("What did you notice about the imagery of the poem?").

Observations go between the naive and the critical response. Like the first, they are charged with the excitement or pleasure of discovery. But they also begin the analysis, the loosening of the order of the work the student is reading. The primary, participating response follows the order of the work. The critical response is marked first by the fact that it does not. It follows another order. In the beginning that order is seen as a personal order, an order of recognition. But by the time the student has written his paper, that order must be seen by others as one of the possible orders of the work itself: what happens when the play is over, when we finish the poem or close the novel — the emergence of the simultaneous order that lay beneath the linear order of the work.

The order of observations, which is at first the order of the observer's attention, frees the student from the linear order of the work and so frees him to find the order of an idea. It anticipates that order. It is not only useless, then, but distracting to tell readers what to look for. When the teacher imposes the order of his observations on students, he is really imposing his idea on them. Order *is* idea.

At the same time that observations are personal, they are also public, as students discover when we impose on them the discipline of separating observations from inference. Once observations have been made, everyone recognizes them. Some fact rises clear of the distractions of private opinion or taste and can be named by everyone in class (though not necessarily with the same name). When this happens, the incoherence of private "impressions" is lifted for a moment, and a perception appears. A bounded perception, yet more full of possibilities. We are freed from this sort of thing: "The poem ["Three Years She Grew"] has a sort of mysterious tone," and we get instead this sort of thing: "The poem begins with verbs in the past tense, shifts to verbs in the future tense, and ends with verbs in the past tense again, without ever having gone through a present."

What do we tell students about making observations? We have discussed that in Chapter 5, so we will summarize here.

1) Observations are concrete — something you can see that we can all see.

2) Observations are what you notice — what strikes you or what you remember when you close the book.

3) What you notice may seem "obvious." That's good. The obvious is always important — probably something we took for granted without ever thinking about it. It's a good idea to put the obvious down first.

4) Observations never occur in the order of the work you have read. You can return to the work later, but for now write as many observations as you can in the order in which they occur to you without looking at the text.

5) To express your observations, you'll be using the language of description. You may notice the tenses of the verbs, or which pronoun the author uses or how he shifts from singulars to plurals, what kind of connections he uses, whether the sentences are long or short — These are not points you have to cover for every work, just samples of what might strike your attention. Don't worry about names. If you notice a poet uses a lot of "-ing" words, you can just say that.

You may not be interested in verbs and pronouns (too bad). You may be noticing another sort of thing: how much abstract or concrete there is; what sort of repetitions there are; whether there's a turn in what goes on; beginnings and endings. *Note:* We do not say this if students have never worked at observations before.

6) Observations don't summarize the work and don't interpret it.

We would begin every writing course with the writing of a few fables so that writers learn directly and have a common focus on the essential things about writing. Observations about the fables will bring out most of the points under 5. But if students have never practiced making observations before, we do not say anything except the first four things. *After* plentiful observations is the time to point out that observers have been noticing such things as tense/time and pronoun/point of view (the grammatical structures) and such other things as repetitions, abstract/concrete, beginnings and endings (the rhetorical structures). As students notice these things, we reinforce the idea that these terms are the terms of literary description and analysis — indispensable for the foundation of a good paper.

Students always notice grammatical and rhetorical structures without any prodding. It's important that they do so spontaneously, to demonstrate for themselves, unimpeachably, that they have the capacity for critical thinking — that the roots of that thinking are very simple. We have been saying that observations are public — true. But *public* here means recognizable by others, not an objective body of materials that we apply to the literature like litmus paper or cell stains. A poem cannot be run through a series of categories (as the inevitable arrangement of a poetry text book would seem to suggest), as if it were a humor like urine, blood, or phlegm, to be tested for sickness or greatness, for tone or metaphor, by a standard experiment. We do not derive the poem from grammar or rhetoric, but grammar and rhetoric from poetry. In fact, the most economical way to learn grammar would be by studying poetry and writing it, poetry and grammar being the two parts of a language that cannot be translated into another language.

Let us say, for the purposes of describing the process, that we are beginning literary work with a poem. The next step after the slow reading we have already described, is to write observations for fifteen minutes. Again, it is crucial that the teacher write. When the teacher does not write, but sits watching, the observed (who are attempting to be observers) become self-conscious, and the exercise appears stilted. With the teacher writing, a form of studying he is well used to and probably very good at, the exercise becomes a necessary form of attention, which the *discipuli* are learning from the *magister*. (You may notice that if you are accustomed to use yellow legal-sized pads, such tools will make a scattered appearance throughout the class.)

Written language differs from spoken (for one thing) because it makes itself evident as something substantial. So the first thing that writing observations does is to make us realize that we are passing from the instinctive to the critical.

Our burst of writing is nonstop, unsorted out, without apologies, censorship, or editing. We must continuously be slipping past the blocks to writing that continuously appear. And we must do it without fussing or calling attention to what we are doing, so that writers get used to this almost insignificant, but potent little resource. This is the second benefit of writing observations.

We say, Begin with the obvious. We want writers to get right to the order of attention. If anyone "finishes" before the time is up, he is to keep on writing, setting down even the "trivial" and the "homely." We know we will all be surprised to hear later what someone else considered obvious. In fact, people frequently make their most interesting observations in that time after they have "finished" and before the time is up. Out of this comes a third benefit: finding out how to use time to increase writing, and writing to increase time.

Later we will be extending this period of writing of observations. After students get used to this and see what it produces, we have some things to say to them about running-writing. We do not say them all at once, but we say them all finally:

1) There are two things we all know about the mind. First, it loves to work without strain. It likes to daydream or worry. It's hard to make yourself do intellectual work with an unwilling partner. But the second thing about the mind is that it hates to be bored. As you try to rouse your mind by writing, it may sulk and give you only boring things to write for five or even ten minutes. It is saying, Go away and leave me in peace. But 12 to 15 minutes is about all the mind can stand of boring itself. So, if you keep on writing, it will give you something good.

2) There is a secret every writer knows: we get our best ideas near the bottom of the page (or when we just about run out of time). Writers turn the paper sideways and squeeze writing between the lines to get the idea down on its essentials, as if there were no more paper. Whatever this power is that setting limits gives us, think about it. We have been using it in class. Use it at home too. Take a

page (a page is nothing) and say, I'm just going to fill this one page with everything essential that I know about this poem. Then write — but leave big margins.

3) Now that you have written nonstop for 20 minutes, look at how many pages you have written. Has there been any other 20-minute period today or yesterday that you have so much to show for?

Of course, this is all one thing said three ways. But they are simple, useful things to say.

Reading observations around the classroom shows the merit of making them. We have said, Begin with the obvious. We find now that every observer has something to contribute, an error-free contribution. If it is an observation, it can't be wrong. Nor can it be too homely or trivial, as Thoreau reminds us:

> We require that the observer be very firmly planted before the facts which he observes, not a mere passerby, hence the facts cannot be too homely.
>
> (*Journal,* November 20, 1857)

There will be many surprises, however. We have not looked at the poem as we wrote so that we would not be attracted by its linear order and start making notes on parts instead of perceiving the whole — or at least finding out the order of our own attention and memory. And the fact that the visible poem was not there made the less visible poem emerge. The order of sound, we find, takes a little precedence over the order of words. Images brighten or ramify. Ordinary words are heard again in a new way. Memorable phrases are remembered. In short, what we didn't know we noticed comes to the surface.

But there will be a few thorns among the blossoms. Talk is a problem: it seems to be continuous by nature, and it is certainly fueled by contention and opinion. Moreover, mixed with good observations will be vague impressions or displacements: things going on in the student that he thinks he noticed going on in the poem. For example, "It was boring," which means, "I was bored," or "It was shocking," which means, "I was shocked." It may even be that the teacher herself or himself has monologuist tendencies or an occasional mulish streak.

Fortunately, we do not have to meet any of these problems head-on. For some of them, we invoke the ground rules already laid down:

1) Observations are concrete: *i.e.,* "There are only two abstract words in the poem: *age* at the beginning and *plenty* at the end."

2) If anyone doesn't see what is supposed to be an observation, and if the observer can't point to the fact in the poem, then it is probably not an observation. The observer can probably take it back to something simpler and find its basis.

3) One objection to any "observation" is enough.

For monologue or contention (in self or others), we invoke the rule: Writing is remedy. When tempted to jump in and do up the poem ourselves, we take notes on what students are saying or jot down our good thoughts. When bickering threatens, we divert that energy into further writing.

In fact, one burst of writing observations will not be enough for class work. When observations are going beautifully, when students are discovering that no observation is singular, but one relates unexpectedly to another because the poem itself is a complex unity, and as the excitement of discovery mounts — that is the very time to break off discussion and turn that energy into writing. This is the time to reorder observations, to jot down new ones, to set down questions which are rising fast, and express the inferences that are occurring. To break off a good discussion may go quite against a teacher's instincts. But the aim of these classes is to send the writers home with many pages of notes, queries, and inferences to push them off to a start on their essays. The best state for the writer will be a state of dissatisfaction with what was said in class.

Teachers know that each class develops a "character" or has its own tendencies when its members have been working with each other. In the tempering of their minds that goes on in intellectual work, class members have instinctively tested those minds against each other. One class develops an interest in irony and drama; another takes up metaphor or scene: demonstrations of the ease and understanding with which they work together. They have taken something from each other and not only from the teacher. Sometimes a class veers away from what the teacher considers important; other times students may say something that gets close to what the teacher knows is important in the work. It's hard not to try to turn the first sort of class around, or, with a little poking or a few artful questions, to push the students who are "getting warm" more steadily toward the promising area.

But we take a morning vow not to do this. We remember that the play, poem, or story has a concentrated integrity. We have chosen it precisely for that. Observations can only lead observers into that, never away from it. A class, ignoring what we know to be important, turns out to be going toward another point, and from that vantage gets a pretty good perspective on important things after all. We haven't discovered ways of getting students to write good papers out of anyone else's reading of the work.

In sum, observations give writers literary knowledge that is personal because empirically founded and personally ordered, but also public because based on concrete, verifiable descriptions. And an essay springing out of real knowledge, personally discovered but socially recognizable, showing some play or tension between instinct and fact, inference and emotion, evidence and judgment, and therefore some energetic alertness in the writing, is a good essay.

II: Observations and Inferences in the Making

We have been describing in a schematic way a discipline for reading and studying. Here are two segments of class work that show some of the things that happen after a class has written its observations.

The course was a sophomore-level class, though two students were seniors. About half the class members were English majors. It was the fourth week of a 14-week term. Before this meeting we had all read (among other things) the *Iliad*. We had not studied it, but just read it over a weekend, rapidly and naively. We talked about it naively, telling each other stories from it: stories about gods and stories about men. We wrote observations briefly, but without trying to develop them. Now we were about to read two English poems in which gods appear: "Leda and the Swan" and "The World Is Too Much With Us." The first segment concerned "Leda."

LEDA AND THE SWAN

A sudden blow: the great wings beating still
    Above the staggering girl, her thighs caressed
By the dark webs, her nape caught in his bill,
He holds her helpless breast upon his breast.

How can those terrified vague fingers push
The feathered glory from her loosening thighs?
And how can body, laid in that white rush,
But feel the strange heart beating where it lies?

A shudder in the loins engenders there

The broken wall, the burning roof and tower
And Agamemnon dead.

Being so caught up,
So mastered by the brute blood of the air,
Did she put on his knowledge with his power
Before the indifferent beak could let her drop?

WILLIAM BUTLER YEATS

After the students had copied the poem from the board, read it several times and written observations about it for ten minutes, we began.

R: Well, what did you notice?

Brian: There were three questions in the poem.

R: Yes.

Brian: Two of them are rhetorical and one is a real question.

R: And by *rhetorical* you mean . . .?

Brian: Not a real question — doesn't need to be answered.

Sandra: The poem seems to be a description of an action, but then, at the end, the poem addresses *us.*

Kasuko: The tense changes. Most of it is present tense. But then with "Being so caught up . . . did she" the tense changes.

Amelia: What tense is it?

Mary S: Past?

R: (Unable to stay out of it) And does the tense change where Sandra sees that the poem is an address?

Pat: The change — the direct address — makes that last question the real question.

Amelia: Whose point of view is the poem written from?

General answer: The girl's.

Jo: I'm not sure about that.

R: Then we'd better think more about that.

Ed: You see the action as she sees it. You only see *parts* of the bird. You hardly know it's a whole bird.

Pat: It's identified in the title, though: swan.

Mary: But the first mention of the girl in the poem tells the whole thing that she is: "girl."

Pat: She's not named in the poem.

Dena: The swan is Zeus and he's never named, either in the poem or the title.

Mary: After "girl" you just get parts of her. Finally she's just "body." She goes from "Leda" to "girl" to "body."

(Pause. Everyone is looking at the poem and taking this in.)

Micheline: The bird is personified for us in "brute blood of the air."

R: Maybe it would be better not to call that *personification* because it doesn't show him as a person. He's greater than a person and less than a person. A person is exactly what he's not.

Micheline: "Brute" is not a person, but "blood" . . .?

R: It's a way of speaking of the part as if it were the whole.

Margaret: He doesn't treat the girl as a person either. Look at his "indifferent beak."

Bill: It's not just Leda he's indifferent to. He's indifferent to Agamemnon dead and to the broken wall, the burning roof and tower.

(General pause while we take this in.)

Kazuko: What about "feathered glory"? Is that the same as glorious feathers?

Everyone: No!

Micheline: "Feathered glory" goes with "brute blood of the air."

R: Why?

Micheline: You won't let me call them personifications.

R: (to herself): You muffed that one.

Connie: The words of the poem are simple.

Sandra: "Knowledge" and "power" are *not* simple.

Pat: They're simple at first.

R: Why?

Pat: They're words everyone uses. We think we know what they mean.

Connie: The poem starts out riming, but in the second part, it doesn't rime.

R: There, tower, up/air, power, drop. Why don't we notice the rime, I wonder.

Connie: I don't know.

R: Look at the poem and see where the pauses come. If the pauses coincided with the rime words, you'd notice them.

Connie: They mostly don't.

R: The way one line runs over into the next line without a pause is called "enjambment."

Pat: Isn't "body" a funny thing to say?

Mary S.: Yes, you'd expect it to be "her body." I kept reading it and catching myself putting "her" in.

Margaret: She's lost it. It's just body.

(Pause.)

Mary S.: What about "strange heart"?

R: Yes, what's so strange about that heart?

Gordon: It's strange to *her.*

Jo: It's a bird's heart.

Gordon: It's not a human heart.

Margaret: But she can feel it.

Amelia: It's natural for a bird.

Mary S.: But it's not natural for a bird to rape a girl. You can't picture that happening in nature. That's *mythological.*

Ed: "Shudder" goes with "sudden."

R: Why?

Ed: Same sounds?

Gordon: They both belong to the bird?

Ed: The words for the bird suggest attack and surprise and . . . and power.

Kazuko: "There" means in the body.

Grace: Doesn't "put on" suggest something that's not really a part of you?

R: Something that can be put off too, like a garment?

Grace: Yes.

Bill: But she *does* have some of his power. It is "engendered there" — those things are going to happen.

(Pause.)

Dena: The first line in the poem I thought about was "And Agamemnon dead." There he is dead, and he hasn't *come* yet!

Pat: *That's* not the girl's point of view.

Sandra: We see that.

The next segment from the following week's class is about "The World is Too Much With Us."

THE WORLD IS TOO MUCH WITH US

> The world is too much with us; late and soon,
> Getting and spending, we lay waste our powers:
> Little we see in Nature that is ours;
> We have given our hearts away, a sordid boon!
> This Sea that bares her bosom to the moon;
> The winds that will be howling at all hours,
> And are up-gathered now like sleeping flowers;
> For this, for everything, we are out of tune;
> It moves us not,—Great God! I'd rather be
> A Pagan suckled in a creed outworn;

So might I, standing on this pleasant lea,
Have glimpses that would make me less forlorn;
Have sight of Proteus rising from the sea;
Or hear old Triton blow his wreathéd horn.

William Wordworth

Bill: There are a lot of little words in this poem that I don't understand.
R: Give us a sample.
Bill: "Late and soon." I don't know what that means.
Mary S.: It means "always."
Margaret: I don't think so.
Bill: I don't know what "world" means either.
No one in class could decide what "world" means, but agreed that its opposite word in the poem is "Nature."
Ed: It's hard to think of even a small point between "late" and "soon." And that goes with "glimpses."
R: Wait a minute. What did you say? Why does "glimpse" go with that?
Ed: Well, a glimpse is a kind of small point.
Brian: Lines 5 and 6 go with lines 13 and 14.
R: Why?
Brian: They're both sight followed by sound. "Sea" is in both lines 5 and 13. The sound in lines 6 and 14 is the same kind, kind of a wind blowing.
R: Wind or breath, yes.
Bill: There are a lot of "-ing" words in the poem.
(The class talked about the participles for a while. They noticed that the words occurred in pairs and how they were distributed through the poem.)
Pat: There's a lot of movement in the poem.
R: What do you mean?
Pat: Well, the present participles mean something keeps going on.
Sandra: And the tense changes.
Gordon: And the clauses and phrases keep moving along. The lines keep moving.
R: Fascinating. And look what the speaker's complaint is.
Margaret: (reading) "It moves us not."
Sandra: It starts out — the poem — in the first person plural and then shifts to "I."

Pat: There are a lot of words of — that show possibility. Look at "might," "would," "will." And maybe you could put "glimpses" with them.

R: Why?

Pat: A glimpse is a sight that's just possible.

Gordon: Yeats is quite concrete, but the poem ends with an abstraction — "knowledge" and "power." Wordsworth is abstract at first but ends with something concrete — a vision — sight and sound.

Jo: Yeats doesn't end with abstractions, though. It ends with the bird letting the girl drop.

Ed: "Out of tune" and the rape are both a kind of violence.

R: "Violence"?

Ed: The human suffers in both.

Mary S.: Yes.

Ed: Wordsworth's poem is written in the first person and Yeats' is in the third person. And Yeats' words like "strange," "indifferent," "vague" go with the third person point of view.

R: Why?

Ed: They . . . I don't know. They're detached.

Grace: There are vast images in Wordsworth: *sea, wind.* They're the opposite of "glimpses." Yeats begins with glimpses — the parts of the body — and ends with what's vast.

Ed: Wordsworth shifts from the first person plural to singular first person. The plural uses phrases of regret. The first person singular breaks away from those phrases. That's where the words of possibility come in.

(Pause.)

Mary: Wordsworth uses lots of possessive pronouns. There's *our, our* again, *ours* — then he rimes *ours* with *hours.* They're joined with words that say there's no power or motion. In Yeats, the power is being used. Power belongs to one being.

Sandra: Yeats goes from the individual to history. At first the particular power of the god. Then he ends with power as an abstraction.

R: But not really history.

Sandra: Why not?

Mary S.: It's *mythology.*

(Pause.)

Ed: You can't tell whether "Getting and spending, we lay waste our powers" is cause and effect or not. "Late and soon" turns things around too.

R: Why?

Ed: You don't expect to *begin* with "late." The first clear statement in the poem is "not." But Yeats shows events as causes, and then shows the effects.

Gordon: Look at all the contrasts. The one that gets me is "Great *God*! I'd rather be/A *Pagan* . . . ."

R: I never noticed that.

Gordon: Isn't that something! "Great *God*! I'd rather be/A *Pagan*!" There are lots of other contrasts too: "Late and soon,"/"now" and "will be,"/"howling" and "up-gathered." "Howling" is so wild, and "up-gathered" is so quiet.

Brian: In the first world . . . .

R: "The *first* world"?

Brian: There's what he calls "the world," right? Then there's a second world where he can see the god come out of the sea.

R: OK.

Brian: In the first world, the power is wasted. In the second world, the *gods* are not shown as acting in power. The power is in the observer.

R: What? Say that again. Don't change it. Just say it again.

Brian says it again and adds: In Yeats, Zeus — the god — has the power.

R: And in Wordsworth, the human observer has the power??

Brian: That's right.

R: Have you been studying the Romantic Movement?

Brian: Nah. I'm a psychology major.

III: Toward the Essay

Each of these segments breaks off at a good point to return to writing. There are new observations to jot down and old ones to sort out or underline. Inferences are rising fast and must be caught in the fluent language that expresses the liveliness of their source. Topics for papers present themselves now too. Most observers will want to write for at least twenty minutes on the patterns they are beginning to see in their observations. Observations are public — one writer may need an observation that a colleague has made — but now is the time to express any important observations in a language of one's own. The observers' minds are full of thought, all alive with the energy of discovery; it is the time to put thought in writing.

While we don't have students' pages of running-writing, we can see the elements of the final essays emerging in these segments of class work. First there are plentiful observations expressed in the language of literary analysis. These represent the students' knowledge of the poem and will appear in their papers as the evidence for their idea about the poem. Some observations are already coming together in patterns, the bases of their assertions about what they see in the poem. Then there is a new order of response, no longer tied to the order of the poem. Finally, many inferences are emerging. At first, because each student had a page or two of observations freshly written and was eager to contribute them, students did not respond to each other's observations. But occasionally a dialogue-discussion formed, and at these points, frequently, inferences came into the light. Most of them were not challenged or questioned for a reason we shall return to later.

The difference between analysis and paraphrase (or paraphrase-with-commentary) is quickly seen in the order of the literary essay. When the writer follows the order of the work he is studying, he will not get beyond paraphrase. The order of his paper must be the order of his own idea. Unless the literary work is extremely difficult, the student is not expected to retell or narrate it, but to analyze it. He must loosen the order in which the work is presented by its author and draw out another order — reduced and simplified — that he presents himself. The loosening that is characteristic of analysis is marked first of all by this new order.

The critic uses two languages right from the start: the language of analysis and the language of response. Those two languages are the subject of this chapter. We cannot tell students how to write a good literary essay much beyond those practices that lead him to the invention of his ideas. But we can say something about the languages a literary critic uses.

The language of analysis is the language of literary definition and description, which is basically grammatical and rhetorical, noting such things as tenses (controlling time), pronouns (controlling point of view), number, and voices; and parallels, position, repetition, diction, tropes, images. When we analyze, we change the order and move away from the language of what we are analyzing.

We note that we have not said anything about a more special or technical literary language embracing such terms as *peripeteia, iamb, epistolary, heroic couplet.* There is no sense in learning these first, like the table of elements, because such a task distracts the student from the task of learning to read literature, and may even make him suppose that learning them is equivalent to learning to read. They are easily conned by a bright parrot, and, like jargon, can be dropped into sentences to suggest more intimacy than exists. Of course, the students must have such terms when he needs them, but before that, he needs the exercise of describing what he has seen out of his own knowledge of language and rhetoric.

We notice in our class segments that observers are speaking the language of analysis freely. Brian has abstracted the pattern of three questions and classified them. Sandra, Kasuko, and Pat, together with Brian, have observed a coincidence of changes in "Leda": in the kind of question asked, in the emphasis or focus (from action to question), and in the tense. For the Wordsworth poem, Sandra, Pat, and Ed have again observed a coincidence of changes: from first person plural to singular, and from words expressing regret to words expressing possibility. Ed sums up the changes as he adds his own observation: "The plural uses phrases of regret. The first person singular breaks away from those phrases. That's where the words of possibility come in." In another intelligent fusion of observations at the end of the first segment, Sandra and Pat come round to answering a question raised at the beginning. Then most of the class had thought the dominant point of view is that of the girl. But Sandra and Pat saw one implication of Dena's remark: that another point of view controls the poem (though they do not identify it). In all this what the observers have to say is simple and clear because they know how to speak the abstract language of analysis, here the language of literary description.

But the critic does not always analyze. He also speaks the language of the poem. He cannot help it, if he is deeply familiar with what he is talking about. In our segments, we see observers acknowledging first of all that they cannot translate even such apparently simple words as *knowledge, power, late* and *soon, world* and *nature.* This is more interesting than anything else that went on in these sessions. It means that the tendency to interpret the poem by changing its terms into general terms, to refer it to another context than its own, is corrected by returning to the language of the poem; and it means a recognition that that language, like the language of any world, expresses the coherence or "meaning" of that world.

Our class spoke the language of the poem less freely than they analyzed, not strange if we are right in thinking that the language of the poem is the sign of familiarity. Two inferences of Bill's are crucial to our point:

> It's not just Leda he's indifferent to.
> He's indifferent to Agamemnon dead and to the broken wall, the burning roof and tower.

> But she *does* have some of his power. It is "engendered there" — those things that are going to happen.

These remarks struck the class into profound pauses. They go beyond observation, extending our realization of what the poem says. And because the inferences were expressed in the language of the poem, no one objected. Indeed, there was surprise and assent on every face.

We make it a principle, then: In poetry, we can't substitute our own words for the poet's words. We respond to and work with his words.

To do otherwise distorts poetry to fit it into another world, with the implication that such violence is justified by the greater importance or centrality of that other world. Or the distortion fits the literature to our own present capacity. But we are not yet what we may be by studying this very work. Writing about literature is learning. Learning what? The only thing we can learn to begin with: to speak its language, a language as important to learn as Latin or German. The real way to increase the power of our own language, or even our "vocabulary," is not to write essays with the aid of a thesaurus, but to learn other languages. And we learn other languages not so much that we may translate what we read back into our own language, but so that we may increase our capacity to understand what we hear and read.

When we analyze, then, we use the abstract words that define the qualities or characteristics of language and literature. Here we are talking about things that the poem itself is not concerned with. But when we move to talk about what the poem is concerned with, we move back to the language of the poem, not only in quotation, but to speak it ourselves. What we want to avoid is general language or our own special terms ("Yeats wants his daughter to have an upper-class lifestyle.") Inferences expressed in general terms refer understanding outside the poem; expressed in the language of the poem, they open the poem familiarly to the student.

All writers take language in this familiar way from each other, especially poets: we see *surmise* and *darkling* go from Milton to Keats to

Hardy, *forlorn* from Wordsworth to Keats, and *propped* from Wordsworth to Dylan Thomas. Our greatest teachers have done so. It was one mark of their authority that they spoke the languages of the authors they taught. One of the greatest of them spoke not only the languages of Shakespeare and Spenser but the language of the Renaissance in England. Perhaps some teachers do not. They may find it easier to speak one language — a special language such as that of psychology or sociology, or a general language — and accommodate what they are teaching to their students' understandings. We prefer not to encourage students to behave like Americans who go to Europe and speak American to everybody, simply raising their voices when they think they will not be understood. To speak the language of the poem in the literary essay is the one mark of authority any teacher will instinctively recognize, the sign that the student has been there, in the country of that poem, and has heard it speak. The language of the poem is the language of response.

When literature teachers talk about analysis, they are suggesting an analogy with science. They mean they want critical papers to have some of the verifiable, public quality that good science has. But finally the literary work is not an object like the objects of science, not something "out there" to be weighed and measured. We try to comprehend it, but, in an important way, as Frye tells us, it comprehends us. We use the language of literary description for the analytical part of our writing, when we want to point to the evidence of observations that everyone can recognize: the patterns of syntax and the patterns of emphasis. We use the language of response whenever we talk about what the poet is saying. We have no other way of talking about it, because it does not exist anywhere outside this author's work and the minds of those who know it. The language of response is the token of our recognition of the authority of the author in his world.

But it is more than that for the student writer. I have found that learning to speak the language of the work is the single most important thing students learn when they try to write about literature. That is what makes the measurable difference by the end of the course. It is the way students truly move into the work before and as they learn to analyze it. It is the way they can express all their intuitive knowledge of the poem. If they can't find some way to work with that while they are struggling with analysis, they will lapse into summary or paraphrase. At least, they sense, this keeps them close to what they are studying. Summary is a damaging closeness because it follows the order of the work and makes analysis even harder. When they are encouraged to use the language of the work as they think about it, they find their understanding of the work leaping forward.

We can see this process taking place in the following paragraph from a student paper. At first the writer is summarizing and quoting a good deal from the poem. Then, as if this had all been fuel, she ends the paragraph with a remarkable sentence, her own sentence, but one which has taken hold of the language of the poem. That language enters into and enormously expands her power to write.

> The ring was given to her mother by her father as an expression of first love, specially made to be brilliant. It was "recklessly cut," "careless of weight," sacrificing "carat-points for [its] bright state." Her mother gave it to her daughter when she died, but the daughter says, "it is yours still, and I go talismanned. . . ." Her mother's life is now the diamond, and the daughter now uses this ring as her source of light that will help her to remember and "name the flight of what [they] meant while [they] were together to create." She sees the diamond on her hand as the "imagined world"where her and her mother were "whole." Now the light, which is the diamond, has come out of the darkness where it was created, and exchanged places with her mother, who was created in the light and is now in the dark among "boxed bones, pine roots and Queens sand."

We tell our students, then, "When you are trying to formulate an idea for a paper or to open the idea up, begin with plentiful observations. Those are going to be the evidence for what you assert in your paper. Then pick what speaks to you as the most interesting or luminous observations. Do at least half an hour of prolific writing on that observation (or cluster) to get out on paper a body of language in which you can look for an expression of your idea. Don't be afraid to use the language of the work."

When students are ready to write, we tell them there are two "never's." "Never begin writing about the work by writing about its beginning. Always begin with what you think is its heart. Never follow the order of the work. Don't worry about covering the work completely. Do speak the language of the work. Along with observations, this is the way to know the work. In the first version of your paper, or as you begin, you may find that you are quoting phrases a good deal. Eventually you'll move past this into an easy and familiar use of that language as if it were your own. Analysis teaches you the parts of the work. Speaking its language will make you aware of relationships among the parts.

You need to know both to explain your idea about how the literature works and what its special unity is."

One difference we all notice between observations and idea is that observations are recognizable by others, but an idea needs to be explained. Or, to be more exact, the critic's idea needs to be explained; the poet's idea needs to be presented or embodied. The first response to an idea is, Explain that; tell me more. Idea shares with observation the sense of discovery; that is the link between them. But idea differs from observation because it is invention.

When anyone writes about literature, then, it is his own idea he is explaining, not the poet's. The poet's idea has been embodied; it does not need to be explained. Critics' ideas are interpretations of their observations about the poem, not interpretations of the poem. Keeping this clear saves a lot of trouble in writing. The student finds it a relief to realize that his writing must comprehend not the whole poem, but the whole of his idea about the poem.

We have been working throughout this book to help inexperienced or unconfident writers acquire certain habits of reading and writing, the bases of a writer's instinct, a sort of writer's sense of direction that tells him where he is, how to move toward where he wants to go, and how to get back home. We have also set forth a few principles to be the guides of instincts, for not the best-endowed or best-trained instincts always tell the right way. When we emerge from the theater at night, if our instincts tell us to turn right, we remember that we turned right when we came in and must therefore now turn left. We move best by a learned instinct, but we must sometimes check ourselves or persist by reasons.

As we come to the point where teaching stops, the point of the author's ideas, on which his writing moves and rests, it may be comforting (or bracing) to point out the double nature of idea. Idea motivates us and tests us. It supports the beginning of writing, but must itself be supported before the writing is finished. Idea is imaginative, a convincing or believable image in the mind's eye. That means ideas are projective; they do not actually exist, but they can be brought into existence.

Because they are *in potentia* — Coleridge calls them "generative seeds" — ideas are exciting and motivating. They ask to be acted upon. Of course, they can't simply be reproduced, like the print from a negative. But the student who has a "great idea" for an essay need not be disappointed when his finished essay does not have all the shine of the original idea, because it will be good for other papers. Like all potential, an idea cannot be exhausted. If the student is faithful and pays enough attention to his great idea, it will be even better fifteen years after he began to express it. And if he has energy, patience, and luck, his whole life may express it.

These are the benefits of ideas, and the tests of ideas rise from the same source. The projective is always doubtful — that is why satirists have so much fun with "projectors." The need to establish what is doubtful keeps the writer making plentiful observations, and separating them from inferences. But even with such support, ideas are never beyond doubt, and writers, whether they are teachers or students, need to remember this. Every idea is fragile and vulnerable. (And woe to the teacher who crushes the unfledged idea: cursed and barren will he be.) Ideas lack the power of judgment (you can be sure you have an idea if the response to it is, "not practical"), and they lack the power of carry-through. By experience and the exercise of intelligence, we acquire judgment, and by training we forge the habits to support ideas.

Still, the writer needs not only power, but belief and hope. He can rely on his ideas to motivate him and on his training to strengthen him. In addition, then, he needs to know that the fears that assail ideas are the products of the same imagination that produced the ideas and are no more nor less real than the ideas themselves, the reality of either a fearful or a hopeful idea being dependent on the time and body that the writer gives it. As for the doubts, they are prompted by reason and are therefore respectable. The writer who expects them as the commonplace attendants of ideas will learn when to check them, when to move past them, and how to take them into account as the tests all ideas meet.

14 | Polar Powers: Abstract & Concrete

We have been addressing teachers and presenting the writer to them in the acts of writing. We seem to have been talking more about writing than teaching because we have talked about inductive teaching. We have been addressing the writer in the teacher. But we have said that induction would not make sense or be constructive if it weren't based on a deductive scheme or idea. That idea is implied in everything we do, and now it is time to make it explicit.

One of the tests of that scheme of ideas is whether it meets the problems of teaching a college course without a subject. The difficulties of teaching an art like writing in an intellectual milieu are enough to floor any teacher. That writing in college is an intellectual enterprise doesn't make it less practical; it only means we can't set it aside with the swimming classes and teach it in the same way. That writing is a required course — not only in college but, we believe, in civilized life — also makes it harder to teach. It is no wonder that some hard-pressed teachers lecture at students while others think up (disconnected) gimmicks to "motivate" them.

Most teachers have an ex post facto view of writing; they try to use ways of analyzing writing to talk about it to students. But writing can't be made systematic, can't be taught as a science. What usually happens is that writing is taught as some sort of analysis, and not an original one but an outline from a textbook.

The only analysis we ever read in a textbook that also could be worked out inductively was *Modes of Rhetoric* by Leo Rockas. The first time the present writer taught a composition course with his book was the first clearly successful writing course she had taught in ten years of trying. Not only the book but its effect gave the teacher something to think about. In its inferences, discussions, its learning and reasoning it is a supremely intelligent book. What made it work inductively was that its analysis produced a set of observations about each mode. Definitions and descriptions are so clear that students can follow them like directions and not go wrong. This showed us the possibility of having a core of real work that could not be done wrong.

It was Leo Rockas who showed us how important to writing is the idea of the abstract and the concrete in his first chapter, "Abstract and Concrete Sentences." He made us realize that, "The most useful knack to readers and writers is the ready apprehension of the concrete in the abstract and the abstract in the concrete" (p. 8).

His book showed that it was possible to teach writing inductively and it suggested that the idea of abstract and concrete was one of the keys. They would keep us to perception, the work of the imagination, to language and to community. He showed that abstract and concrete are polar powers that interplay in thinking and writing. This unity of a double power means that we can teach writing as an art, teach it inductively to a community of individual writers, and give a course of writing an intellectual structure.

In the beginning we distinguish the polar powers. The abstract belongs mostly to the teacher, and the concrete to the student. The teacher makes a gift of the abstract to the student. By the end of the course, students will be conscious of the abstract in the concrete and the concrete in the abstract: to their capacity they will all receive and be full.

The terms that concern us are *concrete, abstract, general.* We are not trying to reduce, with these few terms, a subject which has epistemological, psychological, and aesthetic aspects (at least). But we don't want jargon, language "more technical than the ideas it serves to express," as Susanne Langer puts it. We want a language "just adequate" to express our concepts *(Mind,* I, 36).

Simply, then, the concrete is the perception of sense. It would be easier to start with the verb form of these words, but we have no useful verb form of *concrete* because sensation and feeling are continuous. They do not occur or begin. They go on with life itself and occasionally rise into consciousness above a threshold which varies individually. If you lay your hand on your arm and keep it there, you won't feel it after a time. You are clothed and do not feel your clothing. But when you read these words, you feel it. Most sensation and feeling is immediate, and we aren't conscious of it until it is mediated, as language mediates it in this paragraph. This is why we say the concrete is the *perception* of sense: *blue.*

To abstract is to draw off, separate, or detach from a thing some attribute or quality of it in order to consider that characteristic apart from the thing: *blueness.* An abstraction gives us something we can define. It is a mental construct, not just structure but the perception of structure.

There are levels of abstraction, *justice* being more abstract than *blueness*. Abstraction has to take place before we can classify. When we have abstracted the qualities of things, we can place things with similar qualities together in classes or groups. To put things in larger and larger classes is generalizing. "A class is general when the things in it share a majority of their qualities (people); a class is abstract when the things in it share a minority — perhaps only one — of their qualities (all brown things)" *(Modes of Rhetoric,* p. 2).

Abstraction and concretion are polar powers of perception, then. Leo Rockas says, "I consider perception to head in two directions recognized by philosophers for centuries, abstraction and concretion." He notes, of course, that neither "process can occur alone." Even to perceive the concrete requires the mediation of some structure, like language. And "you can't abstract unless you can tell which qualities to dismiss because of their novelty. . ." (p. 2).

When we say that the abstract and the concrete are perceived, that means that we intuit them, spontaneously and naturally. No teacher has to incite that or coax it. "All cognition of form is intuitive" (Langer, *Feeling and Form,* p. 378). It is especially important for us teachers that abstraction is intuitive, for we have thought out the abstract part of the writing course and embedded it in every kind of concrete: assignments, class conduct, observations, rewriting, etc. We know we can get students to produce the concrete directly, but not the abstract. We are bringing students to the abstract. We can do that continuously and without strain because everyone intuits form or structure. If the form is there, then, students will apprehend it swiftly and instantly. The teacher's job is first, to put it there, and second, to bring it to consciousness.

Before we say more about this, we need to establish one point about concrete and abstract: their relation to thinking. Thinking and language both begin in perception. That is why we can keep thinking and writing together, teach students how writing is the instrument of thought. This idea, in modern times, goes back to Cassirer.

Most people are agreeable to the idea that the perception of the concrete is intuitive, but the abstract seems to them to belong to philosophy, mathematics, science. They see that they can get students to write concretely, but they suspect abstraction is beyond most of us. But abstraction in itself is a power of perception. "All cognition of form is intuitive; all relatedness — distinctness, congruence, correspondence of forms, contrast, and synthesis in a total *Gestalt* — can be known only by direct insight, which is intuition." Langer says this clearly. "Both abstraction and interpretation are intuitive. . . . They lie at the base of all human mentality, and are the roots from which both language and art take rise." Language and art, yes, and "all discursive reasoning would be frustrated without it. The simple concatenation of propositions known as 'syllogism' is only a device to lead a person from one intuition to another" *(Feeling and Form, pp. 378-9).*

What gets in the way of the ordinary person understanding this? The ordinary misconception that identifies thinking and logic. Everybody knows that thinking and logic aren't the same, but in schools a kind of miasma of method arises. We're afraid that it may be so. Perhaps, we suspect, a thing is not honorable if it is not systematic. So it ought not to be necessary but it is to say this:

> Thinking employs almost every intuitive process, semantic and formal (logical), and passes from insight to insight not only by the recognized processes, but as often as not by short cuts and personal, incommunicable means. The measure of its validity is the possibility of arriving at the same results by . . . demonstrating formal connections. But a measure of validity is not a ground of validity. Logic is one thing, and thinking is another; thought may be logical, but logic itself is not a way of thinking — logic is an abstract conceptual form, exemplified less perfectly in our cerebral acts than in the working of computers which can outdo the best brains a thousand fold in speed, with unshakable accuracy *(Mind,* I, 148-9).

Everyone recognizes this passing "from insight to insight," especially the "short cuts." Perhaps most people are too modest to realize that this is thinking. Thinking does have to be measured and tested, especially in schools, so it is not surprising that the test intimidates the act of thinking itself. It's a nice irony that the philosopher measures an assertion about logic with logic: "a measure of validity is not a ground of validity."

Identifying thinking and logic not only makes thinking the privilege of the specialist, but separates thinking from the imagination, the prime agent of human perception. When we have done that, we have reduced imagination to making ornaments or to frosting the cake: "Oh, I've written the story," said Mary McCarthy's old student, "Now I just have to go home and put in the symbols."

This is a chapter about polar terms; they express the polarity of our method. The teacher and the student are polar powers. In the beginning, the abstract belongs to the teacher, and the concrete to the students. The abstract, all the embedded structures of the class, represent our knowledge. The concrete is the students' experience. That solves the dilemma of the college writing course, an art in a world of study, a course without a subject. Instead of making composition the subject of the course, or giving the student subjects to write about, we have given our course an abstract shape, the shape of perception coming to consciousness by generating writing that has structure. Our course has not an intellectual content but an intellectual shape.

All experience is concrete structure. The student begins with her experience. In our class, she is working with the abstract and the concrete as polar powers. We have abstracted a structure from literature and suggested it to her. The structure as she begins to perceive it, calls experience to her mind. She imagines these experiences in shapes that are versions of one of of our six essay shapes. She imagines it as:

1) two contrasting or similar perceptions of her own.
2) a misconception of her experience which she can answer.
3) an experience other than her own but complementary to it.

Or she imagines:

4) a significant extension or effect of that experience.
5) weighing it as choice.
6) a deeper structure of value within it, and she identifies that value.

Let's say that when she has finished her last essay, we all see that her experience is a kind of family experience. She classifies it as a family experience. When she can do this, she has taken another step of abstraction. She has detached from her experience another structure and one that leaves more of the concrete part of that experience behind. She is now in a position to generalize her new abstraction. The term *family* helps her to put what she knows in a larger class of experiences.

If ours were a sociology class, she could carry out this generalization by referring her experience to a body of studies, data, facts. Then she could make a generalized assertion about it. To support this assertion, she needs (as usual) concrete evidence. But she does not draw this entirely from her own experience because her sociological abstraction has left that behind. She draws her evidence now from the body of sociological knowledge. And, to write about this assertion and negotiate this evidence, she must speak the language of sociology, which is composed of 1) terms, definitions of concepts. They represent the abstract structures of this science; 2) descriptive language, which refers to the facts and data of the body of knowledge.

In this sociological essay, our putative student has made a different structure out of her experience by means of a new abstraction. She has also generalized it, because she has other knowledge of it, knowledge of it as other than her single experience. Successive abstractions and generalizations like this have given us the great abstractions of science and its great laws: "Gravity falls off as the square of the distance" — but not without the assistance of genius and study.

But if we remain in our composition class, a class in writing without a subject, and ask a student to write a less "personal" and more general essay, she cannot follow this procedure. She cannot generalize, because she does not have the knowledge. Though she cannot generalize, she can formulate in language a generalization. Of course, the generalization is empty because there is no body of knowledge — no abstract structures, no concrete data — in the student's mind to which her language refers. So what she produces is a simulacrum of a scientific generalization. What we, experts in language, are asking for is a forgery in language. We have asked the student to make a generalization without her being able to generalize. We don't notice or don't mind the grossness of this, because our own knowledge of the subject is shallow. We're encouraging students to opinionate about bodies of learning for which a century's work has made the opinions impertinent. When the student actually enters a sociology class, the teacher will have to work to get those notions out of her head.

But we haven't done ourselves a favor either by assigning a subject to the student, even though we were only trying to make our composition class intellectually respectable. Having been given a subject and being unable to generalize, she must and does forge a generalization. Then she is faced with the impossibility of originating language to assert it, articulate it, or support it. The awkwardness of trying to go through the motions of thinking in language not truly abstract (because she can't define her terms) and not truly general (because it refers to no knowledge of her own) makes her break out in a fever of errors, whose symptoms usually are:

1) misspelling (the nervous stammer of writing);
2) shifting pronouns and vague reference of pronouns (flatulent pronouns);

3) unidiomatic language, syntax askew, and jargon (she has broken her native tongue and is trying to speak a foreign language).

But, doctors of language and literature though we may be, we cannot read the wrong behind these symptoms. We consult our *Physician's Desk Reference,* our handbooks, and prescribe some drugs to cure the symptoms.

The course of sin, however, is not so short as this makes it out to be. When students come to us in literature classes, a subject we do know about, we discover that they have no instrument for the knowledge we are prepared to give them. They can't write in an easy, colloquial way, they have become fond of jargon and indifferent to the referential and unifying power of pronouns, they care nothing for evidence and consistency, and, though they wish they could spell, they cannot use writing to think and solve problems. Naturally this is a disappointment, and we mutter to the student, *"Who* was your English composition teacher?" It is the question of David to Nathan, and the answer is the same, "Thou art the man (or woman)."

In the face of these difficulties, we call on our forces and the students' to work together in an interplay of powers. Our purpose is to generate writing with structure. The shape of the course is writing coming to consciousness.

Structure comes first for the student. Our principle is that all experience is concrete structure. That starts us where intellect and sensation are working as one, though we can distinguish parts. We want to distinguish so that we teachers will know what we are doing, and start students off on the right track: enabling them to write efficiently (though writing can't be done systematically), letting them succeed, so that they will arrive at the teacher's consciousness of writing. We are handing over to the students as much as possible so that they can begin at a point where they can carry it out: generate it, order it, and finally understand it in their own terms.

We are conscious of structure in a way that students are not expected to be. So we begin by making a gift of structure to the students, selecting for them structures that we know work. In the beginning, the teacher is conscious of structure; the students are becoming aware of the concrete. The more fully they work with it and become conscious of it, the more inevitable will be their need for structures.

To begin with, we let students be naive as one way of freeing those intuitive powers of perceiving abstractions and reproducing structures, without which the abstract will never come to consciousness. That is why we are interested in forms from oral literature. But we are not really going back to the original ages of the world. Most writers work intuitively and never need a consciousness of abstraction. But college writers are going to be discursive writers, and their writing must meet tests. It must come to a standard of truth or verifiability. Eventually they must be able to generate and criticize their writing.

With the conscious power to abstract structures emanating mostly from the teacher, then, and the power of perceiving the concrete working in the student, we begin in a well-balanced way: with naive and source-experience, and consciousness.

We must give students structures to begin with, even though we say that structure is latent in experience, because green writers don't realize that one has to *give* a structure to writing. Their experience has for them a kind of objective reality. It is *there*. Some of them can hardly bring themselves to put it into words. Shape or form is not implicit in experience for them, but out there. They either get it or they don't. A great deal of structure in writing is tacit, so in reading, one overlooks it. But the great obstacle to structuring is the impulse to chronicle writing. If you think of your experience as a series of events, then the obvious thing to do for it is to chronicle it.

How is it that anyone learns to structure material consciously? One notices finally that that is what sticks to the mind. That is what we can remember. In a semester of reading essays aloud, listening to them, and making observations, students become conscious of what makes them notice and remember.

The structures we give students act in two ways. The first is to call material out of the plenum of experience. Second, they act on it: hold it, shape it, make thinking about it possible, and make it possible to change the way the writer thinks about it. Why not then make our seed sentences more schematic? If, as we assume, the essay is the sentence writ large, why not sort out the forms of reasoning in paradigms like: "What X teaches us is Y"; "Q and Z are similar because_____"; "The most important thing is _____ because _____"?

The abstract is coming to consciousnesss in our class, but does not announce itself in this way. Such sentences would be another way of analyzing writing to teach it to students. An analysis may be presented as a structure — though not an abstract structure. Such an analyzed structure is a model. We need an abstracted structure, because its power lies precisely in the fact that it has been perceived by someone. Perception, we said, is the interplay of polar powers. The concrete, the perception of sense, is the generating pole; the abstract, the perception of structure is the shaping power. In Blake's phrase, their power lies in their "conversing" as "forms dramatic."

"The use of a model," as Susanne Langer says, "belongs to a higher level of conception, the level of discursive thought and deliberate analogical reasoning" *(Mind,* I, 63). A model tells us the *principle* of how something works, but it does not *present* the thing working. A model would tell students how a sentence works, but it would not generate writing. A model permits us "to match the factors of the model with respective factors of the object according to some convention. The convention governs the selectiveness of the model. . ." *(Mind,* I, 59).

Our sentences are not models, because they generate images. They are seed sentences. An image is what the imagination makes, the fusing of concrete and abstract, sensation and intellect by what Blake calls the Parent Power. He understood its generative force.

Susanne Langer describes the power of images to present the appearance of a thing and how they "shape it for recognition and memory." Images are "abundant and fragmentary, not single and coherent like a model. We use and discard them prodigally" *(Mind,* I, 59-60). That prodigality is their virtue for teachers. "The high intellectual value of images, however, lies in the fact that they usually, and perhaps always, fit more than one actual experience" *(Mind,* I, 60). "Knowledge begins, then, with the formulation of experience in many haphazard ways, by the imposition of available images on new experiences as fast as they arise; it is a process of imagining not fictitious things, but reality" *(Mind,* I, 63).

It is certainly a high intellectual value that images fit more than one actual experience. That makes them work efficiently in assignments for a whole class. If we have an intellectual term and a sensational term, then a model is closer to the intellectual term, and an image is closer to a sensational term. Our seed-sentences do not serve as models. We cannot claim they are images, but they provoke images for students. They keep the initiative of imagining reality with students.

This is how structure comes first for the students. We set them to work abstracting and embodying these structures in language, in essays. We expect that if they keep on composing, hearing in-class readings of all the versions of a structure, making observations, trying to realize their idea in rewriting — in all the ways we have described in this book — that gradually a consciousness of abstract structure will arise.

The process of thinking in language works readily through abstract and concrete because they are contrary and complementary. Like the poles, they are apart but related by the world of perception they both embrace. Each implies or contains the other, as greenness contains green, and green contains greenness. Each is distinct and complete: the idea of justice can be thought about in the absence of a just society, and a just society can exist without discussing the idea of justice.

Neither exhausts the other. No abstraction wears out the concrete, which is rich, the principle of the prolific, producing endless embodiments of the abstract, il*lustra*ting it in the sense of making it shine. Nor is the concrete there just to serve the abstract. It is what needs no explanation, what is evident.

In its most highly developed form, the abstract grows by lines of reasoning which cannot be improved or added to by the concrete. A large whole system may be abstract, as western philosophy is; or concrete, as is that Japanese system involving architecture, landscape gardening, ceramics, personal and social development — all associated with tea — for which we in the West have no name.

Abstract and concrete show students the polar functions of language: to make permanent and to keep tentative, making thinking/writing both clear and flexible. Abstract language is the tool of analysis, puts into play the loosening, dissolving power of thinking that makes change possible. Abstract order is the order of purpose or intention. The concrete is "sticky" — like honey, pervasive and sweet, the cohesive and attractive force in writing, making the structure of thought appear. By its expansiveness and cohesiveness, it encourages development in writing. The order of the concrete is the order of emphasis or attention.

The structure of the whole idea is expressed in abstract language; the cohesion of the whole is in concrete language. Structure and cohesion together make what we call coherence.

Abstract and concrete work together to make identity — a unity in variety and a variety in unity. They limit and complete each other. The concrete limits the speculativeness of the abstract and develops its schemes; the abstract structures the exuberance of the concrete and develops its implications. The abstract reduces the concrete, but also frees it from a general or predetermined form. The concrete enlivens the abstract and stabilizes it. Together they make up the identity of an idea and express it as description and definition — perhaps even a truth embodied or an accurate sweetness.

Outside of the class, the abstract and the concrete can work like this for a writer in the polar skills: prolific writing, which generates and sustains writing; and rewriting, which makes the writer conscious of the demands of structure. We work at these skills in class, but they are also what a writer can practice alone. The other skills work in the class and because of the class, so that the teacher can reach all the students.

Teachers often say that it is hard to teach a large class, that they would love to teach "on a one-to-one basis." That is supposed to be good for students too. But teaching a good-sized class is hard only when we make it a unit, everyone doing the same thing or discussing the same subject or trying to see the same thing the teacher sees. We are working with exactly as many individuals as there are in the class, not teaching the class as if they were all the same. At the same time, we are profiting by the community of the class. Instead of putting information into students, we are putting work — exercise — into them.

In the variety of their developing perceptions, students are able to do for each other what no teacher could do for them all. Some students realize what they are doing more quickly than others. They can go on working at their skills and take them as far as they can. Their development helps to quicken and carry on the development of their colleagues. Each understands her work in her own terms; each is autonomous; each composes the community. Practicing skills together, students are each becoming more individual, realizing their identities. And that is, finally, what brings them to consciousness.

The unique and the common, then, are another pair of terms for us. The common, the community, is abstracted from all those unique powers and experiences of individuals.

But these ideas are not the end of the book. No ideas will make a writing class good without writing. The question to be asked of any writing class is not, what are the ideas behind it, but how much writing does the teacher assign, read and annotate intelligently, and return to the writers the next time they meet. This is the one thing necessary, and without this everything else is empty. To end the book, then, we give a detailed syllabus, day by day and hour by hour, of assignments and the rhythm of each day's work. Teachers who do that will, like the members of the class, learn something in their own terms, come to a consciousness of teaching in different terms than ours, throw this book away, and write their own.

15 | Exercising Writing: Syllabi

A Syllabus for a Basic Writing Class

Since principles are abstract and can generate any number of concrete proposals, any number of syllabi might be designed to carry our principles into action. Here is one well-tried working syllabus for a basic class of inexperienced writers. It is a combined sequence of prolific writing, two whole structures from the tradition of oral literature, and three-part expository essays so ordered as to practice writing both at will and on demand.

We offer it as a sample of syllabus design and as a practical way for a teacher to examine through experience how far our principles can take a class of readers and writers.

It is timed to fit a class meeting twice a week (in sessions here labeled A and B) in 75-minute sessions during a fourteen-week semester.

WEEK 1

WEEK 1

1A We play the Grandma Game, going twice round the room to learn   1A
each other's names. (25 min.)

I write correctly punctuated examples of direct discourse on the board. (5 min.)

According to directions I give, we all write a six-paragraph dialogue and several aphorisms, in the shape of a fable. (20 min.)

We read what we have written aloud to each other. (25 min.)

Assignment: I sign up as many as I can to meet with me during this week for informal conferences. As many as five may come together for informal conversations about the work we will do. I ask them to bring me copies of their schedules so that I may arrange future conference times with each of them.

They are to write another fable in the shape we have just written and read (dialogue and aphorisms), using any animals as characters.

Each reads the assigned fable aloud, one after the other, right around the room. (35 min.)

1B Each rereads the aphorisms. From each set I choose one or two to   1B
write on the board, grouping them according to sentence type — sim-

ple, compound, and complex. I point out the identifying characteristics of each type, and remark on other noticeable rhetorical devices as they appear. (35 min.)

Assignment: Write Fable 3. Bring in a sewn-bound notebooks.

WEEK 2

2A   With the class divided into small groups of six to eight, we read Fable 3 to each other. (20 min.)   2A

We all write the names of two animals on two bits of paper which we fold and pile in one place; each draws two papers and will use the creatures they name as characters for the assigned Fable 4. (5 min.)

In sewn-bound notebooks, we write nonstop for ten minutes. We read what we have written to each other. (45 min.)

I return Fables 1 and 2.

✳ *Assignment:* Write nonstop for ten minutes. This assignment is to be carried out every day for the rest of the semester.

Write Fable 4.

2B   One person reads an assigned Fable 4. I distinguish, roughly, in one or two sentences, between observation and reaction. We write nonstop for three minutes to say what we have noticed in the fable. We read our observations to the author. (20 min.)   2B

In small groups, we read our fables one by one. After each reading, members of the groups write observations and read them aloud. (35 min.)

Each selects a day's prolific writing and reads it aloud to the small group. (15 min.)

I return Fable 3.

Assignment: Write Fable 5. Go through the prolific writing produced so far and mark in the margin phrases or sentences of special interest.

WEEK 3

3A   One person reads an assigned Fable 5. We write nonstop for three minutes to say what we have noticed, and read those observations. (20 min.)   3A

In small groups, we read Fable 5, writing and reading our observations after each one. (35 min.)

We write nonstop for ten minutes on the experience, so far, of writing and reading fables and observations. (10 min.)

We read a few of these, as many as we have time for.

I return Fable 4.

Assignment: Write Fable 6.

3B   Someone reads an assigned Fable 6. I put one of the aphorisms on   3B
the board. We all rewrite it in three or more versions. (15 min.)

We read the rewrites aloud. I sort the sentences into types as I write
them on the board, again remarking on successful rhetorical features.
(25 min.)

We rewrite another of the aphorisms in three or more versions, and
read them aloud. (25 min.)

I return Fable 5.

Assignment: Rewrite in three or more versions one aphorism for
each Fable 1-5.

WEEK 4   *WEEK 4*

4A   In small groups, Fable 6 is read aloud; we write and read observa-   4A
tions for each. Then we rewrite one of the aphorisms and read them
aloud. (45 min.)

I put a simple, a subordinated, and a coordinated sentence on the
board. I ask for others of each kind to be read and write them in the
appropriate places. Students are encouraged to save the ones they enjoy
by copying them into their notebooks. (25 min.)

Assignment: Choose your favorite among the fables you've written;
rewrite it, and make a fair copy.

Bring notebooks of prolific writing, some of which I'll collect for review.

4B   I talk about family stories, tell one or two, then ask everyone to turn   4B
to prolific writing as a way of getting at such stories from their own
experience. We write nonstop for fifteen minutes. (25 min.)

We read the results aloud. (If there is time, we write nonstop again,
on this theme.) (45 min.)

I return sets of rewritten aphorisms, and collect five to eight (or
more) notebooks of prolific writing. (The number depends in part of
class population; ideally, three weekends of five to eight notebooks
each will cover the class.)

Assignment: Write Family Parable 1.

WEEK 5   *WEEK 5*

5A   We read our family parables aloud. (50 min.)   5A
Someone rereads a parable; we write nonstop, to say what we have
noticed; we read as many as these as there is time for. (20 min.)

I return the rewritten fable, and the notebooks of prolific writing.
Assignment: Write Family Parable 2.

5B   In small groups, we read Family Parable 2. After each, we write   5B
and read our observations. (50 min.)

Still in small groups, we each choose a day's prolific writing and
read it aloud. (20 min.)

I return Family Parable 1, and collect five to eight notebooks.
Assignment: Write Family Parable 3.

WEEK 6   *WEEK 6*

6A   In small groups, we read Family Parable 3. After each, we write   6A
and read our observations. (50 min.)

✱ (In bare outline, this procedure may by now sound monotonous; yet
in practice — we can't refrain from noting — it establishes a rhythm
both enlivening and dependable, as well as providing what every
writer most desires, an attentive and responsive hearing.)

I take a sentence at random from a parable, put it on the board, and
ask everyone to rewrite it. Since only a few will know the context, it is
a straight exercise in exploring the possibilities of the sentence. We
read aloud as many of the rewrites as we have time for. (20 min.)

I return Family Parable 2 and five to eight notebooks of prolific
writing.
Assignment: Write Family Parable 4.

6B   One person reads a family parable. I ask everyone to write three to   6B
five adjectives which describe the action of the main character, the
character who makes a difference to the way the story moves. As these
are read aloud, I put many of them on the board, using at least one
from each reader. I choose one adjective from the list and change it into
a noun which I write on the board. (25 min.)

We each write at least two elegant sentences which begin with that
noun followed by "is," and read them aloud. (15 min.)

Another person reads a parable; we write adjectives as above and
read them; I select one, transform it into a noun, and we again write
sentences. We read as many aloud as we have time for. (30 min.)

I return Family Parable 4 and collect the remaining notebooks of
prolific writing.

Assignment: Write three to five adjectives suited to the action of
your Family Parable 4. Choose one; transform it into a noun; use it,
followed by "is" to begin a sentence for which you write at least three
different predicates.

7A   Everyone reads one of the assigned sentences aloud. (10 min.)   7A

Two to four people read Family Parable 4, then read the adjective and the noun derived from it, followed by the sentence that begins with that noun. (15 min.)

I write one of those sentences on the board and ask its author to re-read the parable from which it was derived. We all write two or three sentences which expand the idea of the sentence on the board in the direction of the parable. We read these paragraphs aloud. (25 min.)

I write another of those sentences on the board; the author reads his parable; we write subsequent sentences, and read as many of them as we have time for. (25 min.)

I return the notebooks of prolific writing.

Assignment: Write such a paragraph for your Family Parable 4.

7B   In small groups, we read Family Parable 4 and the paragraph de-   7B
rived from it. We write nonstop what we have noticed, and read what we have written. (30 min.)

As a single large group, we listen to someone read a paragraph followed by a parable. We then write new paragraphs which show the concept of paragraph one as it has been developed by the parable. We read these paragraphs. When all have read, the author rereads the paragraph beginning with an abstract word, the parable, and the new paragraph which derives from both of them. It is an essay with a beginning, middle, and end. (40 min.)

I return the adjective/noun/defining sentence assignment.

Assignment: For one of your Parables 1-3, write a set of adjectives about the action of the character who changes the story. Choose the most suitable. Turn it into a noun. Write a sentence beginning with that noun followed by "is." Write a few more sentences about the idea. To this opening paragraph, add your family parable as a concrete example or illustration of the meaning of the abstract word. Then write a concluding paragraph which expresses the effect of the example on the idea.

8A   I present them with Rosemary Deen's definition of an expository es-   8A
say as a piece of writing which supports the idea it asserts.

We read Essay 1. (I mention that the definition we began with is an abstracted idea, and each of our essays is serving as a concrete support for understanding that idea.) (50 min.)

We write nonstop for ten minutes in search of yet another family story. We read as many of these writings as there is time for. (20 min.)

Assignment: Write a three-part essay using a family parable as the middle part. Follow the procedure of the previous assignment for Essay 2.

8B One person reads the assigned essay. We write, nonstop, what we have noticed, and read those observations. (25 min.)

In small groups, we read our essays. After each, we write and read our observations about it. (45 min.)

I say a few brief sentences about how I grade, and announce that I will regrade rewritten essays. (I have already said as much in individual conferences with each student.) I return Essay 1, which has been given a grade.

Assignment: Choose your best-written family parable, rewrite it, and make a fair copy.

WEEK 9

9A I put an opening sentence from an Essay 2 on the board. We rewrite it, in two or three versions each, using the abstract word but free to place it anywhere in the sentence and follow it with any verb. We read our sentences. (25 min.)

Each chooses a version of the sentence, and writes nonstop for fifteen minutes on any experience it calls to mind. We read as many of these as there is time for. (45 min.) I return Essay 2.

Assignment: Starting with a sentence rewritten in class, write a three-part essay, Essay 3.

9B We read our essays in small groups. We write and read what we have noticed about each of them. (35 min.)

I put an abstract noun on the board. We all write sentences beginning with it and followed by "is." We read the sentences. I write another abstract noun on the board, and we repeat the process. (35 min.)

I return the rewritten family parables.

Assignment: Using one of the sentences written in class, write Essay 4.

WEEK 10

10A One person reads an Essay 4; we write and read observations about it. (25 min.)

In small groups, we read Essay 4, writing and reading what we have noticed about each essay. (45 min.)

I return Essay 3.

Assignment: Write a defining sentence for each of ten abstract words I put on the board. Rewrite each of these for elegance.

10B   Each reads a favorite sentence from the assignment. I write these on   10B
the board, sorted according to their types, so that there are good sentences, correctly punctuated, on view. (20 min.)

I put a few abstract nouns on the board as well, and ask them to write a 50-minute essay, Essay 5. They may begin from one of the abstract nouns or from any one of the sentences. (50 min.)

I return Essay 4.

Assignment: Using another choice from the material on the board, write another 50-minute essay, Essay 6, in three parts.

WEEK 11   *WEEK 11*

11A   We read our essays in small groups; after each, we write and read   11A
what we have noticed about it. (45 min.)

I distribute a mimeographed sheet of quotations, one or two sentences in length, of the kind that are often presented on examinations as topics or subjects for essays. Someone reads the first quote. We all write two or three abstract words which seem to express the sense of the quote, and read these aloud. We each write a sentence for one of the words, and read as many of these as we have time for. (25 min.)

I return Essay 5 and the sets of elegant sentences.

Assignment: Write five first-paragraph sets of sentences for any five of the quotes on the mimeographed sheet. Use one of them, and write Essay 7. . . . But put the concluding paragraph on a separate page.

11B   Each reads one set of first-paragraph sentences from the assign-   11B
ment. (15 min.)

One person reads an Essay 7, omitting the concluding paragraph.

We write our observations about the two first parts of the essay, and read them aloud. (25 min.)

We each write a paragraph in conclusion to the essay, and read them aloud. (30 min.)

I return Essay 6.

Assignment: Exchange Essays 7, except for the page on which your conclusion is written. Write a conclusion to your colleague's essay. Rewrite it for elegance.

WEEK 12   WEEK 12

12A   Three or four authors of the final paragraph read Essays 7, with   12A their conclusions, followed by the author's reading of the original conclusion. (20 min.)

From quotes and words on a mimeographed sheet, all write a 50-minute essay, Essay 8, in three parts, with special attention to the power of concluding well. (50 min.)

Assignment: Use another of the quotes on the sheet to write a three-part essay, Essay 9, in 50 minutes.

12B We read Essay 9 in small groups; we write and read what we have observed about it. (40 min.) **12B**

I return Essay 8, and we read them aloud. (30 min.)

I return Essay 7; each author gets a colleague's conclusion along with his own. (If I can, I combine comments on Essays 7 and 8 in observations and comparisons I write on Essay 8.) I collect five to eight notebooks of prolific writing.

Assignment: Write another three-part essay, Essay 10, on your own subject or one chosen from the sheet.

WEEK 13   WEEK 13

13A I put two quotes on the board. We choose one and write a 50-minute **13A**
essay on it, Essay 11. (50 min.)

We read as many of these aloud as we have time for. (20 min.)

I return Essay 9, and five to eight notebooks.

Assignment: Write Essay 12 on your own subject or one chosen from the sheet.

13B In small groups, we read Essay 12; we write and read our observa- **13B**
tions about each. (40 min.)

We rewrite our last paragraphs for Essay 12, and read as many of these as there is time for. The rewrites are handed in with the essay. (30 min.)

I return Essay 10 and 11 and collect five to eight notebooks.

Assignment: Write Essay 13.

WEEK 14   *WEEK 14*

14A For assigned Essay 13, we write nonstop for ten minutes in search of **14A**
an experience which would amplify the development of the middle section. We rewrite these, so that there are two experiences related to demonstrate the same idea as expressed in paragraph one. (Some students will probably have begun to do this in essays they are handing in. If so, I comment on that and ask them to read the essays in which more than one concrete and cogent experience is developed.) We read three or four beginnings and amplified middles aloud. (45 min.)

We rewrite conclusions for Essay 13 to incorporate the sense lent by the expansion of the middle. We may have time to read one or two of these new versions of Essay 13, which I collect along with the original. (25 min.)

I return Essay 12, and five to eight prolific writing notebooks.

Assignment: Write Essay 14.

14B   Write the final in-class essay.   14B

I return Essay 13, and collect the remaining notebooks of prolific writing.

English 1: Writing Assignments

Week   1. Practicing elemental skills. Fables, aphorisms rewritten.
Week   2. Essay   1: "Once/Now." Rewritten aphorisms.
Week   3. Essay   2. Another "Once/Now." First stint of daily prolific writing due.
Week   4. Essay   3: "The Opposing Voice." Rewrite of Essay 1.
Week   5. Essay   4: Another "Opposing Voice." Rewrite of Essay 2.
Week   6. Essay   5: "Two Voices." Rewrite of Essay 3.
Week   7. Essay   6: Part I of Research Paper: A Descriptive Report. Second stint of prolific writing due. Rewrite of Essay 4.
Week   8. Essay   7: "Hindsight." Rewrite of Essay 5.
Week   9. Essay 8: Part II of Research Paper: A Research Report. Rewrite of Essay 6 due.
Week 10. Essay   9: "Foresight." Prolific writing due. Rewrite of Essay 7.
Week 11. Catch-up: Research and rewriting.
Week 12. Essay 10: The Research Paper. Prolific writing due.
Week 13. Essay 11: "Insight." Rewrite of Essay 9.
Week 14. Rewrite of Essay 10.

For those who can write consequential sentences, a second course: essays of from 300-500 words, grading resting on a core of seven rewritten essays (writers can choose their best seven), with a total of 3500 words.

Class work: a modification of the work described for inexperienced writers (omitting the class essays), consisting of reading all essays,

written observations, reading observations, prolific writing, and preliminary writing for the next assignment.

16 | A Sense of the Whole

To set down here the practical and theoretical parts of our work, we have divided what we know best as a whole. Chapters focus on one thing at a time, though much of what they describe goes on all at once in class. Yes, we do prepare for a semester by writing syllabi in which first things are first, and such ordering of basic moves is vital. Yet, of course, in every class hour we work on all five essential skills, often simultaneously.

But sometimes we see beyond syllabi, beyond the matter of this book; we see neither map-lines parting the whole nor densely concrete experience overwhelming those lines. We sense the whole in its ramifications; we try to situate in imagination what we have undertaken.

The bounding line of the undertaking is what our profession commits us to value: the world of literature and the work of students as writers within it. We believe that writing the literature of exposition is a valuable human ability. We believe that students are able to practice it. We think that writing and recognizing honest exposition are tasks belonging to the university.

Exposition is the literature of rational discourse; it is characterized by the disinterested discovery of ideas defended only by the cogent evidence. In exposition, it is full, fair, and accurate demonstration that persuades. (When we — unclearly — tell students to be clear, we are perhaps thirsty for the separation and order of unmistakable proof.) The idea of the university is that reason can develop and make public what can be so proven. That is the research for which this society still gives us leisure. We claim it by right, though off campus we may recognize that it is by its rarity a privilege.

Exposition, like the university, lays claim to the service of reason. The expositor sets out an idea and upholds it democratically by a reasonable address to the reasoning capacity of other human beings. It is not a primitive genre of literature any more than democracy — to which it is profoundly connected — is a primitive form of government. (Nor is either always faithful in act to the qualities of its bravest definition — but that failure doesn't negate the worth of those qualities.) What we have in mind when we teach expository writing is not what pays, not what we feel we feel, not obedient memorizing of formulae or data characteristic of undergraduate work in math or science. We aim at the well-conceived, the coherent, the accurate, the disinterested.

And we aim at it for all our students, not alone the bright, quick ones who need chiefly to practice fair-mindedness. That is why we start with forms, not formulae, as seed sentences for expository essays: though not everyone's reason ranges equally fast or free, everyone is imaginative. For an idea the writer imagines, she can find appropriate reasonable support. The difference between assignments already analyzed and explained — someone else's idea — and assignments of seed sentences which evoke imagined wholes is clear when we read the results. Essays writers have imagined do not sort out into those done right and those done wrong. They are all right, instead; the essays divide a class of writers into a democracy of differences, interesting because individual. In all of them, facts must check and reason be reasonable — and any writer can meet these requirements when working with them on behalf of a thought of the writer's own.

Exposition properly calls on writer and reader as individuals. It does not simply report. Nor does it charm, goad, or frighten readers into group reactions. It does not want to. Its explanations and their argument intend to sustain a public truth.

The humanities have a part in the truth the university stands for. Freshman composition classes present students with their share of the work in that part. It is right that they are the most nearly universal undergraduate required course.

No wonder we like to teach writing.

Afterword

Throughout this book we have talked about teachers' responses in class to student writing. Teachers' written responses are marked by the same characteristics and intentions:

1. to help the writer work from strength,
2. to identify and define the literature in the paper,
3. to encourage a writer's distinction between first version, rewrites, and revision,
4. to pass the initiative for rewriting to the writer by making observations, rather than inferential or judgmental statements, about problems in the writing,
5. to maintain a sense that what is written can be easily, profitably, pleasurably rewritten.

Though everyone knows them, two other things must be made explicit:

• All prepared papers must have written comments. For this no class comment, even the teacher's, can substitute.

• Papers collected in one class session are to be returned in the next one. (Failing these two things — it's not too much to say — everything else is a lie.)

There are questions of what comments go on finished papers and what are fair standards of grading. Though they are outside the scope of this book, they are easier to ask when writers succeed in practicing lots of writing and rewriting.

Teachers' responses at every stage of writing show what only teachers can say. A writer's Aunt Em can say, "That's well organized" (or "not well organized"), but only the teacher can express the component observations that will make writers renew instead of give up their attention to their own writing. We teachers read everything for literary evidences, as Thoreau does in this passage:

> Labaume says that he wrote his journal of the campaign in Russia each night in the midst of incredible danger and suffering, with "a raven's quill and a little gunpowder mixed with some melted snow, in the hollow of my hand," the quill cut and mended with "the knife with which I had carved my scanty morsel of horseflesh." Such a statement promises

well for the writer's qualification to treat such a theme.

(November 17, 1855)

Not even sympathy for the man can take precedence over respect for the writer.

The classical comment on what the teacher tells the student is well-expressed by Jonson:

> I will like and praise some things in a young writer which yet, if he continue in, I cannot but justly hate him for the same. There is a time to be given all things for maturity, and that even your country husbandman can teach, who to a young plant will not put the pruning-knife, because it seems to fear the iron, as not able to admit the scar. No more would I tell a green writer all his faults, lest I should make him grieve and faint, and at last despair. For nothing doth more hurt than to make him afraid of all things as he can endeavor nothing. Therefore youth ought to be instructed betimes, and in the best things: for we hold those longest we take soonest, as the first scent of a vessel lasts, and the tinct the wool first receives. Therefore a master should temper his powers, and descend to the other's infirmity. If you pour a glut of water upon a bottle, it receives little of it; but with a funnel, and by degrees, you shall fill many of them, and spill little of your own; to their capacity they will all receive and be full.

(Ben Jonson, *Timber*)

To accompany this we set down a few other passages: some are lights on — or excursions from — points we have touched, some are *exordia*, and some, *prise de conscience*.

"You alter your experience by discerning principles in it."

(Hugh Kenner, *Bucky*)

Clarity is not writing so that you may be understood but so that you cannot be misunderstood.

"Demonstration, Similitude & Harmony are Objects of Reasoning. Invention, Identity & Melody are Objects of Intuition."

(Blake, *Reynolds Marginalia*)

"Repeat often what we have formerly written; which beside that it helps the consequence, and makes the juncture better, it quickens the heat of the imagination, that often cools in the time of setting down, and gives it a new strength, as if it grew lustier by the going back. As we see in the contention of leaping, they jump farthest that fetch their race largest; or, as in throwing a dart or javelin, we force back our arms to make our loose the stronger.

(Ben Jonson, *Timber*)

One day the Mully [the Arab folk wise man] picked up a musical instrument and, after trying it a moment, began to play one note over and over. Soon his friends grew weary of this note: "Please, Mully, play other notes! Play chords. Nobody plays just one note!"

"Fools," said the Mully, "they *look* for the note."

"One Central Form composed of all other forms being Granted, it does not therefore follow that all other Forms are Deformity."

(Blake, *Reynolds Marginalia)*

As kingfishers catch fire, dragonflies draw flame:
 As tumbled over rim in roundy wells
 Stones ring; like each tucked string tells, each hung bell's
Bow swung finds tongue to fling out broad its name;
Each mortal thing does one thing and the same:
 Deals out that being indoors each one dwells;
 Selves — goes itself; *myself* it speaks and spells,
Crying *What I do is me: for that I came.*

(Gerard Manley Hopkins)

"The soul has a *logos* which increases itself."

(Heraclitus, *Fr. 115*)

Skills are the point where power passes into identity.

Power over others is more responsibility than anyone can bear or carry out.

"The spirit of improvement is not always a spirit of liberty, for it may aim at forcing improvements on an unwilling people . . . but the only unfailing and permanent source of improvement is liberty, since by it there are as many possible independent centers of improvement as there are individuals."

(J.S. Mill)

"Design solves problems elegantly, but force imperfectly."

(Hugh Kenner, *Bucky*)

Discipline, rigor, strictness are qualities individuals may choose to exercise from within, upon their own acts. All discipline is self-discipline, rooted in inner life. It can't be imposed on others or taught except by example.

"I asked him once . . . if he had got a new idea this summer. 'Good Lord,' said he, 'a man that has to work as I do, if he does not forget the ideas he has had, he will do well. Maybe the man you hoe with is inclined to race; then, by Gorry, your mind must be there; you think of weeds.' "

(Thoreau, *Walden*)

"The ultimate end of criticism is much more to establish the principles of writing, than to furnish *rules* how to pass judgment on what has been written by others . . . ."

(S.T. Coleridge, *Biographia Literaria*)

". . . the omission of act in self & the hindering of act in another; This is Vice, but all Act is Virtue. To hinder another is not an act; it is the contrary; it is a restraint on action both in ourselves & in the person hinder'd, for he who hinders another omits his own duty at the same time."

(Blake, *Lavater Marginalia*)

"Rejection is not a critical act."

(Northrop Frye)

"*Extra vagance*! it all depends on how you are yarded."

(Thoreau, *Walden*)

An analysis of Hamlet's soliloquy: "Shakespear, dispensing with the customary exordium, announces his subject at once in the infinitive, in which mood it is presently repeated after a short connecting passage in which, brief as it is, we recognize the alternate and negative forms on which so much of the significance of repetition depends"! (G.B. Shaw. Quoted by Louis Crompton, editor, in *The Great Composers* [University of California Press, 1978])p.xii.

Shaw, on a piece of pedantic music criticism: "How succulent that is: and how full of Mesopotamian words."

(Quoted by Louis Crompton in the same place)

"Pure and neat language I love, yet plain and customary."

(Ben Jonson, *Timber*)

"Language most shows a man: speak that I may see thee."

(Ben Jonson, *Timber*)

Elizabeth Cowan: One final question. Once you and I were talking about what we would order [for] our last meal, and you said you would order dry cereal so that you wouldn't mind dying. If you were choosing to have this the last time you'd talk to an audience like this, what would be your final words to teachers of English?

Northrop Frye: I think the last thing I would say to teachers of English is to love literature. That is not as I think of it a sentimental or soft focus, because it seems to me that love is a constant source of new discoveries in the thing or the person you love. To say, "Love literature," is an exhortation; some may object that you can't be commanded or exhorted to love, but I don't think that's true: love is the focussing of the creative power within yourself in order to direct it on others and to create a new kind of society out of your relation to them. That would be my last answer — the next thing would be dry cereal.

("Frye's Literary Theory in the Classroom," a panel discussion. *CEA Critic*, XXX, Vol 42, No 2, January, 1980)

Bibliographical Notes

1. Northrop Frye, *The Stubborn Structure* (New York: Cornell University Press, 1970).

2. Susanne Langer, *Mind: An Essay on Human Feeling*, Vol I (Baltimore: John Hopkins University, 1967).

3. Leo Rockas, *Modes of Rhetoric* (New York: St. Martin's Press, 1964).

4. Susanne Langer, *Feeling and Form* (New York: Charles Scribner's Sons, 1953).

5. Northrop Frye, *The Educated Imagination* (Bloomington: Indiana University Press, 1969).

Index

p. 32